ENGELS TODAY

Also by Christopher J. Arthur

DIALECTICS OF LABOUR: Marx and his Relation to Hegel

Engels Today

A Centenary Appreciation

Edited by

Christopher J. Arthur
Honorary Lecturer in Philosophy
University of Sussex

First published in Great Britain 1996 by
MACMILLAN PRESS LTD
Houndmills, Basingstoke, Hampshire RG21 6XS
and London
Companies and representatives
throughout the world

A catalogue record for this book is available
from the British Library.

ISBN 0–333–63324–5 (hardcover)
ISBN 0–333–66531–7 (paperback)

First published in the United States of America 1996 by
ST. MARTIN'S PRESS, INC.,
Scholarly and Reference Division,
175 Fifth Avenue,
New York, N.Y. 10010

ISBN 0–312–16013–5

Library of Congress Cataloging-in-Publication Data
Engels today : a centenary appreciation / edited by Christopher J. Arthur.
p. cm.
Includes bibliographical references and index.
ISBN 0–312–16013–5 (cloth)
1. Engels, Friedrich, 1820–1895. I. Arthur, C. J. (Christopher John), 1940– .
HX274.7.E53E44 1996
335.4'092—dc20 96–14477
CIP

10 9 8 7 6 5 4 3 2 1
05 04 03 02 01 00 99 98 97 96

Printed and bound in Great Britain by
Antony Rowe Ltd, Chippenham, Wiltshire

Contents

Notes on the Contributors

Christopher J. Arthur studied at the Universities of Nottingham and Oxford; he taught philosophy for many years at the University of Sussex. He is the author of *Dialectics of Labour: Marx and His Relation to Hegel* (1986); he edited *The German Ideology* by Marx and Engels (1970), *Law and Marxism* by E. Pashukanis (1978) and *Marx's Capital: A Student Edition* (1992).

Ted Benton is Professor of Sociology, University of Essex. He is the author of *Natural Relations* (1993), *The Rise and Fall of Structural Marxism* (1984) and *Philosophical Foundations of Three Sociologies* (1977).

Terrell Carver is Professor of Political Theory, University of Bristol. He is the author, among other works, of *Friedrich Engels: His Life and Thought* (1989), *Marx and Engels: The Intellectual Relationship* (1983) and *A Marx Dictionary* (1987); he also edited *The Cambridge Companion to Marx* (1991).

Andrew Collier is Reader in Philosophy at the University of Southampton. Among other works he is the author of *Critical Realism* (1994), *Socialist Reasoning* (1990), *Scientific Realism and Social Thought* (1989).

Anne Dennehy is a Research Student in the Department of Social Medicine, University of Bristol.

John O'Neill lectures in philosophy at the University of Lancaster. His publications include *Worlds Without Content: Against Formalism* (1991), *Ecology, Policy and Politics: Human Well-Being and the Natural World* (1993) and *The Market: Ethics, Information, Politics* (1996).

Sean Sayers is Reader in Philosophy at the University of Kent, Canterbury. He is the author of *Reality and Reason: Dialectic and the Theory of Knowledge* (1985) and (with Richard Norman) of *Hegel, Marx, and Dialectic: A Debate* (1980). He was a founding editor of *Radical Philosophy*, of which he is currently book reviews editor.

Lise Vogel, Professor of Sociology and Women's Studies at Rider University, Lawrenceville, New Jersey, was 1994–95 Harris Distinguished Visiting Professor at Denison University. She is the author of *Woman Questions* (1995), *Mothers on the Job: Maternity Policy in the U.S. Workplace* (1993) and *Marxism and the Oppression of Women: Toward a Unitary Theory* (1983).

Introduction

Christopher J. Arthur

Friedrich Engels died in London on the 5th of August 1895, aged 74. At his centenary, it is generally recognized that, whereas he became famous as the 'other half' of 'Marx and Engels' (playing second fiddle as it were), he was in truth a distinct figure in his own right, who made an enormous contribution to the trajectory of radical thought to the present day. In particular, what cannot be underestimated is his contribution to what came to be known as 'Marxism', both at its genesis and in its diffusion after Marx's death in 1883. Indeed, the French Marxologist Maximilien Rubel considers him to be the veritable founder of 'Marxism', so important were his works in establishing the tradition.

Engels was born on 28 November 1920 in Barmen, a town in the Wupper valley. He was the eldest child of a mill-owning family which had connections in Bremen and Manchester, cities with which the young Engels became familiar. Although he did not study for a degree, he took the opportunity of his military service in Berlin to make connections with university circles, notably with the 'Young Hegelian' movement.

From an early date he enjoyed writing for the press and his articles became increasingly radical in content. This radicalism was largely informed by his first-hand knowledge of commercial life. It is said that he became a communist in 1842.

While Marx was editor of the *Rheinische Zeitung* he published articles by Engels. The two met briefly at the Cologne offices of the paper in November 1842; but it was in 1844, at their second meeting (in Paris), that they discovered how much they agreed with each other; the two became lifelong friends.

There is little doubt that Engels was ahead of Marx in his appreciation of the importance of class struggle and in his understanding of the necessity to mount a critique of political economy. The evidence for this statement lies in his masterpiece *The Condition of the Working Class in England* (1845), and in his earlier essay *Outlines of a Critique of Political Economy*. Marx thought very highly of these works and continually cited them in his own writings.

The beginning of the collaboration of Engels with Marx is attested to by their joint works of the 1840s, *The Holy Family* and *German Ideology*. While the final literary form of the *Manifesto of the Communist Party* (1848) was due to Marx, Engels made a full contribution to its content through providing Marx with drafts and advice.

The two men moved back to Germany to participate in the 1848–49 revolution, Engels again contributing to Marx's re-established paper, the *Neue Rheinische Zeitung*. In May 1849 Engels joined the armed revolt that broke out against the Prussian monarchy; this rebellion was finally crushed in July, Engels escaping to Switzerland.

Following the failure of the revolution, both men settled in England for good; but while Marx, in London, set himself to the task of researching his great work on *Capital*, Engels's intellectual work went into eclipse as he concentrated on earning a living (and through this subsidising Marx) at the Manchester branch of the family firm. His main writing during this period concerned military tactics and warfare. His study on the political and military aspects of Prussian relations with Italy, *Po und Rhein*, was very successful, and, being originally anonymous, was widely believed to be the work of a general. Indeed, Engels's expert articles on military affairs, appearing in various publications, earned him the nickname 'General' with the Marx family.

Upon his retirement from business, and his move to London in 1870, Engels was free to devote all his energy to political work, both organizational (he was immediately elected to the General Council of the International) and literary. His great facility with languages gave Engels a continuing role in liaison with numerous European socialist movements.

One of Engels's most influential works, written in the service of the movement, arose almost accidentally. The popularity of works by Dr Eugen Dühring, a new adherent to socialism, caused first W. Liebknecht, and then Marx himself, to urge Engels to refute these unwelcome doctrines. It was with some reluctance that Engels took up the challenge. Since Dühring's work ranged widely over philosophy, economics, history and science, as well as socialist theory itself, Engels found he was imperceptibly constructing an entire 'system' himself.

What began as a chore ended as the most influential textbook on Marxism ever written. As Engels later put it: 'The polemic was transformed into a more or less connected exposition of the dialectical method and of the communist world outlook fought for by

Marx and myself – an exposition covering a fairly comprehensive range of subjects.' (Although it is known that Marx contributed a chapter to the book, the question of his endorsement of its doctrines in full has occasioned much controversy; it appeared in final form in 1878 by which time Marx's intellectual fires were burning low, although his death was still five years away.)

A still greater success than the book itself was a pamphlet consisting of three chapters excerpted from it, namely *Socialism: Utopian and Scientific*; within a few years it was circulating in ten languages, and it sold in tens of thousands.

After Marx's death in 1883 Engels had to take on the burden of editing and publishing the remaining volumes of Marx's *Capital*. But he still found time to produce works of his own, the most influential being his book *Origins of the Family, Private Property and the State*, and his article *Ludwig Feuerbach and the Outcome of Classical German Philosophy*. He often generated propositions subsequently much discussed in the course of letters designed to quell the doubts of correspondents. His posthumously published notes on *Dialectics of Nature* became a source book for Soviet 'dialectical materialism'.

The aim of the present collection of essays is limited. It is unnecessary to attempt a comprehensive coverage of Engels's life and work. There are many books and articles which do this (some of which are listed below). Rather, what we have attempted is to focus on what are still 'live' issues in Engels's intellectual legacy, either because Engels made a still relevant contribution to a topical issue or because there is some aspect of his work and influence that still occasions debate.

One of the fiercest ongoing debates concerns Engels's relation to Marx. He was immensely influential in his role as Marx's editor and primary commentator. For long taken as virtually Marx's *alter ego* Engels is now generally perceived as a force in his own right. This, however, has not been to his advantage because the literature concerned erected a dichotomy between the views of Marx and those of Engels, and charged the latter with systematically misrepresenting the former. This view of Engels became so prominent that a recent work by J.D. Hunley, treating and refuting 'the dichotomist portrait', considered itself to be very much against the stream of scholarly opinion today (*The Life and Thought of Friedrich Engels: A Reinterpretation*, 1991).

The odd feature of this literature, however, is that the authors disagree among themselves on the substantive issues involved, although it is always Marx who is the 'good guy' and Engels the villain. Thus an author with a taste for dialectic will praise Marx's dialectical subtlety, while condemning Engels for his positivism; conversely, an author with a distaste for dialectic will attribute this aspect of Marxism to Engels's metaphysical inclinations, and rescue the sober scientist Marx from its baleful shadow. For example, Lucio Colletti (in his *Marxism and Hegel*, 1969) regrets that Engels inaugurated the tradition of reading Marx as a dialectical materialist, whereas David McLellan in his little book on *Engels* (1977) contrasts Marx's affiliation with Hegel to Engels's Enlightenment naturalism.

While my own contribution below touches on aspects of this issue it is certainly not settled here, and no doubt will always be up for debate. However, it is ultimately less important than assessing the substantive question of whether or not the works of Engels can still provide us with food for thought. We believe this to be the case and offer our essays in this spirit. For, if Engels's legacy became intertwined with the whole intellectual history of the communist movement in the twentieth century, it still today repays attention.

Because Engels's own range of interests was so wide our own assessments therefore cover a wide field, although for the most part they deal with theoretical issues.

Terrell Carver concentrates on Engels's early career in order to show how profound was his commitment to democracy, and to show how anachronistic and mistaken it would be to see that as in conflict with his communism. Carver's paper gains considerable force from his allusions to the events of 1989, with their echoes of the 1848 revolutions in which Engels of course participated.

The following paper, by Andrew Collier, complements Carver's in that it takes up the later work of Engels in relation to his communist politics. Engels played an important role, especially after Marx's death, as mentor of the international socialist movements; thus he became involved in problems such as reform or revolution, for which no ready answers existed. After explicating the Marxist case for revolution, Collier's contribution shows that Engels's approach to the question demonstrates exemplary realism.

In related vein, John O'Neill defends Engels against charges that his advocacy of 'scientific socialism' was responsible for generating a dogmatic Marxism such as predominated in the Second and Third

Internationals. O'Neill's paper argues that Engels defended a fallibilist account of science in general and of historical sciences in particular.

At the time, many radical thinkers were influenced by Darwinism, of course, which was taken to provide the basis of a whole evolutionist world outlook. Ted Benton situates Engels's work on this topic in the ideological context of the time. In addition, Benton's paper demonstrates Engels's importance as a precursor of environmentalist critique in his book on the condition of the English working class.

As we have already said, Engels's first great success was his *Condition of the Working Class in England in 1844* (the 'in 1844' was added to the title for the English translation of 1892). It is now 150 years since its publication. It is especially appropriate therefore for our collection to address it in a special essay; here Anne Dennehy argues that it is of more than historical interest – for the same determinants of class inequality and urban squalor are operative today.

The dramatic rise of a new wave of feminism in recent decades has naturally led to a reappraisal of one of Engels's last works, *Origins of the Family*. Lise Vogel looks back at the context of the composition of this work and offers some reflections on the way it should be read today.

In his later years Engels conceived his task more and more in terms of underpinning Marxism with a philosophy, or world view. Sean Sayers draws on some of Engels's philosophical ideas in his discussion of materialism.

Although, in the division of labour between Marx and Engels, the former dealt with economics, Engels, perforce, as editor and popularizer of Marx's work put his own slant on it. His reading of Marx's critique of political economy has been so influential that it deserves a study in its own right, provided here by me. It is really three papers in one, in that three questions are addressed: Engels's work on Marx's manuscripts, his interpretation of Marx's dialectical method, and his promotion of a reading of *Capital* organized around the concept of 'simple commodity production'. However, these issues flow naturally into one another.

The book as a whole therefore covers a good deal of the legacy left to us by Engels, and the chapters demonstrate that it is of much more than historical interest but germane to radical thought in many fields today.

Further reading

A comprehensive collection of all Engels's works, in reasonable translations with useful notes, is available in the *Marx-Engels Collected Works* (50 volumes) published by Lawrence & Wishart from 1975 on: for example, see Volume 4 for *Condition of the Working Class in England in 1844*; Volume 10 for *The Peasant War in Germany*; Volume 23 for *The Housing Question*; Volume 24 for *Socialism: Utopian and Scientific*; Volume 25 for *Anti-Dühring*; Volume 26 for *Origins of the Family, Private Property and the State*, and for *Ludwig Feuerbach and the Outcome of Classical German Philosophy*; and Volume 27 for *Dialectics of Nature*.

A short anthology of *Selected Writings* of Engels, edited by W.O. Henderson, was published by Penguin 1967.

While each essay in this book has its own references, a selected list of contributions to our understanding of Engels, and the issues he raised, may be useful, as follows. It ranges from McLellan's short introduction, to full scale 'lives'.

Carver, T. *Marx & Engels: The Intellectual Relationship*, Brighton, Wheatsheaf Books, 1983.

Carver, T. *Friedrich Engels: His Life and Thought*, Basingstoke, Macmillan, 1989.

Henderson, W.O. *The Life of Friedrich Engels* (2 vols), London, Frank Cass, 1976.

Hunley, J.D. *The Life and Thought of Friedrich Engels: A Reinterpretation*, New Haven and London, Yale University Press, 1991.

McLellan, D. *Engels*, Fontana / Collins, 1977.

Mayer, G. *Friedrich Engels*, English trans. (abridged) G. and H. Highet, New York, Howard Fertig, 1969.

Nova, F. *Friedrich Engels: His Contribution to Political Theory*, London, Vision Press, 1968.

Rigby, S.H. *Engels and the formation of Marxism*, Manchester, Manchester University Press, 1992.

Rubel, M. 'Engels, Founder of Marxism', ch. 1 of *Rubel on Marx*, O'Malley, J. and Algozin, K. (eds), Cambridge, Cambridge University Press, 1981.

Sayers, J., Evans, M. and Redclift, N. (eds) *Engels Revisited: New Feminist Essays*, London and New York, Tavistock, 1987.

Stedman Jones, G. 'Engels and the History of Marxism', in Hobsbawm, E.J. (ed.), *The History of Marxism, Volume I*, Brighton, Harvester Press, 1982.

1

Engels and Democracy[1]

Terrell Carver

In my view Engels was a democrat, and the tradition would be enriched if he were reclaimed as such. His criticisms of 'bourgeois democracy' were trenchant, and they deserve re-examination to see if there has been any progress since their time. Perhaps there has been less than we have been led to believe, and one reason for this may be that politicians have a vested interest in simplifying and foreclosing what we think democracy might mean. Engels, and of course Marx, are chiefly known as revolutionaries, but I shall argue that this aspect of their theory and practice has been vastly overplayed. This was done by parties whose interests are at odds with, or are at least very marginal to, the sort of democratic politics that most people would find generally tolerable.

Thus one way of thinking critically about democracy in the present is to revisit crucial episodes in the past by looking at the writings and careers of political actors such as Engels. In doing this I shall focus on his early career, which has a liveliness and 'edge' rather more like our present situation than the features and circumstances of his later career. Also, the earlier years are little investigated, and most often viewed as mere 'build-up' to his self-described role as 'second fiddle' to Marx. During the 1840s Engels had a budding career on his own account, and when working with Marx something of the role of gadfly in matters of practical politics. A close look at the historical detail involved will usefully blur the more recent distinction between democrats on the one hand, and communists on the other. The two philosophies had common origins and shared practices, even in revolutionary times, and it is a mistake to read their later sharp divergence (at the end of the twentieth century) back into the more familiar and more interesting type of politics in which the youthful Engels took part.

REWRITING THE PRESENT BY REREADING THE PAST

Since Engels is well known now as a communist, it may sound surprising to relate that he wholeheartedly supported, in theory and in practice, national and international movements for representative and responsible government, which I take here as a working definition of democracy. While it is acknowledged in the biographical literature that he admired the ideals of the French Revolution and was, at least at the beginning of his career, a democrat in some vague sense, the focus among modern commentators is very much on getting him through, over, past or around this 'stage' and into the realm of communist revolutionaries, who are thought to be very different in their doctrine and practice. My point here is that what Engels *shared* with democrats of his own time, and – other things being equal – with ours, has been left unexplored, as it is thought to be obvious or off the point. Neither is true, and the events of 1989 and the following few years highlight this for us quite dramatically.

I would characterize the political changes in East Central Europe as revolutionary reconstructions with large, though varying, amounts of popular participation, and as such they are a further episode in the struggle for truly constitutional governments that dates back most notably to 1789 in France. Moreover the widespread spontaneous character of the popular outbursts in 1989 across Europe is also strongly reminiscent of the revolutions of 1848, and I shall be regarding the decade of the 1840s as particularly important in the development of democratic theory and practice, during which Engels theorized democracy in practical terms. Hence it is also a crucial period for us to revisit, as ideas and movements that are now back on the agenda were scrutinized there with a freshness and vigour – well captured in some of Engels's writings – that belie the deadening effects of twentieth-century history and the rigor mortis of familiar ideologies.

The political activities undertaken in the 1840s by Engels in various European localities – Cologne, Berlin, Brussels, Paris, London, Manchester – were part of the popular, if almost always clandestine, politics that led to the outbreaks of mass anti-monarchical violence that occurred in 1848–49. As a reporter, and as virtual co-editor of a Rhineland newspaper, he was able to relay news items to journals all over Europe and beyond, and to provide his own readers with similar coverage. In mass political action information about the wider world and larger issues on the one hand, and spontaneity related to local concerns and events on the other, are not at all inconsistent. Engels's approach to democratic politics took this for granted.

My interpretive framework for comparing 1848 and 1989, and for analysing Engels's political theory and practice, is necessarily very broad, yet I shall be quite specific in my attention to historical detail and conceptual relevance. I take genuine constitutionalism to mean representative and responsible government, together with periodic elections, multi-party politics, an independent judiciary, and a multitude of rights that allow citizens redress against their rulers: rights to free intellectual enquiry, to uncensored publication on political subjects, to popular participation in all levels of government, to challenge governmental policy in the courts, to protect citizens from religious (or anti-religious) oppression, to self-government independent of foreign control.

That list – which obviously overlaps the People's Charter of 1838 as well as Charter 77 and innumerable other documents demanding popular sovereignty – happens to be derived from Engels's journalism of the early 1840s. There is no reason to assume any cynicism in this whatsoever, though this is not to say that this programme formed the limit of his ambitions, nor is it to deny that some elements of it were transitional in themselves, as he saw the democratic trajectory. How much democracy should there be is itself a question that gets democratic politics going, and democratic politics as such contains no firm boundaries at which citizen participation must end. Rather it is a feature of democratic politics that political actors are allowed to ask this kind of question and to work towards a negotiated solution. This is precisely what Engels was up to, and precisely why he qualifies as a democrat.

An exploration of Engels's early encounters with the practicalities of political action in England, undertaken to further democratization there, reveals the commonalities between communism, as he understood it in the early 1840s, and the outlook of the *Communist Manifesto* of late 1847/early 1848.

ANGLO-GERMAN ATTITUDES

In September 1842, at the age of 21, Engels left Berlin, having finished his national service. En route to his home in Barmen, he visited the

Cologne office of the *Rheinische Zeitung*, a liberal and somewhat persecuted newspaper, where he met the communist Moses Hess. In correspondence of the following year Hess reported on this meeting with one of the paper's occasional Berlin correspondents: '. . . we talked over the issues of the day and he [Engels], a revolutionary of the Year I, departed from me a thoroughly zealous communist.'[2] Engels's 'conversion' to communism is traditionally dated to that meeting with Hess, and it is certainly true that socialist or communist ideas – there was no firm distinction at that time – do not appear in his writings up to then. Hess took credit for such a conversion by implying that he brought Engels forward from a primitive view of social transformation, one characteristic of the first years of the French Revolution, to the most up-to-date ideas of communism, such as his own.

However, it is unlikely that Engels needed much persuading, as he was an almost perfect reflection in himself of the 'European Triarchy' that Hess was looking for: revolutionary sentiments in his admiration for French politics, critical Young Hegelianism in his appreciation for German philosophy, and a perspective on industrialization and class that he could expect to develop in England in connection with his family's business interests. Over the next two years communist ideas crept into Engels's works, and they certainly influenced his choice of subject-matter, but the development from revolutionary democrat to communist was not a dramatic change in outlook.

This was because the communist or socialist outlook was highly varied, and generally visionary, while the movement for democracy was also for many theorists and politicians a doctrine of revolution and not necessarily anti-communist. Theoretical distinctions and battle lines between revolutionary democrats and revolutionary communists were not then sharply drawn, and in any case Hess, Engels and other radicals were inclined to view communism as a stage in European political development that would build on the achievements of democratic theory and practice by pushing them further forward.

Communism was then no simple reversal of democracy, and democrats were potential allies for communists, not enemies. Communism at the time did not mean much more than community of goods, about which theorists of communism developed widely differing utopian schemes. Practical communists sought to find persuadable democrats – revolutionaries of the Year I – to look beyond the political goal of representative and responsible government and to consider in addition the 'social question' raised by the inequality of property in contemporary society.

Engels arrived in London on 19 November 1842, and journeyed to Manchester some days or weeks later. As one of the correspondents in England for the *Rheinische Zeitung* he covered 'the concrete conditions' and 'the existing state of things' in politics, just as his new editor Marx desired, and his treatment displayed a class-perspective that recalled his early journalism – the 'Letters from Wuppertal', written and published in 1839 when he was just 18. His factual study of industrial poverty in the Wuppertal was highly formative, but even as journalism it was rudimentary. During his time in Berlin he had attended lectures on political economy by Leopold von Henning, whose Hegelian view that economic theory was an aspect of developing rationality in history, and that rationality required its practical realization in the political realm of economic policy-making, was clearly inspirational. During his two years in Manchester Engels made startling progress on both a theoretical critique of the modern economy and an empirical account of its effects on the working class.

IDEAS AND ACTION

Engels's articles on England for the *Rheinische Zeitung* were swiftly written without much research, and they were based on very limited personal experience of the English political scene on which he commented. His views were coincident with previous articles in the paper written by Hess and Gustav Mevissen, a founder and shareholder who had himself visited England that summer. Hess had placed the question of revolution in England on the editorial agenda, and Mevissen had provided a class analysis of the current situation, covering landed interests, manufacturers and middle classes, and propertyless workers.

In Engels's time there were obvious, even violent, political clashes to be observed in England, especially the mass strikes in the manufacturing districts that had taken place in mid-1842. The activities of the Chartists and the Anti-Corn Law League both led to noisy meetings, demonstrations, marches and desperate political tensions in Parliament itself. The *People's Charter* had been published in 1838, and it contained demands for universal male suffrage at the age of

21, annual parliaments, salaries for MPs, elections by ballot rather than by public vote, equality in electoral districts, and abolition of property qualifications for parliamentary candidates. The original committee, formed to promote the *Charter* as a parliamentary bill, consisted of MPs and members of the London Working Men's Association. After the failure of these efforts, the National Charter Association was formed in July 1840 in Manchester to organize a mass petition. This eventually attracted 3.3 million signatures, but it was also rejected by Parliament. During the mass strikes of August 1842 an attempt was made to link the struggle for wages to the Chartists' cause, but the strikes were forcibly suppressed, and the two movements – one for better wages and conditions for working people, and the other for a more democratic and representative Parliament – then diverged.

Overlapping those movements to some extent was the Anti-Corn Law League, founded in December 1838 in Manchester, and dedicated to the repeal of the protective tariffs that kept out foreign grain. This policy maintained high prices for domestic corn, because it suited aristocratic landed interests, and conversely it forced manufacturers to pay high wages, because their workers were denied access to cheap foreign foodstuffs. The Anti-Corn Law League wanted a major reform in policy that the ruling Tories, traditionally allied to landed, agricultural interests, would not countenance. One way of achieving this change in economic policy might be to reform Parliament itself in accordance with the *Charter*. The *Charter*, in so far as it promised universal suffrage, might result in a Parliament more favourable to working-class interests and less favourable to agricultural landlords than the current restricted representation allowed. This coincidence of interests did not remove the very real differences between these three groups that a reform of Parliament would inevitably expose. In 1846 the Corn Laws were repealed, a policy change that was to some extent forced on the Tories to counter the threat of reform. Reform of Parliament was not achieved in the 1840s, and the unsuccessful attempt of 1842 to promote a mass alliance of opposition forces was not repeated.[3]

For Engels this was democratic politics on a grand scale far surpassing the political activity that was permitted or even attempted in Prussia. Moreover it was tinged with a kind of proto-communism (as he saw it), in that the interests of the working classes were openly and sometimes violently pursued, though community of goods was not an obvious issue in the struggle. The revolution that he and the

Rheinische Zeitung had in mind was itself a democratic one – the creation, through violent means if necessary, of representative and responsible government. They reasoned that such a government would have to legislate to protect the interests of the broad mass of voters, including workers, rather than the minority of wealthy property-owners.

THE 'SOCIAL QUESTION'

The consequences of industrialization were on display in England to a far greater degree than in Germany, and this, too, engaged Engels's interest. Hess had argued that the industrial poor represented the political issue of the future, and England (by which German communists meant Britain) had more of them than anywhere else. In what sense the industrial poor might themselves be an important political actor before and after a democratizing revolution was left nebulous. But then the democratic model was itself vague about the exact scope of revolutionary, electoral and parliamentary participation that the industrial poor might expect to enjoy in practice, so neither Hess nor Engels must have felt it necessary to define those matters very distinctly. Making the industrial working class a political issue for educated democrats did not explicitly include – but did not necessarily exclude – some conception of industrial workers as an organized force in politics.

Engels's experience as an international trader entered his articles in a striking manner, and in that respect he contributed something of his own to the radical views developed by Hess and others on the *Rheinische Zeitung*. Their perspective had been internationalist in a somewhat mystical way – a Hegelian synthesis of French revolutionary vigour, English industrial might and German philosophy. For what else could Germany, in the eyes of its intellectuals, contribute but something philosophical and synthetic? In Young Hegelian eyes, and perhaps rightly, Germans were international visionaries, as their political and industrial achievements at home were not yet on a European scale to match those of France and Britain.

Engels produced an analysis of England as a trading nation. No doubt the motivation for doing this was his expectation that it would reinforce Hess's conclusions concerning the revolutionary potential of an industrialized country, and those are precisely the conclusions that he drew for the readers of the *Rheinische Zeitung*. But in doing this he challenged Young Hegelians to look beyond democracy in the German context (which was still just an idea, and a proscribed one at that) and to give content to Hess's sketchy internationalism. If they could see industry abroad, and see industrialization as an international force, they could then see the relevance of a powerful new analytical tool – political economy. Almost at a stroke Engels conjoined philosophical politics with social science.

Engels's argument flowed in a chain of empirical deductions quite unlike other Young Hegelian discourse. In part this was because the economic issues relevant to a trading country had not yet been fully aired in relation to Germany, and it is therefore unsurprising that they did not play a significant role in Young Hegelian literature or in the politics of the day from which the movement arose. Engels's achievement within Young Hegelianism was to draw on his unusual background in international trade, his current posting to a job in English industry, and his academic curiosity about economic affairs. His aim was to make significant alterations in his contemporaries' political perceptions about the scope of democratic politics.

Very simply Engels argued that a trading nation such as England must constantly increase its industrial output, or face decline. This was because of the progressive industrialization of the foreign countries which formed its export market. Lower costs abroad would bring a flood of cheap imports, resulting in bankruptcy for domestic manufacturers. Domestic industrialists would consequently demand protective tariffs on foreign goods to protect their position in the home market. This would lead to high prices, to which English consumers would object. Moreover foreign industries would seek barriers to English products, so English export industries would fail and workers would face unemployment. Competition and protection at home and abroad thus formed a two-sided process continuing to infinity, in his view, and those forces would produce an inevitable contradiction in practice.

This conceptual analysis, Engels continued, was also confirmed by direct observation of the existing state of affairs. He took the recent wave of strikes to be a result of changes in the terms of international trade, and an augury of the impossibility for peaceful reform or 'legal revolution'. Because industrialization made more and more people dependent for their livelihood, indeed their very existence, on these economic fluctuations, he predicted a mass revolt against the land-owning nobility and the industrial aristocracy. This would be a matter of political necessity.

Engels's analysis of the political furore surrounding the Corn Laws was straightforward reporting, but it was augmented by a perceptive account of the position of the middle-class party of merchants and manufacturers. He compared their situation in England with the position of similar classes in Germany, who were coincidentally the backers of the *Rheinische Zeitung*. In England he found a relatively enlightened version of the industrialists and traders that he knew from his days in Barmen, and he expected the Whig party of the English middle classes to be forced into just the kind of squeeze that he would like to see developing in Germany. In England this would happen when the working class became more and more imbued with the radical-democratic principles of Chartism and came to recognize those principles as the expression of its collective consciousness. At that point political power would flow to the working class who would have an advantage in terms of numbers and determination over the middle classes. The battle against the old order and its political and economic privileges would be bound to intensify, and middle-class democrats would have to choose which side they were on.[4]

CHARTISTS AND OWENITES

Engels's articles were full of praise for the popular agitation in support of the *People's Charter* that he had seen at public meetings in Manchester and neighbouring Salford. He contrasted English factuality and humour very favourably with French socialism, which in his view was beset with scheming and factionalism, and with German philosophical radicalism, which he considered ill-written and self-regarding. For Engels the Chartist movement for the democratization of Parliament was in a sense a popular front for much more radical schemes for revolutionizing contemporary society, including the destruction of landed, aristocratic interests, which he considered reactionary, and the curtailment of propertied, commercial interests, which he considered exploitative. His highest praise was for the 'founder of the socialist movement' Robert Owen, who wrote badly, in his opinion, but had lucid moments. Owen's views were comprehensive, according to Engels, and he remarked that his writings teemed with outbursts of rage against theologians, lawyers and doctors, all lumped together.

Owenites and their meetings were undoubtedly influential in Manchester, and the heady mixture of groups, interests and ideas within the Chartist movement of the 1840s was vividly pictured by Engels, an eyewitness and partisan. But he did not pay much attention to the leadership of the movement, which stuck to very limited aims and methods in pursuing the national campaign. His characterization of Chartism as English socialism now seems somewhat odd, since the leadership lost confidence in themselves and then the confidence of their supporters. The first mass political movement to include significant working-class participation fell apart long before any very organized form of socialism emerged in England.

Engels, writing for Germans in a Swiss paper, had no English audience among Chartists at this point. As political journalism it was thus doubly removed from real struggles, but his analysis was very confident none the less:

> In the socialists, English energy is very clearly evident, but what astonished me more was the good-natured character of these people. I almost called them lads, which, however, is so far removed from weakness that they laugh at the mere Republicans, because a republic would be just as hypocritical, just as theological, just as unjust in its laws, as a monarchy ....[5]

The oppressed and poor as political actors were coming into focus in Engels's analysis of contemporary English politics. He clearly wanted an alliance of Irishmen and Chartists, converted to socialism, to march on the British establishment and remove it. And he did not want any constitutional backsliding towards monarchy or any other stratagems to defend landed and commercial interests at the expense of agricultural and industrial workers. The French constitutional monarchy of King Louis Philippe was specifically mentioned by Engels as an example of the way in which a mass movement had been betrayed.

Yet Engels's notion of mass political participation in the struggle for democracy was inchoate, so he did not handle the role of leaders at all well, seeing them as either traitors or cyphers. The political process by which the interests of the oppressed and poor were to be pursued and then protected in constitutional political structures received little attention in his writings. Though he supported democratic politics, indeed the whole process of democratization in England, France, Germany or wherever, he also viewed democracy as distinctly limited in what it could achieve with respect to the 'social question':

> But democracy by itself is not capable of curing social ills. Democratic equality is a chimera, the fight of the poor against the rich cannot be fought out on a basis of democracy or indeed of politics as a whole. This stage too is thus only a transition, the last purely political remedy which has still to be tried and from which a new element is bound to develop at once, a principle transcending everything of a political nature.
>
> This principle is the principle of socialism.[6]

The elimination of religious appeals from both kinds of approach – philosophical arguments for intellectuals and factual arguments for others – was crucial to Engels's outlook. Indeed his intellectual strength derives to a large extent from his conviction that arguments from first principles were more convincing, not less, when they proceeded from atheism and applied a dialectical logic to human experience. But there was a certain political weakness in his conviction that arguments from fact could persuade ordinary readers as effectively as the religious enthusiasm so common, and so astoundingly influential, in the early nineteenth century.

PRACTICAL POLITICS

As a communist supporter of democracy, Engels found himself in a tricky political position. The movement for democratic rights to participate in government was only just under way in Europe, and only just beginning to achieve constitutional concessions from which citizen participation in government could be institutionalized. In so far as this movement for representative and responsible government was opposed to established monarchical systems and the remains of a feudal social order, socialists and communists supported it wholeheartedly. And in so far as it expanded the numbers of people involving themselves in political life, organizing to promote their ends and communicating their ideas to an increasingly articulate public, socialists and communists sought an alliance with the democratic movement. In those ways socialist and communists expected to build on the principles of constitutional legality and middle-class politics, accepting them as an improvement on feudal tradition and arbitrary rule. But their position as allies to the democratic movement was somewhat undermined when their socialist and communist principles intruded. In pursuing their defining aims, they criticized democratic principles as insufficient to remedy the 'social question' of endemic poverty and the peculiar ills of industrial society.

Keeping clear of middle-class constitutionalism would perforce condemn the political writing and other activities of socialists and communists to a sectarian ghetto and would make it difficult to attract committed supporters and keep them. But forging an alliance with the democratic movement while maintaining a distinctively socialist and communist identity would inevitably expose them to charges of impracticality in trying to go too far too fast. More seriously it might lead to their expulsion on charges of anti-democratic subversion and socially catastrophic nihilism. In such a position socialists and communists found it easy to make enemies and difficult to keep friends, so throughout most of his life Engels fought his battle for communism in conjunction with a very small group indeed.

Middle-class democrats were committed in principle to freedoms of speech and organization, so socialists and communists could expect some toleration for their critical views and constant agitation. But socialism and communism often jeopardized democratic politics for two reasons: firstly because they appeared too radical for the middle classes on the issue of redistributing property, and secondly because they attracted official repression for their intended subversion of the existing order. Toleration within organizations for would-be allies who sought fundamental alterations from within and attracted destruction from without was consequently limited. But socialists and communists had to align themselves with the democratic movement because it offered them their best access to political influence and practical success.

Engels put his name to a letter to communists in Germany advising them as a matter of tactics to:

> . . . proceed jesuitically, put aside teutonic probity, true-heartedness and decency, and sign and push forward the bourgeois petitions for freedom of the press, a constitution, and so on. When this has been achieved a new era will dawn for c[ommunist] propaganda . . . In a party one must support everything which helps towards progress, and have no truck with any tedious moral scruples.[7]

But as a matter of fact he recognized:

> . . . that even these radical bourgeois here [in Germany] see us as their future main enemies and have no intention of putting into

our hands weapons which we would very shortly turn against themselves.[8]

In politics Engels aimed to be a communist Machiavel, fighting the battle of democracy, but he found his opponents no less cunning. For that reason his political career involved him in considerable frustration.

Though somewhat sceptical of Marx's emphasis on theoretical questions – but highly impressed by his thoroughness in arguing political issues through to basic premises – Engels joined Marx in early April 1845 in an informal political association. This was not an inevitable event, as Engels had previously been much closer to Hess. Indeed Engels had been working with Hess in Elberfeld (near Engels's home town in the Wuppertal), and the two planned for a time to edit a journal together. But Engels had his suspicions that Hess was tending towards philosophical and moral idealism. Even if Marx was not wholly practical in a political sense, he was at least empirical in his interests and razor-sharp in his writings, unlike Hess, who was given to dreamy, ill-defined speculations. Best of all Marx was utterly disinclined to preach any pseudo-Christian, quasi-religious or even moralistic socialism based on love for one's fellows and true faith in a doctrine – approaches to social reconstruction which Engels's thoroughgoing atheism had led him to reject. Engels admired Marx's insistence that the conflicting material interests of class politics formed the basis of the communist critique of existing society. Indeed class analysis was a preoccupation dating back to the 'Letters from Wuppertal'. In Marx's view the resolution of social conflict in favour of the labouring class would become the basis in practice of a new society – communism. For Engels, who had experienced the real world of industry and commerce, here were exciting and realistic premises for political action.

Towards the middle of the 1840s the middle-class movement for constitutional rule took off in Germany. Between late 1844 and early 1848 – while he was in Barmen, Brussels and then Paris – Engels continued with his own topical journalism, always from the communist perspective, and with his overt advertisements for the communist cause. His articles were written for the press in Germany, Belgium, France and England, and the political complexion of the papers that took his work ranged from socialist and communist to respectably reformist. Using German, English and finally French, Engels covered familiar ground in chronicling industrial unrest in

Germany, elsewhere on the continent and in England; protesting at the harassment of communist writers and sympathetic presses in various continental countries; considering the balance of political forces and relative levels of economic development in Britain, France and Germany; addressing the Irish question, the Chartist campaign and the agitation against the Corn Laws; and pondering the implications of the development of European constitutionalism for the future of the working-class movement.

While in Barmen, Engels claimed that the vigour of his own communist analysis – combined with the threat of spontaneous mob violence – could move the middle classes of the Wuppertal to reject the benefits (for them) of private property and to see the virtues (for all) of communal ownership. But he expected even more enthusiasm from the working classes and even less resistance. He acknowledged that there were a number of republicans and indeed communists among the youth of the middle class, but their numbers would inevitably be small. Thus communists could not count on them but would instead look to the 'glorious array of working Democrats and Communists'. In Germany, he commented, 'Democracy and Communism are, as far as the working classes are concerned, quite synonymous.'[9]

Engels took the line that '*Democracy nowadays is communism*', and 'all European democrats . . . are more or less Communists at heart'. This was because, in his view, 'the transition from the absolute monarchy to the modern representative state in no way abolishes the poverty of the great mass of the people', but rather brings to power a new class, the bourgeoisie. By means of its capital this class presses heavily on the 'masses', and hence it is 'the opponent *par excellence* of the Communists, or socialists respectively, as representatives of the mass of the people'. In Engels's view the working class was no beneficiary of the current system and so would hardly want to defend its ideals and institutions.[10]

By the spring of 1845 Engels had himself had practical experience in class politics, and he put this quite pointedly to Marx, saying:

> . . . standing up in front of real, live people and holding forth to them directly and straightforwardly, so that they see and hear you is something quite different from engaging in this devilishly abstract quillpushing with an abstract audience in one's 'mind's eye'.[11]

Engels and his communist associates in the Rhineland, such as Hess, had been holding public meetings arranged on the spur of the moment and without police permission. Organizations to assist the working classes, and thereby circumvent strikes and violence, were being set up throughout Germany in late 1844, as the Silesian weavers' uprising had taken place that summer. Engels reported that 'our own people' had gained access to the local rules committees in Cologne and Elberfeld and that in alliance with Christian rationalists they had defeated pietist conservatives, though he did not say on what issues. The society for the education and relief of workers in Elberfeld was twice addressed by Engels himself, and he sent Marx a report:

> Here in Elberfeld wondrous things are afoot. Yesterday we held our third communist meeting in the town's largest hall and leading inn. The first meeting was forty strong, the second 130 and the third at least 200. All Elberfeld and Barmen, from the financial aristocracy to *épicerie* was represented, only the proletariat being excluded.[12]

Proletarian participation was presumably unthinkable, as middle-class participants would surely have stormed out, and the police would have considered it a disorderly gathering by definition. But for the middle classes – in a respectably organized gathering – Engels reported that communism was a tremendous draw. He considered them to be potentially favourable to the communist cause, as they had been frightened into intellectual curiosity and political action by outbreaks of working-class violence against employers and landowners. Even if the police were successful in banning further meetings as seditious, he expected that communist publications would henceforth be voraciously sought and widely read.

Engels was not yet, however, in direct contact with a working-class audience. 'What the proletariat does we know not and indeed could hardly know,' he wrote to Marx from Barmen. Though he was anxious to show them the communist way towards 'the free development and exercise of their human nature and inborn capacities', he dismissed this for the moment as impossible, presumably because of swift police repression – and an even swifter and perhaps more terrible reaction at home. Instead his audience was drawn from the politically liberal and socially philanthropic middle classes.

Engels's speeches of February 1845 were themselves published in August in a radical Rhineland magazine, and his verdict on the episode was a model of political calculation. He commented that middle-class schemes to dupe the working classes with savings banks, premiums and prizes for the best workers were mere hypocrisy and sham philanthropy, rightly exposed to ridicule by communists who had found a rare opportunity – 'in a country of patriarchal police government' – to gain a public hearing. But in the local societies to relieve working-class distress the twin dangers inherent in the communists' position began to surface. Their rationalist allies deserted them, because the middle classes feared a red revolution, and the Prussian government wound up the groups altogether, because it feared democratic activity.[13]

WIDER NETWORKS

After Engels moved to Brussels in early 1845 the framework for his political activity shifted somewhat. In Belgium he could contact working-class communists and socialists directly, if not always openly, and he could pursue the organizational means to spread communist information throughout the émigré community in Belgium and France. Expatriate German labourers were working in what he considered to be more advanced conditions in industry than those employed in Germany, and so in his view they ought to be more receptive to communist and socialist ideas. Socialist and communist ideas were in any case more sophisticated in France and Belgium than in Germany, so the new class politics would be that much more potent. Émigré socialists and communists, such as Engels, aimed to influence workers in Germany, albeit indirectly for the time being. When the political situation in Germany became favourable, a network of socialists and communists – both middle-class and working-class in origin – could return, and the development of German socialism and communism would then advance in step with the most progressive wings of the movement.

Engels worked with Marx in founding a Communist Correspondence Committee in Brussels in early 1846, and similar committees were founded in London, Paris, Cologne and a number of other towns. The Brussels Committee aimed to contact groups such as the League of the Just. The membership of the League comprised conspiratorial revolutionaries and visionary communists, and its adherents were located in England (where Engels had first made contact) and on the Continent. In turn, the League was closely associated with the German Workers' Educational Society in London, founded in 1840, in order to introduce communism into popular programmes of after-hours study. The League was also a force in the International Society of Fraternal Democrats in London, founded in 1845, which aimed to bring left-wing émigrés into contact with Chartism and middle-class democrats. The Brussels Committee aimed to contact both kinds of group – workers' educational societies and pressure groups for democratic reform.

As Marx was still banned from France, Engels travelled to Paris during 1846 and 1847, and he reported back to the Brussels Committee about his meetings with German workers – cabinet-makers living in the Faubourg St Antoine in Paris. This was a group of 12 to 20, gathering once a week for discussion, at which Engels gave an address:

> Meanwhile I appeared. In order to establish contact with them, I twice discussed conditions in Germany since the French Revolution, my point of departure being the economic relations ... It is a good way of attracting new people for it's entirely public; a fortnight ago the police arrived and wanted to impose a veto but allowed themselves to be placated and did nothing further ... I hope to be able to achieve something with the fellows, for they all have a strong desire for instruction in economics.[14]

Engels's great success with these groups came later in 1846 when he obtained majority support for his definition of communist aims. At these gatherings Engels urged the German workers in Paris to reject mere 'reforms' of production and exchange, which he described as petty-bourgeois panaceas. Communism, which he defined very simply in three points, was the recommended alternative. Communists aimed:

> 1. to ensure that the interests of the proletariat prevail, as opposed to those of the bourgeoisie; 2. to do so by abolishing private property and replacing same with community of goods; 3. to recognise no means of attaining these aims other than democratic revolution by force.[15]

By early 1847 Engels believed that the Paris police, suspicious of his political activities, were watching him with a view to deportation.

He ceased his communist agitation for a time, and by the summer he was back in Brussels where a Democratic Association – similar to the London Fraternal Democrats – was being formed. Writing to Marx, Engels affirmed that 'nothing democratic must be allowed to take place in little Brussels without our participating', and presented the affair as a plot. Middle-class democrats, so he thought, were working against the interests of communists and of the newly formed Brussels German Workers' Society, which was similar to the Educational Society in London. Engels – though professing embarrassment about his youthful appearance – took on the vice-presidency of the Democratic Association, and he and Marx co-operated in publicizing plans – Marx in Brussels and Engels in Paris – for an international democratic congress. The two communists were thus balancing their efforts between working-class and middle-class venues within organizations that were increasingly international – and internationalist – in character. In a letter to Marx, Engels drew out what seemed politically important to him in this Brussels episode:

> The affair [of the Democratic Association] has made a capital impression on the [German Workers'] Society; for the first time they have had a role to play, have dominated a meeting despite all the plotting, and have put in his place a fellow who was trying to set himself up against them . . . They have experienced what it means to be associated . . . The fellows are beginning to feel their own importance.[16]

Through the Brussels Correspondence Committee Engels and Marx were achieving recognition as international communists, and the League of the Just in London approached them proposing membership. They countered with a proposal for reorganization so that the loose conspiratorial group would become an organized political party representing communism as they conceived it. In Engels's phrase their communism was summed up in the 'necessity for revolution by force', very much in the tradition of the French revolutions of 1789 and 1830. In his view this form of mass democratic politics involved constant contact between radical intellectuals and 'the people', *ad hoc* forms of organization changing to meet threats and to consolidate gains, and fierce resistance to counter-revolutionary 'reaction' and backsliding 'liberal' compromises that worked against democracy. At the same time his conception of mass politics excluded plots, conspiracies and ill-prepared insurrections. In a political party – as he conceived it – communism would acquire an organization of dedicated members with as much public presence as possible. Such communists would not be mere 'sympathizers' whose commitments to existing parties of reform would dampen their efforts, nor would they be hare-brained schemers whose antics would lead to mass repression.

An international congress to found the Communist League was agreed, and Engels – as a representative of the German workers in Paris – attended its meetings in London in June 1847. Marx lacked funds to make the journey. Engels arrived with a draft 'confession of faith' or revolutionary catechism, a type of work that was useful in converting workers to the communist cause. Discussions of the 'confession' and draft rules took place after the first congress among members of the League and other communists working within the various local workers' societies and correspondence committees. Engels rewrote his draft as a declaration of the 'principles of communism' in October, retaining the simple question-and-answer format. In November, having returned to Paris, he was elected once again to be a delegate from there to the second congress, as Marx was for Brussels, where his Correspondence Committee had spawned a new section of the still-gestating Communist League. About the mechanics of his own election Engels was honest but not self aware, turning up contradictions but not seeking resolutions. Two questions in particular – the place of intrigue in democratic organizations, and the role of the middle classes in a workers' party – did not detain him in his thought and action:

> After an extremely muddled session I was elected with a 2/3 [majority]. This time I had engaged in no intrigues whatsoever, there had been little opportunity for any. The opposition was merely a fiction; a working man was proposed for appearances' sake, but those who proposed him voted for me.[17]

The second international congress of communists was held later that month in London. Engels wrote cheerfully to Marx about their plans to attend the sessions together, and said, 'This congress must be a decisive one, as this time we shall have it all our own way.' And he took Marx into his confidence about the policy document that he was still drafting for the Party, albeit behind the backs of its general membership in Paris:

> *Strictly between ourselves,* I've played an infernal trick on Mosi [Hess]. He had actually put through a delightfully amended confession of faith. Last Friday at the district [committee of the Communist League] I dealt with this ... I got them to entrust me with the task of drafting a new one which ... will be sent to London *behind the backs of the [communist] communities.* Naturally not a soul must know about this, otherwise we shall all be unseated and there'll be the deuce of a row.[18]

Later he wrote more specifically to Marx about his revisions: 'I think we would do best to abandon the catachetical form and call the thing Communist *Manifesto.* Since a certain amount of history has to be narrated in it, the form hitherto adopted is quite unsuitable.' Engels informed Marx that he had begun with the question 'What is communism?' and had then gone straight on to discuss the proletariat – its history, how it differs from earlier workers, its antithetical relationship with the bourgeoisie, the development of economic crises and, finally, the communists' party policy, 'in so far as it should be made public'. He described his present version as 'wretchedly worded' but said, 'I think I can get it through in such a form that at least there is nothing in it which conflicts with our views.'[19]

As it happened Engels could make certain of this, because at the second congress, where he acted as secretary, he and Marx were charged with preparing a final version, and the two worked together when they were back in Brussels in December. Engels returned to Paris later in the month, and Marx – after repeated entreaties and threats from communist leaders – sent the final manuscript to the printers in January 1848.[20] Because the title substituted 'Party' for 'League', it represented something of a coup for communists such as Engels and Marx, who had steered clear of 'the Just'. The *Manifesto of the Communist Party* was published in London in February 1848 at a printshop owned by a German émigré, and the German Workers' Educational Society covered the costs.

The outbreak of revolution on the continent in the early weeks of 1848 did not so much overtake the *Manifesto* as sweep it up in events. Its co-authors returned quite unexpectedly to Germany. Copies of the document were shipped over from London, and Engels and Marx moved back into communist politics in the Rhineland, editing the *Neue Rheinische Zeitung* from Cologne.

REVOLUTIONARY DEMOCRACY: THEN AND NOW

In 1848 a flysheet based on the *Communist Manifesto,* in which Engels had had a very large hand, listed 17 demands and was widely circulated in Germany and in the German press, reaching an audience from London to the lower Danube. Engels (and Marx) signed the document, which called for a range of reforms amounting to a revolution, all of which were consistent with the political experiences and goals of the early 1840s. These were: a unified German republic, parliamentary government, universal suffrage, free legal services, an end to feudal obligations, complete separation of church and state, free education, nationalization of productive resources such as mines and transport, state mortgages and tenancies, state control of banking and currency, guaranteed livelihood and provision for the incapacitated, curtailment of the right of inheritance and the introduction of graduated rather than flat-rate taxation.[21]

However, what is generally not detailed now, as it was much more obvious to democrats of the time, is the nature of the enemy: authoritarian, non-constitutional monarchies. Among the myriad German states only four constitutions survived the post-Napoleonic reaction, and one of those was abrogated summarily in the 1830s. Otherwise monarchical or clerical authoritarian rule was the norm, sometimes dressed up with appointive or non-popular elective bodies with a 'consultative' role, but no real control. There was censorship, religious interference with conscience and education, arbitrary arrest and punishment, and a stifling conformity and stupidity that was both deeply resented and widely supported. These creaky structures were not up to the horrors of twentieth-century Stalinism, but they are not at all loveable in retrospect merely for the contrast. I think it safe to generalize that in 1848 as in 1989 they were perceived as outdated, inefficient and embarrassing by democrats, inconsistent with the ambitions of nationalists, and a focus for all kinds of discontent. All the 1848 revolutions were in a sense unsuccessful, in that reactionary, authoritarian or only mildly reformed regimes succeeded the popular meetings and constituent assemblies of the heady days of the '48ers. Constitutional rule did not reach Germany until the 1860s, France till the 1870s, and further east not till after the First World War. It should quickly be said that these constitutions were not especially liberal by late twentieth-century standards.

During the 1840s Engels and Marx did not merely write but also spoke, and not just to workers. In fact workers were a difficult audience to reach as meetings were regularly broken up by the police (whether of Prussia, Belgium or France) as threats to public order. Arguably the more effective politics pursued by the two was with the various democratic societies that they joined and promoted; those societies of 'fraternal democrats' were, of course, semi-clandestine as even semi-constitutional rulers in Belgium and France had little liking for such agitation. Thus Engels and Marx involved themselves in a dual strategy, playing both sides of the class divide.

This is hardly more remarkable than the strategy pursued by other democrats who played both sides of a nationalist divide, making strategic alliances and temporary common cause with 'figures' or 'elements' or even 'cells' working for some form of liberation based on language, 'race' or ethnicity, or historic occupation of territory. This, too, should sound familiar to us as we assess 'what happened' in 1989 and subsequently; anti-Stalinism made common cause temporarily possible among the varied nationalities and political factions of Eastern Europe. Engels, more than Marx, was willing to play a nationalist card politically; but both were about as wholeheartedly committed to popular sovereignty as one could reasonably expect.

Where Engels and Marx differed from most of their democratic allies was in their economic policy, where even in the short term they argued for 'despotic inroads on the right to property'. Most of their strategic bedfellows wanted an expansion of rights to private property at the expense of feudalism both aristocratic and communal, and these propertied democrats were not interested in conceding resources or rights to the poor, working class or otherwise.

Popular democrats, after pressuring their authoritarian rulers, also had a large stake in continuing public order and the legal system, so they had a strong incentive to cooperate with large elements of the surviving political structure; they did not need Engels and Marx or any other working-class communists or radicals or idealists or utopians as allies at all in any continuing sense. This should also sound familiar in the present context as reformed and renamed communist parties and familiar political figures reappear in Eastern European politics with popular support or acquiescence, and as a sense of betrayal develops among those who had hoped, like Engels and Marx, to move the political agenda smartly forward in the direction of egalitarian and cooperative structures in the economy, or those who, rather unlike Engels and Marx, had wanted to push nationalistic demands for border adjustments and ethnic recognition or autonomy in cultural matters.

Constitutional government is difficult to achieve, yet solves few real problems. But without it we get 'Absurdistans', which may have had written constitutions; one very common thread of popular complaint during the recent risings in Eastern Europe was 'they treated us like fools', as respect for the ruled and redress against rulers was notably absent, and public untruth was the norm. It is heartening, and quite amazing, that people will turn out in large numbers and take ultimate risks to defend their dignity, and to interpret the recovery of that dignity in terms of participation in constitutional politics. The August 1991 demonstrations in the Russian Republic demonstrated this yet again.

Of course economic hardship, lack of material prospects and anger at falling behind in every way played a part in provoking mass action, as did the geopolitical shift represented by Mikhail Gorbachev's evident intent to dispose of the Soviet Union's European annex. But Soviet tanks were not the only threat to life and limb – many died in Romania, and economic decline can rumble on for centuries without widespread mass reaction. No rational calculator of self-interest in Eastern Europe could possibly have deduced an increase in individual economic advantage from turning out to support the candlelight demonstrations, human chains or mass occupations of public buildings. Constitutionalism implies power-sharing with citizens, and that implies respect for them and their views.

Any coalition for genuinely constitutional rule is very broad but necessarily temporary; Engels and Marx are correctly located within one, and their differences with their various temporary allies are no stranger or more sinister or outlandish or significant than the similar differences – over economic and nationalistic issues – that arise today. Participants in Civic Forum, New Forum, Citizens Against Violence, or any number of other pressure groups for genuinely constitutional rule, were quite justified in having secondary agendas of their own and admitting to a merely temporary suspension of differences. Many of these coalitions were self-proclaimed 'non-parties' headed by 'non-politicians'. Some of these groups and some of the leaders made a transition to partisan politics; others did not. That was to be expected, and it casts no doubt on the original 'non-party' orientation, which was sincere enough and quite effectual. Engels and Marx considered the Communist League disbanded or necessarily moribund during the events of 1848, as they and their associates practised the kind of open-air, public-meeting, non-sectarian politics associated with the struggle for constitutional rule. At least one of their associates was elected as a deputy in the Frankfurt Parliament, which sat as a constituent assembly for Germany. Only at the end of the struggle, in the spring of 1849, did Engels and Marx take a partisan line, and then only in advising self-defence when workers' interests, and constitutionalism itself, were about to be engulfed by monarchical restoration. The knives were out at that point, and Engels and Marx freely vented their rage on democrats who struggled insufficiently or ineffectually against monarchical reaction, and then cravenly sought to protect themselves and what remained of their secondary agendas by compromising with or capitulating to the *anciens régimes*. But it is surely a disastrous oversimplification to see them as sectarians all through the process, and to disregard their respect for the political as well as the economic achievements of the somewhat liberal if thoroughly commercial classes that influenced the movement for constitutional government.

It must be said, however, that Engels and Marx themselves did little to remind anyone of their political practice as democrats or to incorporate much of their democratic views in their political writings. The theoretical support for constitutional democracy was embedded in their journalism, which presumed that the basic groundwork for constitutionalism was already receiving adequate publicity and that readers of the *Rheinische* or *Neue Rheinische Zeitung* wanted or needed a radical but not impractical gloss on events and a stimulus to further direct action. Whether temporary coalitions for democracy succeed or fail, after the event the participants are more likely to be known for their differences than for their areas of substantive agreement; after all, controversy makes more interesting reading and exciting tale-telling, which is how 'history' reaches us. Narration has a logic or structure of its own, independent of 'events', even as these are conceptualized at the time. Writing 'history' from the point of view and state of knowledge of actual participants is an impossible task; participants do not know who is going to do what next, and no one knows how they are going to function in a narrative plot constructed years later when 'history' actually appears.[22]

After 1849 the situation with respect to the political theory and practice of Engels and Marx as democrats becomes even more difficult to assess, as effectively they cut themselves off from the coalition politics and mass action and publicity in which it would be visible. Neither functioned as a direct participant in the constitutional struggles in Prussia in the early 1860s, by which time some of their younger associates were standing for elected office and beginning to win seats, and many others were pressuring politicians and parties for liberalization of the political system, often through the trade union movement. Engels and Marx had little occasion to repeat the basic justifications for constitutional rule, as they did not participate in the coalitional politics necessary to get it going and promote the further erosion of monarchical rights that genuine constitutionalism requires. Instead they gave advice at a distance through sectarian channels, that is the workers' movements, national and international, and the nascent socialist parties of continental Europe and occasionally elsewhere. While in residence in England they contacted native socialists, but stood aloof from progressive coalitions, feeling unwelcome as foreigners. Circumstances were against their return to Germany; they had problems with citizenship, with finances, with family in England and in Prussia. They found it easier to stay on as émigrés in England and to visit Germany just occasionally for non-political reasons.

Frankly, though, had Engels and Marx had the will to get back into German politics, they could have found a way. They could have pursued a non-party line on constitutionalism, as in 1848, or a partisan line within representative institutions, or a sectarian line as agitators pushing the political agenda towards economic issues related to class inequality – and pulling it away from the nationalist sentiments that cross-cut social class. Instead they offered advice by correspondence from London, a useful meeting place for international socialists needing encouragement, and theoretical works of uncertain political value. In truth Engels and Marx had no theory of the party in or out of revolution, no theory of leadership partisan or otherwise, no theory of the state or administration; nor is there any body of practical decisions taken or followed by them from which their views could be adduced. There are a few angry articles, occasional sketches, specific bits of advice and enigmatic generalities.

This can all be explained away, of course. Had they been practical politicians Marx would never have written his books (as much as he did), and Engels could not have supported him financially (and kept himself in the style to which he had become accustomed). Both were bitter about what they regarded as betrayals in the politics of 1848–49, and neither wanted anything further to do with parties.

Their participation in the German socialist movement, before, during and after its period of illegality, was distant and minimal, consisting of advice, mostly by correspondence. Probably Marx did not want to put his wife and children through any more upheavals, expulsions and police surveillance; Engels never broke with his parents and siblings and seems to have had a fine regard for their feelings as burghers of Wuppertal. Increasing age was perhaps a factor, though the foundation of the non-Lassallean and pro-Marx German Social Democratic Party in 1869 coincided with Engels's retirement from business – at 49 years of age, and Marx was then 51. This is not to berate them for the choices that they made, but to emphasize that their views – as they survive in the written record – must be read against a political background that includes their somewhat peculiar circumstances. From our point of view these texts are in a dialogue with a 'silence' that requires interpretation; 'reading the words on the page' is never sufficient.

Constitutionalism, however popularly supported, is not going to satisfy everyone in terms of economic policy, nationalistic aspirations and the mechanics of power-sharing. But it seems to me to be the key to the upheavals of 1989 and 1848, and altogether unfortunate to take it for granted. Anti-Stalinist it is, but it is no creation of the last fifty years. What disappoints me particularly is that there is so little consideration, in the literature on Eastern Europe or elsewhere, of what might be done in specific terms to make constitutional rule more workable. Parliamentary systems and partisan politics are rather taken for granted, whereas they could be more excitingly redefined. Voting procedures, the mechanics of representation, unified or devolved government, referenda and consultation, the number of offices open to election – these are what matter in practical politics in democratic countries. But too frequently constitutionalism is ossification, and the documents as negotiated represent a low common denominator of agreement among partisan representatives. Party politicians are necessarily concerned to exclude citizens from the powers and rights that they wish to share out, concurrently or alternately, among themselves. The law of oligarchy is not necessarily an iron one, but it seems depressingly resilient. While the enthusiastic agreement on generalities that characterizes mass politics must inevitably give way to disagreement on specifics, there ought to be some way to fuel compromise with idealism rather than cynicism.

I have argued that Engels and Marx were democrats of a largely undiscovered and somewhat reticent variety. Did their work undermine constitutionalism? In their own time, they supported it and probably had some effect; their criticisms of it were not influential on anyone with any great prospects for undermining it. Later, of course, their criticisms of 'bourgeois democracy' were highlighted at the expense of their support for constitutional politics as such. As this was done by other people for reasons of their own, Engels and Marx can hardly be held responsible. Yet they did argue that emerging forms of constitutional rule would prove inadequate in economic terms, as class struggle would be sharpened; yet class struggle within a democratic framework could also force or win an amelioration of working-class poverty, and Engels and Marx promoted a socialist politics in their own time on this basis. The extent to which constitutional democracy is consistent with or indeed requires the unregulated, semi-regulated or welfare-supplemented market economy was the problem that preoccupied Engels from an early age, and it is still the pre-eminent issue today.

Notes

In the notes below the following abbreviations have been employed:

MEGA² Karl Marx and Friedrich Engels, *Gesamtausgabe* (Berlin: Dietz Verlag, 1972– (series in progress)).

CW Karl Marx and Frederick Engels, *Collected Works* (London: Lawrence & Wishart, 1975– (series in progress)).

1. This chapter is derived from revised and rewritten material previously published in Terrell Carver, *Friedrich Engels: His Life and Thought* (London: Macmillan, 1989), Chs 4 and 6, and 'Marx, Engels and European Democracy: 1848/1989', *Political Theory Newsletter* (Canberra), pp. 130–7.
2. I/3-Apparat MEGA² 685.
3. W.O. Henderson, *Life of Friedrich Engels*, 2 vols (London: Frank Cass, 1976), Vol. 1, pp. 20–6. I/3-Apparat MEGA² 1051–85.
4. 2 CW 368–82.
5. 3 CW 389.
6. 3 CW 513.
7. 6 CW 56.
8. 38 CW 172.
9. 4 CW 647.
10. 6 CW 5, 75–6.
11. 38 CW 23.

12. 4 CW 237–40; 38 CW 10, 22–4.
13. 38 CW 30, 569.
14. 38 CW 61–2.
15. 38 CW 81–2.
16. 38 CW 128.
17. 38 CW 143.
18. 38 CW 138–9.
19. 38 CW 149.
20. For a textual comparison of the *Manifesto* and Engels's drafts, see Terrell Carver, *Marx and Engels: The Intellectual Relationship* (Brighton: Harvester/Wheatsheaf, 1983), pp. 78–94.
21. 7 CW 3–7.
22. For a wide-ranging and polemical discussion of some of these issues, see Alex Callinicos, *Theories and Narratives: Reflections on the Philosophy of History* (Cambridge: Polity, 1995), Ch. 2.

2

Engels: Revolutionary Realist?

Andrew Collier

By the time of his death in 1895, Engels was a revered elder statesman of the Second International. The SPD in particular took his opinions seriously, accepting, if somewhat reluctantly, his amendments to its party programme at Erfurt in 1891. Yet this party, and most of the other supposedly Marxist parties in the International, behaved as reformist parties, supported their national governments in mutual slaughter in 1914, and survive today as parties dedicated not even to the reform of capitalism, but to its management. Was Engels himself implicated in this process? Some things that he said in his later years can be read as a retreat from the revolutionary politics in which he had been engaged in 1848; in his 'Introduction' to Marx's *Class Struggles in France* he certainly pleaded for a realistic recognition of the tendencies adverse to revolution in contemporary history. Was this the beginning of the slippery slope (or first rung of the ladder, depending on your point of view) that led to the 'new realism' of modern social democracy? In this essay I will first analyse the structure of the Marxist case for revolution and the way the argument has been 'played backwards' by social democrats; then I will look at the text of Engels's 'Introduction' to see what he is arguing there; I shall then relate this to his most systematic account of the projected revolution, in *Anti-Dühring*; finally, I shall ask what relevance this has for socialists today.

I

The structure of the Marxist case for revolutionary socialism seems to me to be as follows:

Desideratum 1 (humanitarian position): Capitalism has produced enough wealth for poverty to be abolished if it were used properly – so it should be used in such a way.

Obstacle 1 (economic constraint): This can't be done, since the laws of the market determine a different distribution and use of that wealth.

Desideratum 2 (interventionist position): Then the government should interfere with market mechanisms to ensure that the wealth is not used and distributed in accordance with their dictates, but on humanitarian lines.

Obstacle 2 (class rule constraint): The government can't do so, because the power of vested interests over it is too great.

Desideratum 3 (socialist position): Then the vested interests must be expropriated, and democracy armed with economic power.

Obstacle 3 (political constraint): An elected government could not do so, because the unelected parts of the state apparatus – army, bureaucracy, police, etc. – are more powerful than any elected assembly, and are tied by internal structure and class interest to the vested economic interests; they would overthrow the elected government rather than let it expropriate those interests.

Desideratum 4 (revolutionary socialist position): Then anyone committed to the foregoing desiderata must be prepared to fight, to defeat the state apparatus and replace it by an inherently democratic one (workers' councils, people's militia and so on) which could not be used against the people.

In order to be convincing, this argument needs some factual backup: first of all, poverty needs to be described to show that it is clearly an evil; secondly, the three constraints must be shown to be real by pointing to various historical facts about economics, sociology and politics, and by analysing the causes of these facts. I am confident that any decent person who has kept their eyes and ears open could be convinced of these points quite easily.

But even so, the case for revolutionary socialism is not watertight; it collapses if it can be shown either that revolution is not possible, or that while possible it would lead to greater evils than it was designed to suppress. Once one is convinced of one of these points, the argument for socialist revolution gets played backwards – and this reversed argument corresponds fairly closely to the stages through which social democracy has passed: (a) the parliamentary road to socialism is tried, but the political constraint prevents it; (b) the social democrats retreat to an interventionist welfare economic policy, but at some point vested interests obstruct this too; (c) the social democrats retreat to a position of 'humane' management of capitalism, i.e. management inspired by humane ideals which they are impotent to implement because of market forces.

At this point an impatient revolutionary socialist may say: never mind the constraints, they do not really exist, they are a reifying illusion; if we just have the *will* to make a revolution, we can: this is the meaning of Gramsci's phrase 'the revolution against [Marx's] *Capital*' which he applied to the Soviet Revolution despite the opinions of its leaders, on the grounds of its supposed voluntarism. There are three things wrong with this voluntaristic defence of the possibility of revolution. Firstly, the constraints are real whether or not you recognize them, as those who ignore them will discover when they collide with them. If pessimism of the intellect is realistic, then optimism of the will is rash. Secondly, if there were no real constraints on what was historically possible the first of the above arguments for revolutionary socialism would not even get started, for they depend at each step on the presence of constraints which only more radical action can abolish; there would be no case for revolution or even for socialism, since goodwill would be enough to solve all our problems. And thirdly, when voluntarism does by chance come to power, it leads to disasters of another kind: 'there are no fortresses that communists cannot storm' – Stalin's slogan that led to more lives being lost in the building of Magnitogorsk than in the Battle of Stalingrad. So socialist politics must answer the question: under what circumstances, if any, is a socialist revolution possible (and, we may add, a lesser evil than its alternatives)? Here Engels has something to say.

II

Engels's 'Introduction' to Marx's *Class Struggles in France* bears the date 6 March 1895, only a few months before his death. Eduard Bernstein saw it as a political testament in which Engels repudiates his revolutionary past and endorses the reformist practice of German social democracy. It had in fact been published with several of the more revolutionary statements cut out by the elder Liebknecht. But even with these restored, it is clearly a defence of the SPD's practice at the time, and a warning against rash revolutionary outbreaks. Yet nothing in it envisages the prospect of the capitalist class surrendering its power without a fight. Its argument can be summarized in six points.

1. *A retrospect on the revolutions of 1848.* It had appeared that although the proletariat was a minority, it was the natural leader of less organized and resolute classes among the oppressed (peasantry and petty bourgeoisie) together with which it formed a majority. But in fact it was nowhere near big enough to lead a revolution. Not until France and Germany were industrialized was a proletarian revolution on the cards. Even a majority proletariat, though, will need allies, as Engels later says:

> By the end of the century we shall conquer the greater part of the middle section of society, petty bourgeois and small peasants, and grow into the decisive power in the land, before which all other powers will have to bow, whether they like it or not.
>
> (p. 189[1])

So by 1895, it seems, the reasons which made revolution impossible in 1848 no longer operate.

2. *The effectiveness of street fighting is symbolic, not military*:

> Even in the classic time of street fighting . . . the barricade produced more of a moral than a material effect. It was a means of shaking the steadfastness of the military. If it held out until this was attained, then victory was won; if not, there was defeat.
>
> (pp. 184–5)

In other words, confrontation with the military can only succeed if the soldiers come over to the side of the people, or at least refuse to fire on them; it cannot come by the superior might of the people. The mystique of 'action not words' which attaches to street fighting is quite misplaced; street fighting is not so much 'direct action' as indirect words, a way of telling the soldiers that the people have had enough.

> For [the insurgents] it was solely a question of making the troops yield to moral influences, which, in a fight between the armies of two warring countries do not come into play at all, or do so to a much less degree. If they succeed in this, then the troops fail to act, or the commanding officers lose their heads, and the insurrection wins.
>
> (p. 183)

But if they fail, it is always defeated.

3. *The shift of odds in favour of the military.* On this issue, Engels – 'the General', as he was known to his comrades – shows how a historical materialist should approach the 'human slaughter industry' (see below); just as the mode of production and the economic relations between classes are forced to change by changes in the technology of production, so the mode of war and the military relations between classes (and one might add, between nation states) are changed by changes in military technology. Marx had once written to Engels:

> Is there anywhere where our theory that the *organisation of labour is determined by the means of production* is more brilliantly confirmed than in the human slaughter industry? It would really be worth while for you to write something about it (I have not the necessary knowledge) which I could insert under your name as an appendix to my book [that is *Capital,* vol. 1 – A.C.].
> (Letter, 7 July 1866, in *Selected Works in Two Volumes,* p. 379)

It is regrettable that Engels, who was the specialist on military matters in Marx's circle (hence his nickname) did not get round to doing this, since it would have gone a long way towards filling the big gap in Marx's political thought – the theory of the state apparatus as possessing its own material substructure in military technology, and its own dynamic in competition between nation states. But at least in this text Engels shows how military technology enters history as an explanatory factor in political struggle:

> By means of the railways, the garrisons can, in twenty-four hours, be more than doubled, and in forty-eight hours they can be increased to huge armies ... In 1848 the smooth-bore percussion muzzle-loader, today the small-calibre magazine breech-loading rifle, which shoots four times as far, ten times as accurately and ten times as fast as the former ... At that time the pick-axe of the sapper for breaking through walls; today the dynamite cartridge.
> (p. 185)

Effective weapons are correspondingly more difficult for civilians to obtain (or at least for propertyless civilians to obtain). This shift has of course gone much further in the twentieth century. On one point, the history of this terrible century has shown Engels to be over-optimistic. He thought that the 'undreamt of efficacy' of weaponry had:

> . . . put a sudden end to the Bonapartist war period and ensured peaceful industrial development, since any war other than a world war of unheard of cruelty and absolutely incalculable outcome had become an impossibility.
>
> (p. 180)

The 'Masters of War' have not been deterred at all by the unheard of cruelty, and not altogether by the incalculable outcome either.

4. *The electoral success of social democracy.* And so to the good news: at every election the SPD had been winning more votes, till it had polled more than a quarter of the votes cast. Even in France, with its revolutionary tradition:

> slow propaganda work and parliamentary activity are being recognised here, too, as the most immediate tasks of the Party. Successes were not lacking. Not only have a whole series of municipal councils been won; fifty Socialists have seats in the Chambers, and they have already overthrown three ministries and a president of the republic.
>
> (p. 188)

For the time being, Engels concludes, this is the sort of work socialists in countries with a wide suffrage must concentrate on. But for how long?

5. *A 'pro-slavery rebellion'?* In his preface to the English edition of *Capital* in 1886, Engels had written that in Marx's opinion:

> At least in Europe, England is the only country where the inevitable social revolution might be effected entirely by peaceful and legal means. He certainly never forgot to add that he hardly expected the English ruling classes to submit, without a 'pro-slavery rebellion', to this peaceful and legal revolution.
>
> (*Capital*, vol. 1, p. 113)

Although by 1895 Engels was extending this possibility to some continental countries, he had not changed his mind about the 'pro-slavery rebellion' (the phrase alludes to the American Civil War). Thus he says that the 'parties of order' were crying:

> Legality is the death of us; whereas we, under this legality, get firm muscles and rosy cheeks and look like eternal life. And if we are not so crazy as to let ourselves be driven to street fighting in order to please them, then nothing else is finally left for them but themselves to break through this legality so fatal to them.
>
> (p. 189)

I think it is clear that Engels means this warning to be taken seriously: the revolution may be *legal,* since an electoral victory may precede it; but it can't in the end be *non-violent,* because the possessing class will not give up its wealth without a struggle – a civil war if necessary.

6. *A historical analogy*. Engels concludes with a surprising historical instance: Christianity in the Roman Empire. It carried on underground agitation, came out into the open when it felt strong enough, survived persecution and infiltrated the armed forces until whole legions were Christian. Diocletian could not stamp it out.

> And it was so effective that seventeen years later the army consisted overwhelmingly of Christians, and the succeeding autocrat of the whole Roman Empire, Constantine, called the Great by the priests, proclaimed Christianity as the state religion.
>
> (p. 192)

The parallel is presumably that in this case an organization of the oppressed endured its tribulations and became an official organization without an insurrection, its numerical predominance within the army being the crucial factor. But of course it did not, as the socialist parties hoped to do, oust the ruling class and reconstruct society. Instead, it was coopted by Constantine to be the religion of the Empire, and adapted to the Empire rather than transforming it as, by its own principles, it arguably should have done. Not that this cooption was easy: the following age was the age of the great Doctors of the Church, who say quite rude things about empire, slavery and private wealth. Augustine – the most politically moderate of them – regarded kingdoms without justice as 'gangs of criminals on a large scale', and his accounts of Roman law courts leave no doubt that this applied to the Empire.[2] He tells us:

> It was a witty and truthful rejoinder which was given by a captured pirate to Alexander the Great. The king asked the fellow,

> 'What is your idea, in infesting the sea?' And the pirate answered, with uninhibited insolence, 'The same as yours, in infesting the earth! But because I do it with a tiny craft, I'm called a pirate: because you have a mighty navy, you're called an emperor.'
>
> (*City of God*, Book IV, Chapter 4)

For the attacks on slavery and private wealth preached by St Basil the Great, St John Chrysostom and Pope Gregory the Great, see Luxemburg's essay 'Socialism and the Churches' (in *Rosa Luxemburg Speaks*). Chrysostom's plea that a Christian empire would be a communist empire is particularly trenchant. Unsurprisingly, he died in exile, although as Archbishop of Constantinople he had been the leading bishop of the entire church.

Nevertheless, the 'Christian' empire remained an empire based on slavery and unequal wealth. Presumably it was not Engels's wish that, on analogy with Constantine's reform, the Kaiser should adopt dialectical materialism as the official ideology to please the socialists in his legions, and retain the monarchy and capitalist economy intact! Yet for the example to be relevant to the point at all, Engels must at least be saying that numerical predominance in the state apparatus, chiefly the army, is crucial to the possibility of revolution.

The central point that comes through Engels's argument is that the paralysing of the military strength of the capitalist state apparatus, either by refusal of the troops to fire on the people, or better by the troops going over to the people's side, is a necessary condition of any successful socialist revolution. His examples suggest three possible ways in which this might be effected: (a) the soldiers are themselves converted to socialism; (b) they will not fire at such large numbers of civilians, whom they recognize as their own people; (c) they doubt the political legitimacy of the counter-revolutionary action. In terms of socialist strategy, the first indicates the recruitment of soldiers, the second the achievement of mass support which cannot be thought to be 'rent-a-mob' or 'a few extremists'; the third suggests that that the old order must be recognized as morally bankrupt – one possible reason being that it had lost the election, and its call for military violence was therefore illegal. Engels speaks at one point of military counter-revolution being possible when the military were 'unhampered by political considerations'. The popular and elected character of their socialist opponents could under some circumstances be a political consideration that would hamper them.

Though we shouldn't reckon on it – the fate of Allende should remind us of that.

Engels in 1895 emerges then as what he was in 1848, a revolutionary democrat:

(a) *revolutionary* in that he did not believe that power could pass from the haves to the have-nots without the haves putting up armed resistance, and that this should not deter us from seeking that transfer of class power, only make us prepare for the showdown. One of the phrases deleted by Liebknecht read 'not to fritter away this daily increasing shock force in advance guard fighting, but to keep it intact until the day of decision' (p. 189);

(b) and *democratic* in that he did not believe in the possibility of a revolution without overwhelming popular support, from the proletarian majority, from broad sections of the intermediate strata, and from a considerable section of the personnel of the state apparatus. Much greater popular support is required to win a revolution than to win an election, which latter can be done in any constituency – in the UK at the time of writing, for example, with the grudging vote of 34 per cent of those who bother to vote at all, if the other two parties are evenly divided.

III

So far I have referred almost exclusively to one text of Engels's, and a critic might retort that this was a short and unrepresentative document, written by a man at death's door and possibly entertaining fond hopes and vain fears which he would have dismissed in his prime. I think on the contrary that in so far as one can deduce strategy or tactics from a theoretical text such as the chapter on socialist theory in *Anti-Dühring*, that strategy and those tactics would be consonant with what Engels says in the 'Introduction' to *Class Struggles in France*. This chapter, reprinted as part of *Socialism, Utopian and Scientific*, is the most concise account of the laws of motion of capitalism, its contradictions and the conditions of their resolution to come from the pen either of Marx or Engels, and it is surprisingly relevant today. In it he traces the origin of two contradictions of capitalism from a common source in the dispersion into private hands of productive resources which are socialized in nature. One of the contradictions is class exploitation and struggle; the other is the contradiction between large-scale planning within each enterprise and the anarchy of the market, through which compulsive laws unintended by anyone assert themselves. Corresponding to these two contradictions, the emancipation projected through socialism has two aspects: it is the emancipation of the proletariat and the exploited classes generally from exploitation; and it is the emancipation of humankind at large from the constraints of market forces, an emancipation which would enable humankind to collectively control its destiny within the limits set by nature.[3] Throughout classical Marxism, but with particular clarity in the chapter referred to, liberation involves the recovery by humankind of forces which were created by human actions, but which have hitherto escaped human control.

> As long as we obstinately refuse to understand the nature and the character of these productive forces – and this understanding goes against the grain of the capitalist mode of production and its defenders – so long these forces are at work in spite of us, in opposition to us, so long they master us, as we have shown above in detail.
>
> But when once their nature is understood, they can, in the hands of the producers working together, be transformed from master demons into willing servants.
>
> (*Anti-Dühring*, p. 331)

Although revolution is primarily the work of the proletariat, humankind in general is in some measure the beneficiary, sharing in the exercise of powers to be acquired by it – powers which are under capitalism the powers of no one, not even the capitalist. A modern instance of this alienation of powers would be what is sometimes called the 'tragedy of the commons', namely that in a society where social powers are dispersed among competing individuals, it is each for himself and *no one* for all: not because the individuals are 'selfish', but because the constraints of individual survival in a competitive world prevent individual competitors from attending to common affairs, and there is no common agency with the power to do so – hence those resources which are inherently common are left unattended to, and wantonly destroyed by the action of competing individuals. Strange as it may sound to some Green comrades, it is not human dominion over our environment which has led to environmental disaster, but lack of that dominion – combined with a great increase in human powers (which, so long as they are dispersed between competing agents, do not amount to dominion, but rather are subject to the impersonal 'dominion' of the market).[4] In terms of economic structure, the dispersedness of powerful competing agents is '*organization of production in the individual workshop and the anarchy of production in society generally*' (*Anti-Dühring*, p. 374).

The recognition of a common human (one might add, not only human) interest in socialism alongside particular class interests certainly does not lead Engels to expect capitalists to welcome socialism – their particular interests far outweigh their share in the common interest. But it may well lead him to expect very widespread agreement about socialist measures, and this is confirmed by his occasional use of society-talk alongside class-talk. When capitalism leads to monopoly '. . . exploitation is so palpable that it must break down. No *nation* will put up with production conducted by trusts, with so barefaced an exploitation of the *community* by a small band of dividend-mongers' (p. 329; my emphasis – A.C.). I wish I could share Engels's confidence in the clearsightedness of the majority. But such passages do suggest that Engels saw socialist revolution as in the interest of a majority larger than the proletariat, and the supposed 'inevitability' of the revolution is simply a function of this overwhelming support, combined with a belief that you can't fool all the people all the time. The model of revolution implicit here is the same as that explicit in the 1895 'Introduction'. Not a minority vanguard seizing power with the passive support of the majority, but an organized proletarian majority, recognized by a majority of non-proletarians (intermediate strata) as representing their interests too, and opposed only by a handful of profiteers unable to command the allegiance of their own state's troops.

IV

How are we to assess Engels's prospectus for socialist revolution? We must ask three related questions. Is his analysis of the tendencies at work a realistic one? Does subsequent history confirm his predictions? And are his prescriptions for socialist revolution acceptable? The third question partly depends on the answers to the first two, but there is one aspect of it that we can answer in advance. One debate among interpreters of Marxism has been about whether it is an essentially democratic political tradition, advocating revolution based on a broad consensus of the popular classes, or whether it aims at the dictatorship of a vanguard party. Most commentators would agree that it is more morally acceptable if the former. And on my analysis Engels at least is part of the democratic tradition. However, for Engels himself, the question was not whether his democratic views got him classed as a 'goody' rather than a 'baddy'. It was not whether the broad democratic revolution was the *best* kind, but whether it was the *only possible* kind. He clearly thought that it was. What, then, does subsequent history show?

Engels makes predictions which can be classified into three types: (a) *tendential* predictions – accounts of already present mechanisms in society which will continue to develop in a given direction; (b) *constraint* predictions – claims about what is and is not possible under specified conditions; and (c) the prediction of proletarian revolution on the grounds of its being in the interest of the vast majority (a 'rational choice' prediction, if you like). There are two main tendential predictions: that the proletariat will grow as a proportion of the population, and that military technology will shift the balance of forces in the state's favour. And there are three main constraint predictions: that socialism cannot be brought about without a revolution, that revolution cannot be made without the organized support of a large majority, and that revolution cannot be made against the military.

The tendential predictions were based on a very plausible analysis of the situation at the time, and they have stood up well in the twentieth century. Despite claims that the proletariat is on the numerical decline – claims that depend for such plausibility as they have partly on concentrating only on the English-speaking world, and partly on defining the proletariat impressionistically (proletarians eat fish and chips, drink beer, wear cloth caps and inhabit Lowryesque landscapes, and so on), rather than structurally as Marx and Engels would – in fact the proletariat has become a majority of humankind for the first time in the last quarter of the twentieth century. And the advent of machine guns, tanks, rockets and warplanes has made both the prospect of civil war immeasurably more horrifying, and the likelihood of victory by the side with the best equipped army immeasurably greater. This would seem to strengthen Engels's case both against premature revolution and for the possibility of broadly based revolution.

But when we come to discuss the actual history of revolutions and failed revolutions in the twentieth century, the tally is rather more complicated. The impossibility of non-revolutionary roads to socialism has been pretty well supported by events such as the overthrow of Cheddi Jagan in Guyana and Allende in Chile, and the non-exceptional nature of these events is indicated by such things as the revelation of plots to start civil war against Tony Benn if he were ever elected Prime Minister; it is further confirmed by the abandonment of their socialist aims by socialist parties that have been elected to office, which may have been motivated by knowledge of the price of fulfilling their pledges. Revolutions against a still functioning national military force have also been conspicuous by their absence. Revolutions have occurred either led by the military, or in the wake of the defeat of the military by a foreign power, or when the military has been demoralized or divided. The only instance which could be claimed as a counter-example to Engels's hypothesis is the success of a few guerrilla struggles against the national army. This has been possible only in predominantly rural countries, where the old regime is so corrupt that it has in some measure been isolated even from the ruling class. It depends on special conditions, both geographical and hence military-strategic, and socio-political.

There have been a few broad, democratic revolutions, for instance against the dictatorships in Greece and Portugal. What there has not been is a proletarian majority revolution leading to socialism. Engels's negative predictions have been well confirmed; his positive hope for a socialist revolution based on an organized proletarian majority has so far not been fulfilled. This sad absence does not refute Engels's tendential or constraint predictions, but I shall return to its significance.

Revolutions which have been described by their leaders as socialist and which have expropriated private capital have occurred in four ways:

(a) in the single instance of Russia in 1917, after the manner of the revolution that Engels had hoped for in 1848, that is with the organized minority proletariat taking the lead, supported by a peasant majority – though, be it noted, in the wake of a national military defeat;

(b) as military coups;

(c) under the lee of the occupying army of an already 'socialist' country;

(d) as the outcome of a rural guerrilla war.

Perhaps what is most noteworthy about all of them, from the standpoint of evaluating Engels's theories, is that they have all occurred under 'exceptional' circumstances – in the wake of a war, or as part of a decolonization process, or against a dictatorship that has lost its class base. What has never happened, or even threatened to happen, is a revolution motivated simply by the interests of a majority proletariat and its allies which have grown strong enough to oust their oppressors. This indicates the real weakness in Engels's theory: he sees revolution as a normal part of historical development.

This is of course an integral feature of his and Marx's account of history, so a few words are required about it here. The classical Marxist model of revolution as a normal part of history is well known: capitalism grows within feudal society, and when it gets too strong to play second fiddle, it bursts its bonds in a bourgeois revolution; the proletariat grows within capitalist society, while capital becomes more concentrated, until the proletariat bursts its bonds in a socialist revolution. The whole of Second International Marxism looked forwards to revolution as its normal future, as becoming a butterfly is the normal future of a caterpillar. It was seen as sudden change brought about by the accumulation of gradual changes until 'quantity is transformed into quality' and a change of kind takes place. Engels's account of the gradual progress of socialist parties can be tied up with his metaphor of universal suffrage as a thermometer: when it registers boiling point, the time is ripe.[5] This makes it clear that the idea of normal progress leading by itself to revolution is not an aberration of the Second International, but an assumption of Engels too (and indeed of Marx). It can be seen in the way they treated French history as the model for the politics of bourgeois society, as they treated England as the model for its economics. It has some plausibility on the basis of a very long-term look at the transition from feudalism to capitalism, because revolutions have been scattered about that history. But each of those revolutions – the Dutch Revolt, England in the 1640s and again in 1689, America in the 1870s and again in the Civil War, France in 1789 and again in 1848 – each case has its 'exceptional' causes, without which it is unthinkable.

If we come to regard revolutions as *always exceptional*[6] do we have to abandon Engels's assumption that they are generated by normal historical tendencies? Not entirely, for these tendencies created the necessary conditions of revolution, and determined what types of revolution are on the cards when exceptional circumstances do arise. Neither do we have to abandon revolutionary aims, since exceptional circumstances can be relied on to crop up from time to time. But we have to abandon the expectation that a socialist revolution will occur in the normal course of events if socialist movements only go on getting more and more supporters more and more organized. Revolutionary situations always come unexpected and unbidden by anyone. At most, socialists can know how to take the opportunity they provide, and what measures will be necessary at the post-revolutionary opening of the socialist road. We cannot have a strategy for bringing about revolutionary situations, but only for responding to them. This suggests that, for all its faults, some of which I have referred to here, the Second International was not wrong in one common aspect of its politics: the distinction between maximum and minimum programmes: maximum – a socialist programme to be pursued in the event of a revolution; and minimum – a programme (necessarily less than socialist in content) to be pressed for in the absence of such a situation.

To summarize: Engels wanted to be a revolutionary realist, avoiding adventurism on the one hand and reformism on the other; he succeeded in so far as his theory of constraints is concerned: he was right about the real constraints which prevent both any non-revolutionary route to fair shares in the world's wealth, and any revolution against an intact state machine. His projection of the tendencies both making revolution easier (growth of the proletariat, concentration of capital) and making it more difficult (advancing military technology) was also realistic. He saw that no revolution could be made without winning over or neutralizing the military, but he failed to see the possibility that this could occur without the commitment of the vast majority to revolution; he therefore failed to foresee revolutions made with minority participation only. In all probability he would not have regarded the outcomes of these revolutions as socialism anyway. And while he was free from the voluntarist illusions that revolutions could be *made*, he failed to see that they are necessarily exceptional since they depend on the prior breakdown of the old regime, a breakdown which cannot itself be created by the workers' movement, however large and well organized.

Despite these oversights, Engels's approach to revolution – his methodology – is exemplary realism: it focuses on the constraints and tendencies generated by real structures, without wishful or wilful thinking on the one hand, or the empiricist assumption that we can't know what is possible until it happens on the other.

Notes

1. All page references for Engels's 'Introduction to *The Class Struggles in France*' are to Volume 2 of the two volume *Selected Works of Marx and Engels*.
2. See, for example, *City of God*, Book XIX, Chapter 6. Christopher Kirwan, in his *Augustine*, reads this passage, in which Augustine laments the practice of judicial torture, as ending in mere resignation. I suspect that he has missed the irony of Augustine's references to the 'wise man' in this passage.
3. That he took the limits set by nature seriously is shown by his remarks in *The Dialectics of Nature*, p. 180.
4. See my *Socialist Reasoning*, Chapter 4, and 'The Inorganic Body and the Ambiguity of Freedom'. See also John O'Neill, *Ecology, Policy and Politics*, pp. 38ff.
5. From Engels's *Origin of the Family, Private Property and the State*:

   > Universal suffrage is the gauge of the maturity of the working class. It cannot and never will be anything more in the present day state; but that is sufficient. On the day the thermometer of universal suffrage registers boiling point among the workers, both they and the capitalists will know what to do.
   >
   > (*Selected Works in One Volume*, p. 589)

6. One of the lessons of Althusser's use of 'overdetermination' is that the 'exceptional circumstances' which give any revolution its peculiarities are not 'exceptional', that is there will never be a revolution without them. But Althusser does not seem to realize that he is arguing against Marx, Engels and Lenin here. See especially his 'On the Materialist Dialectic' in *For Marx*.

References

Althusser, Louis, *For Marx* (Penguin, Harmondsworth, 1969).
Augustine, Aurelius, *City of God* (Penguin, Harmondsworth, 1972).
Collier, Andrew, *Socialist Reasoning* (Pluto, London, 1990).
Collier, Andrew, 'The Inorganic Body and the Ambiguity of Freedom', *Radical Philosophy*, No. 57, 1991.
Engels, Frederick, *Anti-Dühring* (Progress Publishers, Moscow, 1969).
Engels, Frederick, *Dialectics of Nature* (Progress Publishers, Moscow, 1934).
Engels, Frederick and Marx, Karl, *Selected Works in Two Volumes* (Lawrence & Wishart, London, 1942).

Engels, Frederick and Marx, Karl, *Selected Works in One Volume* (Lawrence & Wishart, London, 1968).
Kirwan, Christopher, *Augustine* (Routledge, London, 1989).
Luxemburg, Rosa, *Rosa Luxemburg Speaks*, ed. Mary-Alice Waters (Pathfinder Press, New York, 1970).
Marx, Karl, *Capital*, Vol. I (Penguin, Harmondsworth, 1976).
O'Neill, John, *Ecology, Policy and Politics* (Routledge, London, 1993).

3

Engels Without Dogmatism

John O'Neill

MARX, ENGELS AND CHILDREN'S HOUR

Both friends and critics of Marxism standardly subscribe to what might be characterized as the Andy Pandy theory of the relationship between Marx and Engels. I refer here to a children's programme, thankfully no more, in which the two central characters, Andy Pandy and Teddy, live in the same box and dance the same steps to the same tune: however, stiff limbed Teddy always does so badly, normally falling flat on his face, that Andy Pandy has to be asked to show him how to do it properly. (The only female character, Looby Loo, is silent throughout and moves only when the menfolk leave, but that is another story.) Thus it is with the relationship between Marx and Engels: the stiff and ponderous Engels attempts the same lines of thought as his intellectually more supple partner, but never quite does it properly, producing crude, dogmatic and indefensible versions of the ideas that Marx, especially in his notebooks (and Marx has become a theorist read through his notebooks), defends in more subtle and undogmatic forms. It is not my aim in this paper to show that there is no truth in the Andy Pandy theory: I think it may well be right about a number of common matters on which both wrote. I do want here to show it to be wrong about one doctrine defended by both Engels and Marx, that is their shared commitment to scientific socialism.

Concerning scientific socialism, the Andy Pandy theory of the relationship between Marx and Engels becomes part of a wider story about the decline of Marxism in the late nineteenth and early twentieth century. The story is one of the descent of Marxist theory into dogmatism and dictatorship. Dogmatic Marxism is standardly traced back to the influence of Engels's defence of scientific socialism and rejection of utopian socialism. Engels's influence is taken to be responsible for the dominance of scientific socialism among theorists of the First International. It is often then traced forward to the dogmatics of Stalin, and to the undemocratic politics of the 1930s and 1940s for which they provided the apology. Scientific socialism provides the thread that ties together 'classical Marxism' and 'Soviet dictatorship'. Ball is typical: 'The missing link in the transition from classical Marxian theory to contemporary Soviet practice is to be found in Engels's philosophical labors.'[1] Against this dogmatic and inflexible current of Marxist thought is set the rediscovery of the early humanistic writings of Marx and hence the currents of Western Marxism associated with Korsch, Lukács and the Frankfurt school. The stage is then set for the continued opposition between an open, sophisticated and democratic Marxism that is the intellectual inheritance bequeathed by the unpublished writings of Marx and the dogmatic, vulgar and undemocratic Marxism that was handed down to socialists by Engels.

In this story of Engels's scientific socialism as the missing link between Marxism and dictatorship, the crucial texts that are standardly cited as evidence are those that Engels wrote or began to write during the 1870s: *Anti-Dühring*, the three re-edited chapters of *Anti-Dühring* published as *Socialism: Utopian and Scientific*, and the *Dialectics of Nature*. Thus, for example, Thomas writes:

> 'Scientific socialism' is a phrase used by later Marxists to guarantee methodological certainty and doctrinal orthodoxy of a certain type. The first of these users was Engels, who popularized the phrase in his own essay in *Anti-Dühring* which was published separately as *Socialism, Utopian and Scientific*. Engels was by no means the worst offender, but he may have been the most important . . .[2]

Having thus linked the use of the term 'scientific socialism' with 'methodological certainty' and 'doctrinal orthodoxy' in Engels's texts of the 1870s, the standard move is to distance Marx from those texts. Either Marx is taken to defend a more sophisticated version of the doctrine of scientific socialism, or, more strongly, to have rejected the very concept of scientific socialism.[3] The attempt to distance Marx from Engels's concept of scientific socialism has generated its own detailed historical researches on just how much Marx knew of, or approved of, *Anti-Dühring*: Did Engels 'read the whole manuscript' to Marx as he claimed in the 1885 preface? What evidence is there of a convergence of views in the published correspondence of Engels and Marx in this period? What was in Marx's letters and notes that Eleanor Marx is said to have destroyed because of the possible embarrassment they might have caused Engels?[4] The details about the relationship matter by virtue of the role Engels's scientific socialism plays as the missing link in the larger story of the decline of socialism into dogmatism and dictatorship.

It is this larger story that I want to question in this paper. I do not question the story in order join the ranks of Althusserians in pursuit of the grail of a scientific Marxism purified of humanism and ethical commitments. As I suggest at the end of the paper, one of the major misfortunes for scientific socialism has been its confusion with 'scientistic' socialism, with the consequence that we have to choose either a vision of socialism as just about values or a vision of socialism devoid of any value commitments at all. The Althusserian contrast between the humanistic and scientific Marx sustains the mistaken view that it is this choice that we have to make. The whole project of setting the philosophical Marx of the early writings against the scientific socialism of the later, for the purpose of praising either, is a sterile pursuit and is being increasingly recognized as such. It sheds light neither on the understanding of the development of Marx's writings nor their virtues or vices. Similar points can be made of any simple opposition constructed between Marx and Engels. However, the fine details of the Marx–Engels relationship will not concern me here. My concern is rather to reject the story that Engels's commitment to scientific socialism provides the 'missing link' to dogmatism and dictatorship. The claim that it does is neither philosophically nor historically defensible.

A commitment to scientific socialism has no necessary connection with dogmatic Marxism or with undemocratic politics. The putative connection depends on an assumption of a dogmatic conception of science, that science commits one to 'methodological certainty' and 'doctrinal orthodoxy' to use Thomas's phrases. Not only is that conception of science mistaken, it was explicitly rejected by Engels in the very 1870s texts that are supposed to reveal his orthodoxy and methodological certainty. In both *Anti-Dühring* and *Dialectics of Nature* Engels defends a fallibilist account of science. His defence of scientific socialism in *Anti-Dühring* was aimed precisely against dogmatic conceptions of socialism. Moreover, his discussion of utopian socialism in *Anti-Dühring* is misread if it is understood as an exercise in the straightforward rejection of utopianism. While such a gloss is possible in the later version that appeared, *Socialism: Utopian and Scientific*, in *Anti-Dühring* the discussion of the earlier utopians appears primarily as a work of praise of the 'utopians' against Dühring's dogmatic rejection of their views. Whatever the faults of the texts of the 1870s – and there are many – they are not the exercises in dogmatism they are standardly portrayed as being.[5] In the texts on scientific socialism, Engels isn't always the stiff-limbed partner to Marx he is routinely taken to be.

POPPER, ENGELS AND FALLIBILISM

One of the many myths about the philosophy of science in the second half of this century has been that fallibilism began with Popper, give or take a few philosophical eccentrics like Peirce. Before Popper the philosophy of science languished in the darkness of inductivism and dogmatism. It was believed that there were good arguments called inductive arguments from singular statements describing particular observations to universal statements describing laws of nature. This was believed, despite the acknowledgement that there exists no deductively valid argument from singular statements to universal statements where the quantifier ranges over an infinite domain, and despite Hume's sceptical attack on induction. On the inductivist view, science proceeded by way of the collection of observations from which laws were inferred. This tended to dogmatism, since it appeared to show that you could prove a scientific theory to be true. Then came Popper who 'solved' the problem of induction by dissolving it. While there is no valid argument from singular statements to a universal law that ranges over an infinite domain, there is a deductively valid route to the denial of universal statements from the truth of the negation of singular statements they entail. While there was no good argument from singular statements that could confirm a universal law, there are good arguments for their falsification. With this 'solution' to the problem of induction came a new model of science which was fallibilist. Science proceeds by bold conjectures followed by attempted refutations. So goes the story. It appears in the best of introductions to the philosophy of science.[6]

Consider the following account of the development of science:

> The form of development of natural science, in so far as it thinks, is the *hypothesis*. A new fact is observed which makes impossible the previous method of explaining the facts belonging to the same group. From this moment onwards new methods of explanation

> are required . . . This is not peculiar to natural science, since all human knowledge develops in a much twisted curve; and in the historical sciences also, including philosophy, theories displace one another.[7]

The passage is from Engels's *The Dialectics of Nature*. This fallibilist account of the sciences is also based upon criticism of inductivist conceptions of science.[8] And this is not an isolated exception in Engels's work. Fallibilism permeates the whole of Engels's work on science and philosophy. In particular it is at the heart of the work that is taken to be the classical document of the dogmatism of scientific socialism, Engels's *Anti-Dühring*. His defence of scientific socialism is a defence of open and critical enquiry: 'The knowledge which has an unconditional claim to truth is realized in a series of relative errors; neither the one nor the other can be fully realized except through the unending duration of human existence.'[9] However, while Engels shares a fallibilist account of science with Popper, his starting points are different. Moreover, Engels's position is in the end more convincing than that of Popper.

While fallibilism as such does not start with Popper, the peculiar variant of the doctrine that dominated discussion in the philosophy of science in the late twentieth century does begin with him. Where Popper's fallibilism differs from that of prior fallibilists is in his taking seriously philosophical scepticism. Thus, to fill out the story just told in more detail, Popper's fallibilism begins from a logical interpretation of Hume's sceptical attack on induction. The 'logical' problem of induction, so called, is that it is not deduction: there is no deductively valid argument from a finite set of singular statements, $Fa_1 \rightarrow Ga_1$, $Fa_2 \rightarrow Ga_2 \ldots Fa_n \rightarrow Ga_n$, to a universal statement, $(x)(Fx \rightarrow Gx)$, where the quantifier ranges over an infinite domain. Thus, to quote just one of his many restatements of the logical problem of induction, he writes: 'No number of true test statements would justify the claim that an explanatory universal theory is true'[10] – adding in a footnote that 'an explanatory theory goes beyond even an infinity of singular test statements'.[11] The specific problem of induction that Popper develops from Hume revolves around the non-observability of all spatial and temporal positions. In logical terms, given the infinity of possible temporal and spatial locations of objects and events, we are never justified according to deductive standards in inferring a universal law of nature from singular statements describing those particulars we have observed. Popper 'solves' the problem of induction by denying that science requires induction. There is no good inductive inference. There is no deductively valid path from true singular statements to a universal statement describing a law of nature. There is, however, a deductively valid route from the truth of a singular statement to the denial of a universal law. Given the truth of a singular statement, Fa & -Ga, one can deduce the falsity of the universal statement, (x)(Fx → Gx). The road is then opened to Popper's version of a fallibilist account of science. Science is a form of critical enquiry that develops through conjectures and their refutation. It progresses by the elimination of hypotheses through the most stringent possible empirical tests, and their replacement by new theories that survive such tests and which are then to be subjected to new tests. We learn not through our predictive success, but through the failure of prediction, through error. The elaborations of this account I leave aside. Of interest for present purposes is the route to that theory.

Does Popper solve the problem of induction from which he starts? The answer is that he does not. Popper's 'solution' fails in its own terms, and it fails because of those terms, that is with the attempt to respond to the philosophical sceptic's challenge to induction. If there is a logical problem of induction that is relevant to science it is not the Humean problem from which Popper's journey begins. Popper's Humean problem of induction concerns the uniformity of nature. Given a true universal statement in which the quantifier ranges over a finite domain of instances, i.e. those in the temporal and spatial slice of the universe we have observed, one cannot infer deductively the truth of a universal statement in which the quantifier ranges over all times and places. A universal statement that is true for observed events might not hold at some future moment in time or at some unobserved portion of space. It may be that all the planets of our sun have been observed thus far to trace an elliptical path around the sun: there is no guarantee that tomorrow they might not travel in some other orbit. Nature might not be uniform. Popper's Humean attack on induction is an attack on the rational justifiability of the assumption of the uniformity of nature – that is, that mere changes in space and time are irrelevant to the truth of universal statements. Keynes usefully restates the assumption thus: 'A generalization which is true of one instance must be true of another which *only* differs from the former by reason of its position in time and space.'[12] Popper rejects the rational defensibility of that assumption.[13]

Popper's rejection of the uniformity argument cannot be sustained. The rational pursuit of science according to Popper's own fallibilist canons presupposes the principle of uniformity of nature. It does so in two ways. First, it is assumed in denying that the mere repetition of an experiment is a rational strategy for falsifying laws. The assumption that changes in temporal and spatial position alone could be relevant to the truth of a universal statement is incompatible with what Popper refers to as 'the law of the diminishing returns of repeated tests'. If mere changes in time and space were assumed to be relevant to the truth of a universal statement, then the repetition of an experiment that a putative law has hitherto survived would be a rational strategy in attempting to falsify a law. Nothing rules out the rationality of indefinitely repeating the experiment. There would be no ground for assuming any diminishing returns from repeated tests. Second, without an assumption of uniformity, there is no reason to assume that theory T_2 which has passed the tests which a theory T_1 has failed should be preferred in the future. We do prefer such theories because the failure of T_1 in a certain kind of test context is assumed to carry over to all similar contexts that differ only in time and place, as is the success of T_2 for those tests. Without an assumption of uniformity there is no reason to assume that, for future events, a falsified law should not from now on hold rather than that which has not been falsified. Science as a rational, critical and fallible pursuit cannot do without some assumption of uniformity of nature. If there is a problem of induction it is not a version of Hume's sceptical argument, and to that argument Popper offers no solution.

Not only does Popper not solve the philosophical sceptic's problem of induction, his resurrection of the problem as central to the rationality of science has been in part responsible for the descent of the philosophy of science into forms of irrationalism he sought to escape. There is no good reason to assume that science could proceed very far on the basis of serious *philosophical* scepticism any more than could everyday life. There is a distinction to be made between proper scepticism of specific scientific claims – scepticism founded on other well-grounded beliefs – and a general philosophical scepticism that is founded upon canons of rational assent that no claim could meet. Popper's programme is an attempt to show that science could be done according to deductivist canons of inference which meet the philosophical sceptic's challenge. The failure of that programme has given a quite undeserved intellectual power to the various forms of sceptical relativism espoused from Feyerabend through to recent postmoderns with all the forms of irrationalism these involve. The proper response to the failure of Popper's programme is to reject the very project it set out to complete. The failure of what Neurath aptly calls 'pseudorationalism' in Popper[14] – the belief that scientific argument can be fully captured by a single rational method, a set of deductive rules that eliminates candidates for truth – is not the occasion for a rejection of rational argument: it is the conception of reason that is at fault, not the rationality of science.

Unlike that of Popper, Engels's fallibilism is not founded either on general scepticism about the foundations of knowledge nor on any particular sceptical attack on induction, although he is, as we shall see, critical of inductivist views of science. What then is its source? The answer lies in Engels's own peculiar version of dialectics. That source may look unpromising. The basic picture of dialectics Engels often presents – a kind of super-science that contains all others – is wrong-headed. So also is the related project of forcing scientific and mathematical results into some general dialectical schema, such that the multiplication of two negative numbers illustrates the negation of the negation and so on. I make no attempt to defend Engels's version of the dialectic here: I believe it is indefensible. However, there is a rational kernel to Engels's dialectic when it comes to his account of the nature of sciences themselves: that kernel deserves to be rescued – even where it may be wrong, it is not straightforwardly so.

Like Popper's, Engels's fallibilism involves a rejection of inductivist accounts of science. Whewell's version of the doctrine in particular comes under criticism. And like Popper, the inductivist picture of science is replaced by that of hypothesis and refutation:

> According to the inductionists, induction is an infallible method. It is so little so that its apparently surest results are everyday overthrown by new discoveries.[15]

Thus, Engels claims, theories in physics, chemistry and biology are subject to 'successive revolutions' as new results falsify the old theory. This criticism of induction is not, however, founded on Hume's sceptical attack on induction. Engels's fallibilism, unlike that of Popper, shows no influence of philosophical scepticism. He expresses a healthy scepticism of philosophical scepticism and is willing to accept that there are truths that are beyond normal doubt, although his examples of such established truths are not always fortunate.[16] Engels also explicitly endorses the assumption of the uniformity of nature. Thus, for example, he writes in the *Dialectic of Nature*:

> We know that chlorine and hydrogen, within certain limits of temperature and pressure and under the influence of light, combine with an explosion to form hydrochloric acid gas, and as soon as we know this, we know that this takes place *everywhere* and *at all times* where the above conditions are present . . .[17]

What Engels grants to Hume's scepticism is that mere observation of regularities does not establish causal relationships:

> The regular sequence of certain natural phenomena can by itself give rise to the idea of causality: the heat and light that come with the sun; but this affords no proof, and to that extent Hume's scepticism was correct in saying that a regular *post hoc* can never establish *propter hoc*.[18]

However, this concession to Hume forms part of an attack on empiricism, not on the existence of causal relations in nature nor the possibility of knowledge of them. The point is taken to show that mere observation of naturally occurring relations cannot as such establish the existence of causal relations. Rather, it is through experiment and 'human activity' that the existence of causal relations is established:

> The empiricism of observation alone can never adequately prove necessity. *Post hoc* but not *propter hoc* . . . This is so very correct that it does not follow from the continual rising of the sun in the morning that it will rise again tomorrow, and in fact we know now that a time will come when one morning the sun will *not rise*. But the proof of necessity lies in human activity, in experiment, in work . . .[19]

This criticism of Hume's account of causation has been echoed in recent realist accounts of science.[20] Science does not normally develop through the observation of naturally occurring regularities. In the open systems that occur in nature, the motion of the stars aside, there are very few regularities that are clearly to be observed. For the most part, events in the world are the consequence of the conjunction of a variety of causal mechanisms and display few invariant regularities. It is through setting up experimental arrangements that causal relations are investigated. The importance of experiment lies in the attempt to isolate some single causal mechanism from the variety of interfering conditions in order to test some claim about its effect. To use the more recent language, experiment is an attempt to approximate to a closed system: observed regularity in such systems provides us with information about the nature of the causal relations that operate in open systems. Where proper sceptical worries arise is in the impossibility of ensuring that one has achieved closure. The problems of achieving a fully closed system in experiment provide the basis of Engels's fallibilism.

The argument appears in Engels's work in the first instance in the form of an argument for fallibilism from the 'interconnectedness of nature'. Engels introduces his fallibilism standardly by way of the impossibility of our ever gaining full knowledge of the 'interconnectedness' of nature. Typical is the following passage from *Anti-Dühring*:

> The recognition of the fact that all the processes of nature are systematically interconnected drives science to prove this systematic interconnection throughout, both in general and in detail. But an adequate, exhaustive scientific exposition of this interconnection . . . remains impossible for us, as it does for all times.[21]

One reason why the interconnectedness of nature entails the impossibility of final knowledge is that it entails that we can never be sure of experimental closure: any regularity established in some experimental arrangement might depend on the particular conditions present. The point is exhibited in the following discussion of the status Boyle's law:

> Let us take as an example Boyle's law, according to which, if the temperature remains constant, the volume of the gas varies inversely with the pressure to which it is subjected. Regnault found that this law does not hold good in certain cases . . . Boyle's Law is only approximately true and in particular loses it validity in the case of gases which can be liquified by pressure, i.e. as soon as the pressure approaches the point at which liquidification

> begins. Therefore Boyle's Law was proved true only within definite limits. But is it absolutely and finally true within those limits? No physicist would assert that. He would say that it holds good within certain limits of pressure and temperature and for certain gases; and even within these more restricted limits he would not exclude the possibility of a still narrower limitation or of an altered formulation as the result of future investigations. This is how things stand with final and ultimate truths in physics . . .[22]

The problem of arriving at unrevisable knowledge in experiment is not, for Engels, merely a practical one. It is an impossibility in principle. There is no possibility of controlling for the variety of conditions which might affect the outcome of an experiment because these are, Engels claims, infinite. The infinity in question here is not that of the infinity of possible temporal and spatial locations of an object. There is a potential infinity in the variety of properties one might encounter in the natural world. There are two forms which the infinity of the variety of nature's properties might take: first, a quantitative infinity – 'every quality has infinitely many quantitative gradations';[23] second a qualitative infinity – 'qualities do not exist but only things *with* qualities and indeed with infinitely many qualities'.[24] This infinity in the variety of nature's properties is taken by Engels to rule out, in principle, final knowledge of the natural world:

> If mankind ever reached the stage at which it worked only with eternal truths, with intellectual conclusions that possess sovereign validity and an unconditional claim to truth, it would have reached the point where the infinity of the intellectual world would have been exhausted both in its actuality and in its potentiality, and thus the famous miracle of the counted uncountable would have thus been performed.[25]

It is possible to understand Engels's account of the problem of induction as a version of what Popper characterizes as the logical problem – that of moving from a finite set of singular statements to a universal statement with a quantifier ranging over an infinite domain. However, the infinity of the domain of natural events, objects and processes is to be understood in terms of the infinite variety of properties they can have, not just infinity in temporal and spatial location.[26] The point is succinctly stated by Lakatos, whose own fallibilism has its roots not just in Popper but also in his pre-Popperian philosophical roots in the philosophy of Engels he learned in Hungary:

> As the universe is infinitely varied, it is very likely that only statements of infinite length can be true.[27]

Thus go Engels's arguments for fallibilism, stripped of much of the additional packaging of the dialectical superscience in which it comes. I believe that it represents a defensible kernel to Engels's account of the sciences. To say this is not, however, to endorse all of his arguments. The arguments from infinity in particular have problems. If the assumptions about the infinity of nature are true they are only contingently so, not *necessarily* so. And Engels certainly has some clearly mistaken arguments in their defence. Thus it is certainly false to say, as he does, that '*every* quality has infinitely many quantitative gradations' (my emphasis). Qualities can vary discretely, and the discrete changes might be finite in number – there might exist upper and lower limits to variation. To take an everyday example, the property of 'being monetarily wealthy' is of that kind: for any currency there is a minimum monetary unit of wealth in terms of which wealth changes, and there are upper and lower limits to the wealth any person or institution can accrue: one can be very wealthy, but not infinitely so. More central to the natural sciences, the properties of light as understood by quantum theory do not conform to Engels's dictum. Interestingly, Hilbert has even suggested that the very reverse of Engels's claim is true: 'Wherever the methods of investigating the physics of matter have been sufficiently refined, scientists have met divisibility boundaries which do not result from the shortcomings of their efforts but from the very nature of things ... Hence the homogeneous continuum which admits of the sort of divisibility to realize the infinitely small is nowhere to be found in reality.'[28] Whether or not Hilbert is right about the findings of the sciences in their current state – and as things stand I do not think he is – it is clearly possible that it could turn out that all physical qualities are by nature discontinuous. Whether or not that is the case is itself a matter to be settled by the canons of scientific enquiry, not something that can be assumed at the outset. Neither is there any reason to suppose there *must* be an infinity of kinds of property that natural objects can possess. If it is the case that they do, again it is only contingently so.

However, while the arguments from infinity may not carry the weight Engels assumes they do, the basic points he makes about the sources of fallibility in science in the impossibility of ensuring experimental closure are sound. Moreover they make better sense as an account of the problem of induction relevant to science than does Popper's Humean problem. If there is a problem of induction that is relevant to the sciences, it is not the Humean sceptical problem about the possible lack of uniformity of nature that Popper develops, but rather the problem of the variety and interconnectedness of nature that Engels notes. In particular, as noted above, that account of the problem of induction makes better sense of the role of experiment and the continuation of experiment in science than does the Humean problem. It is the attempt to restrict the possible variety of nature's properties that is the rationale for experimental control and the continuation of experiment. One controls experiments in order to limit the number of non-essential properties that might influence the outcome of an experiment, not to check on the effect of time and place. One replicates an experiment to check for adequate control in the previous experiment, not to increase the number of cases for inductive inference. And one develops new experiments to test a scientific hypothesis in hitherto unobserved conditions, not in hitherto unobserved times and places. The problem of induction relevant to science is the problem of variety and interconnectedness that Engels outlines.

Engels's account also makes sense of the particular fallibility of the social sciences as compared to the natural. It is this special fallibility that is at the heart of the political dimension to Engels's discussion of science in *Anti-Dühring*. The point of the discussion is to highlight the possibility of error in the social sciences and hence to undermine the dogmatism of Dühring's claims to the discovery of 'final and ultimate truths'. While, for Engels, knowledge-claims in all the sciences are fallible and open to revision, the sciences are placed in a hierarchy of epistemological uncertainty. Interestingly, given its recent revival, he defends fallibilism about mathematics: the problems concerning the introduction of infinitesimals are offered as examples that show that 'the virgin state of absolute validity and irrefutable proof of everything mathematical was gone for ever; the realm of controversy was inaugurated. . . .'[29] However, while the fallibility of mathematics is recognized, Engels presents the sciences as increasingly open to revision as one moves from physics through the life sciences to the social sciences. Thus he writes of the other physical sciences that the possibility of non-revisable truth claims is still more remote: 'Things are even worse with astronomy and mechanics, and in physics and chemistry hypotheses swarm around us like bees ... As time goes on, final and ultimate truths become remarkably rare ...'[30] In the life sciences the complexity of the systems analysed and the problems of closure that arise from the 'interconnectedness' of biological processes entail still further room for revisability:

> In this field there is such a multiplicity of interrelations and causal connections that ... the solution of each problem gives rise to a host of other problems ...; besides, the need for a systematic presentation of interconnections constantly makes it necessary to surround the final and ultimate truths with a luxuriant growth of hypotheses again and again.[31]

The development in the biology of cells is offered as an example of this particular fallibility: 'Often enough discoveries such as that of the cell are made which compel us to revise completely all formerly established final and ultimate truths in the realm of biology, and to discard whole piles of them once and for all.'[32]

It is, however, the historical sciences of society that are singled out as exhibiting the highest degree of fallibility. Moreover, the central political point of Engels's discussion is to reveal the exceptional fallibility of the social sciences. The historical sciences inherit all the problems of the life sciences, but possess also additional problems of the non-repeatability of events:

> In organic nature we are at least dealing with a succession of processes which, so far as our immediate observation is concerned, recur with fair regularity within very wide limits ... In social history, however, the repetition of conditions is the exception and not the rule ... and when such repetitions occur, they never arise under exactly the same circumstances ... Therefore, anyone who sets out here to hunt down final and ultimate truths, genuine, absolutely immutable truths, will bring home but little, apart from platitudes and commonplaces of the sorriest kind ...[33]

Engels's comments on the historical sciences deserve some emphasis for two reasons. First, the problems he notes do place epistemological limits on the social sciences which are of significance.

Nothing like the partial closure achieved in experiment in the natural sciences is possible in the social sciences, and the transitory nature of social structures and events render them inaccessible to the techniques of investigation possible in the non-experimental natural sciences. These are real problems with the social sciences that render them forever more controversial than the natural sciences.[34]

Second, the political lessons Engels draws from this special fallibility highlight just how far the programme of scientific socialism is set precisely *against* the dogmatism and methodological certainty it is standardly accused of fostering. Engels's purpose of stressing the extent to which the social and historical sciences are susceptible to epistemological uncertainty is to underline the importance of tolerance and openness in political argument. The discussion of the increasing epistemological uncertainty serves to undermine the strategy of shoring up claims to certainty in the political sphere by appealing to the existence of established truths in the exact sciences:

> That twice two makes four, that birds have beaks and similar statements are proclaimed as eternal truths only by someone who aims at drawing the same conclusion that there are also eternal truths in the sphere of human history . . .[35]

By showing that even the mathematical sciences are not free of revisability in belief, and by then highlighting the special epistemological problems of the social and historical sciences, Engels aims to subvert any tendency to dogmatism in socialist debate and to replace it with 'critical and scientific examination and judgement'.[36] The point of stressing the continuity of the social with natural sciences is to highlight their particular fallibility. The argument for scientific socialism is precisely an argument against the belief in the possibility of 'methodological certainty' and the forms of orthodoxy that this belief fosters. The fallibilism about science has a political point.

ENGELS AGAINST DOGMATISM AND ORTHODOXY

The central theme in the political epistemology of *Anti-Dühring* is opposition to the tendencies to dogmatism and orthodoxy in socialist debate that Dühring represented. The central purpose of the book is to reject Dühring's 'methodological certainty' and the consequent orthodoxy. Whereas the 'ordinary philosopher and socialist ... merely expresses his ideas and leaves it to the future to judge their worth',[37] Dühring claims infallibility and 'offers us beliefs which he declares are final and ultimate truths'.[38] The view has political consequences: a belief that one is in possession of a doctrine which is 'the one way to salvation and simply must be accepted by anyone who does not want to fall into the most abominable heresy'.[39] The aim of Engels's work is to defend the openness of the socialist movement to argument and debate, and against dogmatism.

In this respect it is worth noting that in *Anti-Dühring* one of Engels's purposes in discussing the utopian socialists is to *defend* them against the attacks made upon them by Dühring. His account of their ideas is, and is meant to be, sympathetic. The whole tenor of his discussion is that of praise. Typical are the following. He writes of Saint-Simon: 'a masterly breadth of view, by virtue of which all the ideas of later socialists that are not strictly economic are found in him in embryo';[40] Fourier is praised not only for his 'criticism of the bourgeois form of the relations between the sexes': 'He was the first to declare that in any given society the degree of woman's emancipation is the natural measure of the general emancipation',[41] but also, a little implausibly, for his account of history: 'It is in his conception of the history of society that Fourier appears at his greatest';[42] and of Owen he writes: 'Every social movement, every real advance in England on behalf of workers is linked with Owen's name.'[43] Engels's discussion is an account of their virtues, of utopians who were 'utopian because they could be nothing else at a time when capitalist production was as yet so little developed'.[44] His main purpose in *Anti-Dühring* is to rescue them from the dogmatic attacks of Dühring: 'These are the men on whom sovereign Herr Dühring looks down from the height of his *"final and ultimate truth"*, with a contempt of which we have given a few examples in the "Introduction".'[45] In both the Introduction and Part III of *Anti-Dühring* it is the possibility of debate against dogmatism that is defended, to the extent that even Dühring's treatment of Marx's opponent, Lassalle, becomes an object of Engels's criticism.[46] Unfortunately, Engels's concern to defend the utopians in his discussion of the utopian socialists in *Anti-Dühring* is less apparent in the later pamphlet *Socialism: Utopian and Scientific*: in editing out passages specifically about Dühring, including those in which the last two quotations appear, the later text omits the central anti-dogmatic themes of the *Anti-Dühring* version, and the title of the pamphlet suggests a straightforward opposition between utopian and scientific socialism that the text itself belies. The consequence is that the widespread misconception of the work as itself a move towards dogmatism is more easily maintained than it would otherwise have been, as is the equally mistaken view that it is the scientific turn that is responsible for that dogmatism.

In *Anti-Dühring* the defence of scientific socialism is linked to a defence of openness in socialist debates: both are founded on a fallibilist conception of science. Against the 'final and ultimate truth' offered by Dühring Engels offers a model of scientific enquiry as open and revisable. The purpose of that defence of scientific socialism is to encourage a spirit of open debate amongst socialists. Neither, it should it be noted, is that linking of scientific socialism and anti-dogmatism limited to Engels. The same themes permeate a great deal of socialist writing in its classical Marxian period. It is, for example, central to the philosopher who was the classic autodidact and at the centre of the autodidactic working-class movement, Dietzgen. That feature of Dietzgen's is highlighted in the 1902 introduction of *The Positive Outcome of Philosophy* written by the most scientifically literate of the Second International socialists, Pannekoek. For Pannekoek, the work of Dietzgen differs from previous philosophy precisely in the degree to which it stressed its own fallibility, recognizing that it gives, at best, only a partially correct view 'to be improved and perfected by successive investigations'.[47] The commitment to scientific socialism is a commitment to openness in political debate. The comparative openness of debates in the classical period of the Marxism of the Second International was in part a consequence of a commitment to a fallibilistic account of social scientific enquiry. Whatever other faults the socialism of the Second International might have had, the common appeal to science, and in particular to social science, to inform political activity was not a source of dogmatism but rather the opposite. The closure of that debate and the development of an orthodoxy in both political and social scientific studies was a later post-Leninist phenomenon.

SOCIALISM: SCIENTIFIC, SCIENTISTIC AND UTOPIAN

One of the great myths about scientific socialism, a myth very much in keeping with the anti-scientific attitudes of our 'postmodern' times, is that science entails orthodoxy and dogma. The claim is neither philosophically nor historically defensible. Given that this is the case, and given the clear textual and philosophical case for a relationship between scientific socialism and the rejection of dogmatism, why the resistance to scientific socialism, and the continuing popularity of the unhelpful contrast between scientific socialism and humanistic and ethical socialism of the early Marx?

Part of the reason both for the fashionable rejection of scientific socialism among socialists and the more general anti-scientific trends in radical politics is the conflation of science and scientism, that is the doctrine that only the natural sciences are candidates for knowledge and that anything that cannot be reduced to the natural sciences – including ethical and intentional statements – should be rejected. Both friends and critics of scientific socialism have failed to distinguish sufficiently between scientific and scientistic socialism. By scientific socialism I mean an account of socialism founded on analyses of social relationships that follow the canons of rational enquiry embodied in the natural sciences. By scientistic socialism I mean that account of socialism which rejects the possibility of rational dialogue of values and presents a case for socialism as relying on no ethical commitment. Scientistic socialism is, like any other version of scientism, indefensible. Unfortunately, both Engels and Marx in places slip into anti-evaluative modes of speech that are quite open to scientistic interpretations. Moreover, it is possible to see how scientism *does* lead to a certain kind of dogmatism. It silences whole modes of ethical and intentional discourse as illegitimate. However, that criticism cannot be levelled at the programme of scientific socialism as such.

The proper criticism of scientistic tendencies in socialism can and should be kept distinct from criticism of scientific socialism. And this is true more generally. The increasingly anti-scientific tenor of much radical political discourse – socialist, green, feminist, anti-racist and anti-colonial – represents a growing intellectual retreat in such movements, a retreat which carries its own dangers of collapse into forms of dogmatic assertion beyond rational debate. That dogmatism is fostered by current postmodernist intellectual fashions. The intellectual virtues of classical scientific socialism, its anti-dogmatism, its rejection of orthodoxy and its insistence on debate that meets the standards of rational enquiry, are now as much in need of being rescued as central virtues of political radicalism and socialism as they were when Engels originally espoused them.

Notes

1. T. Ball, 'Marxian Science and Positivist Politics', in T. Ball and J. Farr (eds), *After Marx* (Cambridge: Cambridge University Press, 1984). For similar lines of argument see also J. Femia, 'Marxism and Radical Democracy', *Inquiry*, Vol. 28, 1985: 293–319.
2. P. Thomas, 'Marx and Science', *Political Studies*, Vol. 24, 1976: 1–23, p. 2.
3. Thomas continues the passage quoted above by claiming that the phrase 'scientific socialism' 'had nothing but the most odious connotations to Marx himself' (ibid., p. 2).
4. The most thorough of such researches is probably Carver's: see T. Carver, *Engels* (Oxford: Oxford University Press, 1981), Chs 6–7; T. Carver, *Marx and Engels: The Intellectual Relationship* (Brighton: Harvester, 1983), Ch. 5; and T. Carver, 'Marxism and Method', in T. Ball and J. Farr (eds), *After Marx* (Cambridge: Cambridge University Press, 1984). See also the remarks on the relationship in P. Thomas, 'Marx and Science', *Political Studies*, Vol. 24, 1976: 1–23, and T. Ball, 'Marxian Science and Positivist Politics', in T. Ball and J. Farr (eds), *After Marx* (Cambridge: Cambridge University Press, 1984).
5. There are writers who do not subscribe to the standard caricatures, most notably, perhaps, Putnam. See, for example, his comments on Engels in B. Magee, *Men of Ideas* (London: BBC, 1978), p. 237.
6. It forms, for example, the basic plot of the excellent A. Chalmers, *What Is This Thing Called Science* (Milton Keynes: The Open University Press, 1976).
7. F. Engels, *The Dialectics of Nature* (Moscow: Progress, 1954), p. 241.
8. Ibid., p. 228ff. I discuss this further below.
9. F. Engels, *Anti-Dühring* (Peking: FLPH, 1976), p. 108.
10. K. Popper, *Objective Knowledge* (Oxford: Clarendon Press, 1972), p. 7.
11. Ibid., p. 27 n. 12.
12. J.M. Keynes, *A Treatise on Probability* (London: Macmillan, 1921), p. 256.
13. K. Popper, *Objective Knowledge* (Oxford: Clarendon Press, 1972), pp. 97–9.
14. O. Neurath, 'Pseudorationalism of Falsificationism', in R.S. Cohen and M. Neurath (eds), *Philosophical Papers 1913–1946* (Dordrecht: Reidel, 1983). Neurath's criticisms of Popper in 1935 anticipate many of Feyerabend's later criticisms of Popper without falling into the irrationalism of Feyerabend's position.
15. Engels, *The Dialectics of Nature*, pp. 228–8.
16. Consider, for example, the ill-chosen geometrical examples in the following: 'But then are there any truths which are so well established that any doubt about them seems to us to be tantamount to insanity? That twice two makes four, that the three angles of a triangle are equal to two right angles, that Paris is in France, that a man who gets no food dies of hunger and so forth? Are there then *eternal* truths? Of course there are' (Engels, *Anti-Dühring*, p. 109). While the examples are badly chosen here the central point made remains

a sound one – that there is a perfectly good sense of 'doubt' that is distinct from philosophical doubt such that it is possible to say that certain claims are beyond doubt.
17. Engels, *The Dialectics of Nature*, p. 234.
18. Ibid., p. 230.
19. Ibid., pp. 229–30.
20. See R. Bhaskar, *A Realist Theory of Science*, 2nd edn (Hemel Hempstead: Harvester Wheatsheaf, 1989), and *Scientific Realism and Human Emancipation* (London: Verso, 1986), Chs 1 and 2.
21. Engels, *Anti-Dühring*, p. 45.
22. Engels, *Anti-Dühring*, pp. 114–15.
23. Engels, *Dialectics of Nature*, p. 232.
24. Ibid., p. 232. For a development of both this assumption and that of the interconnectedness of nature see D. Bohm, *Causality and Chance in Modern Physics* (London: Routledge & Kegan Paul, 1957), Ch. 5.
25. Engels, *Anti-Dühring*, p. 109.
26. I restate Engels's problem in such terms in J. O'Neill, 'Two Problems of Induction', *British Journal for the Philosophy of Science*, Vol. 40, 1989: 121–5.
27. I. Lakatos, 'Necessity, Kneale and Popper', in J. Worrall and G. Currie (eds), *Lakatos, Philosophical Papers 2* (Cambridge: Cambridge University Press, 1978), p. 123.
28. D. Hilbert, 'On the Infinite', in P. Beneraceff and H. Putnam (eds), *Philosophy of Mathematics* (New Jersey: Prentice Hall, 1964), p. 136.
29. Engels, *Anti-Dühring*, p. 110.
30. Ibid., p. 110.
31. Ibid.
32. Ibid., p. 111.
33. Ibid., pp. 111–12.
34. For a useful recent discussion of this point see A. Collier, *Critical Realism* (London: Verso, 1994), Ch. 8.
35. Engels, *Anti-Dühring*, p. 112. By 'eternal' truths I take it that Engels means statements that will be believed to be true for all time, that do not turn out to be false.
36. Ibid., p. 113.
37. Ibid., 'Introduction', Ch. II, p. 37.
38. Ibid., p. 37.
39. Ibid.
40. Ibid., p. 333.
41. Ibid., p. 334.
42. Ibid.
43. Ibid., p. 339.
44. Ibid., p. 341. This is part of the passage that was edited out of the later *Socialism: Utopian and Scientific*.
45. Ibid., p. 339.
46. Ibid., p. 40.
47. A. Pannekoek, 'Introduction', in J. Dietzgen *The Positive Outcome of Philosophy* (Chicago: Kerr, 1906), p. 28.

4

Engels and the Politics of Nature

Ted Benton

INTRODUCTION

Marxists have responded slowly and uncertainly to the rise of ecological politics since the 1970s. Some have seized on the 'Limits to Growth' debate as confirming classical Marxist expectations that capitalism would ultimately collapse under the weight of its own contradictions. Others have burrowed back into the writings of Marx and Engels to discover that they were the original political ecologists. Others in the Marxist tradition have taken a more hostile stance. They have noted the claims made by green activists to have gone beyond the class politics of left and right, in proclaiming a universal interest of human kind. They have also noticed the relatively privileged social position of many environmentalists, and have found it easy to represent environmental campaigns to protect unspoilt countryside as attempts to protect middle-class lifestyles at the cost of homes and jobs for working-class families.

There is, however, a growing convergence between the political left and radical ecological politics, based on a recognition that environmental protection and social justice must be sought together if either is to be achieved (see RGSG, 1995). The purpose of this chapter is to explore Engels's engagement in nineteenth-century debates and conflicts over our relationship to and understanding of nature. Though I think it is very important to recognize the historical distance between Engels's time and our own, I think it can be shown that there are enough commonalities for the effort of reconstructing Engels's work to be worthwhile. My concern, more specifically, will be to consider what Engels's work might have to offer for our current interest in a realignment between green and socialist politics.

I shall be considering two contributions to the nineteenth-century politics of nature made by Engels. The first is his early, classic work

The Condition of the Working Class in England (Engels, 1969a). That work is of special interest today because of the ways in which Engels makes links between the environmental conditions and health of the industrial working population on the one hand, and their working conditions and class relations on the other. The suggestion that there might be a separation between the politics of the environment and questions of class domination and economic exploitation would have seemed an absurdity for Engels.

The second contribution I'll be discussing was a continuing interest of Engels's, but one on which he came to concentrate his attention from the early 1870s onwards. In the division of labour between Marx and Engels, it fell to the latter to engage with current developments in the natural sciences, and to engage in battle with rival philosophical 'systems'. The importance attached by both thinkers to the work of Darwin is well known, but Engels, especially, continued to take a keen interest in developments not just in evolutionary biology but also in physics, chemistry, astronomy, geology and other disciplines. As we shall see, Engels published on such matters with considerable reluctance, and only because he felt constrained to do so by the popularity at the time of philosophical system-building, in which contemporary scientific ideas were used to justify a huge diversity of different moral and political conclusions. As I shall suggest, Engels's later writings have much to offer both by way of example and in their substantive content. In our own day the natural sciences have immense cultural importance, in addition to their incorporation into capitalist labour processes, consumer-technologies, weaponry development and so on. Engels's broadly optimistic view of science in relation to potential human well-being is in sharp contrast to the outright hostility, or, at best, ambivalence shared by today's green movement (see Yearley, 1991: Ch. 4), as well as much of the radical left. Engels's work is an assertion of the political importance of intellectual work which contests reactionary and ungrounded appropriations of scientific ideas. But Engels's approach to this task is one which combines together a view of science itself as a cultural practice with a recognition of the value of its status as knowledge. In the context of today's rivalry between 'realist' and 'constructivist' approaches to science, such a combination has become all but unthinkable. I'll be focusing, here, on two themes in Engels's work on the sciences of his day: first, his critique of the mechanical, or 'reductionist', metaphysical materialism which was popular in radical circles in Germany around the mid-century, and, second, his long-standing engagement with the politics of Darwinism and, later, 'social Darwinism'.

THE CONDITION – A FOUNDING WORK OF ECOLOGICAL SOCIALISM?

Engels's *Condition* is widely recognized as one of the founding texts of the Marxian tradition, and a classic work of social history. He begins with an account of the Industrial Revolution, and the historical formation of the modern industrial proletariat in England. Though rural relations are not completely neglected in the work, Engels's primary interest is in the growing concentration of the industrial population into the great towns and cities, and in the conditions prevailing there in the early 1840s. Many of Engels's sources of evidence are the official reports of the time, journalistic accounts and so on, but some of the most powerful descriptive writing in the book comes from Engels's own first-hand experience, especially from his explorations of the poorest districts of Manchester and industrial Lancashire.

Despite the harrowing content of his descriptive material, Engels does not represent the industrial workers as passive victims: their conditions of life also include resources for the formation of collective efforts of resistance, self-understanding and social and political transformation. However, what marks out Engels's approach from much subsequent Marxist (not to mention non-Marxist sociological) class analysis is his attempt to link together the occupational situation (position in the labour market, employment relations, working conditions, labour process technologies and so on) with a whole range of other features of the lives, individual and collective, of industrial working-class families. The result is a remarkable synthesis of broadly environmental with social relational/historical analysis.

Engels offers vivid descriptions of the conditions of life of slum dwellers in the industrial towns and cities, pausing at intervals to note common features. He pays attention to the physical organization and spatial distributions of these districts. Not only is there a residential segregation between the classes, but building around the main thoroughfares is so disposed to 'conceal from the eyes of the wealthy men and women of strong stomachs and weak nerves the misery and grime which form the complement of their wealth'

(Engels, 1969a: 80). Within the working class districts, too, there are differentiations of housing condition: Engels shows, with the help of diagrams, how contractors maximize the profitable use of space in the design of terraces which can command different levels of rent according to stratifications among the working-class families. In the poorest districts are also concentrated the lodging houses. Engels quotes a contemporary report on these dwellings in Birmingham:

> They are nearly all disgustingly filthy and ill-smelling, the refuge of beggars, thieves, tramps and prostitutes, who eat, drink, smoke, and sleep here without the slightest regard to comfort or decency in an atmosphere endurable to these degraded beings only.
>
> (Cited in Engels, 1969a: 70)

Despite these differentiations, however, there are features common to all the working-class districts:

> The streets are generally unpaved, rough, dirty, filled with vegetable and animal refuse, without sewers or gutters, but supplied with foul, stagnant pools instead. Moreover, ventilation is impeded by the bad, confused method of building the whole quarter, and since many human beings here live crowded into a small space, the atmosphere that prevails in these working-men's quarters may readily be imagined.
>
> (Engels, 1969a: 60)

Engels notes the connection between the lack of sewers, gutters and 'privies', together with the practice of keeping pigs in the courts between the cottages, and the piles of rotting refuse in the immediate vicinity of the dwellings, as well as the pollution of local rivers and streams, and so of domestic drinking and washing water supplies. These external conditions, together with the poor construction, the filth and overcrowding inside the working-class dwellings, and the often weakened condition of the people themselves, take an immense toll in terms of health and mortality. Engels follows the recent report on the sanitary condition of the labouring poor by Edwin Chadwick in making these links:

> All putrefying vegetable and animal substances give off gases decidedly injurious to health, and if these gases have no free way of escape, they inevitably poison the atmosphere. The filth and

stagnant pools of the working people's quarters in the great cities have, therefore, the worst effect upon the public health, because they produce precisely those gases which engender disease; so, too, the exhalations from contaminated streams.

(Engels, 1969a: 128)

But Engels is concerned not only with the effects of these environmental conditions on the health and mortality rates of the urban industrial poor. He also echoes, sometimes in a different register, the concerns of more respectable social reformers for the moral and psychological well-being of those condemned to live in this squalor. How can family life and personal decency be maintained in these conditions? Should anyone be surprised if theft, prostitution, drunkenness and sexual 'excess' prevail?

Not content with this analysis of the residential conditions of working people, Engels goes on to illustrate the multitude of ways in which the diet of these families is insufficient in quantity as well as poisoned and adulterated. Finally, the whole is further combined with a systematic, industry-by-industry, study of occupational diseases and hazards. Here there is a special focus on the combination of the working and living conditions of working-class children and the maldevelopment which results.

Despite the obvious limits of its historical period, there is much in Engels's approach that is relevant to our current debates about environmental issues. Very roughly, one can classify the currently dominant perspectives into three broad divisions (see Benton, 1995, for a more extended account). The first, technocratic and managerialist approaches, tend to take for granted the persistence of existing power relations and institutional structures. Environmental problems are seen primarily in terms of potential exhaustion of material resources and the risk that waste emissions will exceed the capacity of global 'sinks'. A combination of 'top-down' legal regulation, fiscal incentives and inter-governmental negotiation is expected to provide the policy framework and the necessary technical innovations for 'sustainable development'.

A second cluster of approaches, which we might, following Dobson (1990), refer to as 'ecologism' tends to think of humans as a part of nature, rather than set over and against it. For this way of thinking, our ecological crisis is a consequence of the modern scientific and technological worldview, and the runaway dynamic of industrialism which it has spawned. The technological/managerialist response to the crisis threatens to take us further in the same catastrophic direction, and fails to recognize the urgent need for a deep cultural reorientation to the natural world, with consequent transformation of our whole mode of life. This perspective shares the widespread scepticism and even hostility to modern science, though this is rendered problematic by continued dependence on ideas drawn from scientific ecology, and selective endorsement of orthodox environmental science when its message is congenial to green arguments.

The third group of approaches has arisen relatively recently from within the social sciences and some humanities disciplines. These disciplines have turned their attention to the rise of public concern about ecological questions in the wake of a widespread shift in their dominant intellectual paradigms. This shift has taken place unevenly and has taken different forms across the different disciplines, but in each case there has been a heightened tendency to treat knowledge-claims with deep scepticism, and, in some disciplines, a move to abandon the search for true accounts and explanatory theories altogether. Attention has become focused upon 'discursive' processes through which the objects of more traditional social scientific enquiry have been 'constructed', and analysis has become governed more by analytical procedures drawn from literary and other forms of critical practice than by the traditional empirical methods of the social sciences.

In its more extreme manifestations this has produced some paradoxical results when social scientists have come to address environmental issues. Questions about our relation to non-human nature have tended to be translated into questions about how different discourses 'construct' 'nature' ('nature', 'real' and 'true' always, of course, in scare-quotes), while the original questions are not only lost to view, but are rendered unaskable on epistemological or methodological grounds. The paradox in all this is, of course, that environmental issues have become important for all of us, including social scientists, precisely because they pose the problem of the substantive relations between human social (including discursive) practices and the discourse-independent processes and causal mechanisms which are their conditions of possibility. Sociologists of science working in the field of sociology of environmental science from this 'constructionist' perspective have not surprisingly been accused by environmentalists of offering comfort to those powerful political and industrial institutions which have a manifest interest in discrediting scientific knowledge-claims about global warming and other issues.

I shall focus later in this chapter on Engels's ways of dealing with a remarkably similar set of issues in nineteenth-century debates about science. For now, however, I will concentrate on Engels's approach, in *The Condition*, to the social and historical study of environmental problems. First, his concern is not primarily with resource exhaustion, nor does he, in *The Condition* at least, concern himself with the wider question of the limits to growth. The Malthusian question of population in relation to food supply is raised, but reinterpreted as a consequence of capitalist property relations, the concentration of the population in the cities, and the effects of machinery and economic cycles on employment and so on the opportunity to *purchase* food. Here, as elsewhere in Marx and Engels's writings, the critique of Malthus, while fierce and unremitting, is confined to a rejection of the status of the 'law' of population as a universal relationship. Neither Marx nor Engels denied the pertinence of the relationship between food and population, but they insisted on the historical and social variability of its forms, so invalidating the conservative political implications drawn by the Malthusians. In our contemporary debate, this points to a development of Engels's approach, as a way of resisting the conservative, and implicitly racist, forms of 'neo-Malthusian' environmentalism which focus on (third world) population growth at the expense of other arguably more significant causes of ecological degradation. This approach would not *a priori* deny the significance of population, but would insist on the necessity of an integral socio-environmental analysis of the relations between food production and distribution, food security, gender relations, family forms, labour markets, income distribution, education, welfare provision for the elderly and so on.

Against environmental managerialism, an 'Engelsian' approach would focus on features of urban design, housing provision and construction, land tenure, access to clean water and fresh air, and safe and healthy working relations and conditions in their relationship to the human, social and developmental needs of individuals and families. Though many of the extremes of degradation Engels described were addressed by subsequent waves of environmental reform (Engels himself commented on this in the preface to the 1892 English edition of the work) and wider social and industrial regulation, the general approach remains highly pertinent for several reasons. One is that comparable conditions do still exist in many third world towns and cities, and there are worsening conditions of endemic unemployment, infrastructural decay, homelessness and social fragmentation in many 'first' and, now, 'second' world cities. The widespread identification of radical environmental politics primarily or exclusively with rural preservation has been a serious obstacle to broadening its appeal.

A second valuable contemporary message of Engels's analysis is his firm and carefully evidenced association of the environmental costs of industrialization with social class. Residential segregation and urban design in general enabled the beneficiaries of the new industrial capitalist order to shield themselves both from the direct environmental destruction it left in its wake, and from the disturbing sight of the human price paid by others for their affluence. For Engels, there were clear, if complex, causal connections between industrial wage labour, hazard at work, poor and adulterated diet, inadequate clothing, air and water pollution, overcrowded, damp and unhygienic housing, anxiety, demoralization, sickness and early death.

By contrast, much managerialist environmentalism dissociates measures aimed at environmental regulation from questions of distribution and social justice. Either intentionally or by design, the least well off bear both the burden of the environmental degradation and the costs of policies designed to alleviate it. More 'ecologistic' approaches also tend to under-represent the significance of class in their concern to appeal to a universal human interest in environmental well-being, and in their tendency to locate responsibility for the environment at the level of individual lifestyle choice. Engels, by contrast, often seems to share the Victorian moral distaste for the lifestyles of the poor but argues eloquently that they are not voluntarily chosen but engendered by circumstances of life. These latter are clearly attributable to a specific mode of class domination.

Of course, it may be argued that while Engels's connection of environmental degradation with class was appropriate in his day, our own world is very different. Partly this is a matter of a supposed decline in the salience of class relations themselves, and partly a matter of the changing nature and distribution of environmental damage and risk. This is not the place to enter into the thickets of the class debate, but suffice it to say that there have been massive shifts in the international distribution of labour and in the global fluidity of capital. These have been among the causes of large-scale shifts in the occupational structures of the 'first world' countries, and the associated weakening of their labour movements. Many commentators have taken a manifest decline in traditional forms of class struggle as a symptom of the decline of class relations themselves. An alternative approach, consistent with the spirit of Engels's work, would be to remain committed to the idea of class relations as structural features of capitalist societies, and to investigate the formation of new patterns of consciousness and action, both nationally and internationally.

So far as the redistribution of the environmental costs of industrial capitalist accumulation is concerned, a global perspective reveals a scene broadly comparable with that exposed by Engels in his own day: socio-economic deprivation tends to be strongly associated with environmental degradation. Influential writers on contemporary environmental problems, such as Ulrich Beck (1992), who emphasize the universality of the environmental threat, do have some powerful arguments on their side. The combination of the sheer scale of industrial activity with the transformative power of modern technologies has produced a range of environmental problems which do, indeed, threaten human (and non-human) populations at the global level. It is true that the well off cannot buy their way out of the longer-term consequences of global climate change, oceanic pollution, ozone depletion or biodiversity loss. At least, it seems obvious that the residential segregation of the social classes which sufficed in Engels's day is no longer enough!

But there are more continuities than appear at first sight. First, as Engels makes clear, the consequences of the environmental conditions of the poor could not, even then, be confined to the working-class districts:

> I have already referred to the unusual activity which the sanitary police manifested during the cholera visitation. When the epidemic was approaching, a universal terror seized the bourgeoisie of the city. People remembered the unwholesome dwellings of the poor, and trembled before the certainty that each of these slums would become a centre for the plague, whence it would spread desolation in all directions through the houses of the propertied class.
>
> (Engels, 1969a: 97)

The mere fact that the propertied class was at risk from the consequences of its own privilege did not, for Engels, in any way detract from the necessity of a class analysis. However, the fact was of very great importance for understanding the bourgeois politics of environmental and public health reform in the nineteenth-century, as Engels himself noted in his 1892 Preface to the English Edition (1969a: 24).

Something similar could be said of the environmental politics of our own day. The global environmental issues which dominate our contemporary perceptions constitute an 'official' agenda which is connected only very indirectly with the conditions which affect the quality of life for most people at home and work. It is an agenda which has been constructed 'over the heads' of such people, and their everyday concerns do not figure significantly in it. The international concern over biodiversity loss, for example, has more to do with the demands of pharmaceutical and agribusiness transnationals for access to raw materials for the new biotechnologies than it does with the needs of indigenous forest peoples or low-income farmers (see Shiva, 1991).

In this setting, the firm links that Engels asserts between living and working conditions, health, diet and moral and psychological well-being are the basis for an intellectually and politically more defensible agenda for environmental politics than the northern-dominated and technocentric construction of the issues. Engels's approach also offers an unequivocal corrective to the danger inherent in some versions of ecocentrism to prioritize nature conservation over human interests. Moreover, in making links, through the concept of class, between living and working conditions, Engels points up the possibility of a framework for overcoming the separation between production-centred labour movements and other social movements addressing issues of health, ecology, gender, sexuality and so on (the so-called 'new' social movements (see RGSG, 1995)).

However, there is a wide gulf between Engels's position and that of a large section of today's green movement on a central issue of environmental philosophy. There is no suggestion in Engels's text that non-human nature is a proper object of moral or political concern independent of questions of human well-being. For ecocentrics, who insist upon the inherent value of non-human, and even non-living, things and beings, Engels thus appears as an 'anthropocentric' thinker, and so as part of the problem, not the solution. Robyn Eckersley (see, especially, her 1992) is an ecocentric theorist who criticizes Marx and Engels and their followers for their anthropocentrism, though she recognizes in their work significant contributions towards an ecocentric emancipatory perspective.

Eckersley's criticism is illuminating in that she recognizes diversity within the general category of 'anthropocentrism'. In particular, she distinguishes the 'resource conservationist' version, which I have associated with technocentrism, from the broader 'human welfare' version of which Engels is a clear example. For both versions, non-human nature is valued solely by virtue of its relationship to human needs or purposes, but human welfare environmentalisms are open to a much wider range of human needs in relation to non-human nature. As we have seen, Engels links a whole spectrum of forms of human suffering from infectious diseases, physical deformities and premature mortality through to perpetual anxiety, moral degradation, and social disintegration to environmental conditions. There is, too, evidence of a recognition in Engels of aesthetic and what we might call 'identity' needs in relation to the environment. His characterizations of the filth and stench of the districts he explores suggest a primarily aesthetic revulsion, and an implicit view that personal and moral degeneration are associated with aesthetic degradation, independently of the more directly 'material' dimensions of poverty, disease and overcrowding. This is confirmed by his discussion of the implications of the compulsion to engage lifelong in monotonous and 'unmeaning' work, leaving the worker 'scarcely time to eat and sleep, none for physical exercise in the open air, or the enjoyment of nature, much less for mental activity, how can such a sentence help degrading a human being to the level of a brute?' (Engels, 1969a: 149).

Besides his recognition of aesthetic and other 'non-material' needs in relation to nature, Engels was also rather more inclined than was Marx to acknowledge human material dependence upon nature and its laws, for all his recurrent celebration of scientific and technical advance. So, for example, in 'The Part Played by Labour in the Transition from Ape to Man', Engels wrote:

> Thus at every step we are reminded that we by no means rule over nature like a conqueror over foreign people, like someone standing outside nature – but that we, with flesh, blood and brain, belong to nature, and exist in its midst, and that all our mastering of it consists in the fact that we have the advantage over all other beings of being able to know and correctly apply its laws.
>
> (Engels, 1968: 361–2)

This is certainly not the unqualified Prometheanism sometimes attributed to Marx and Engels, but it still falls short of the ecocentric insistence on inherent value in non-human nature. What remains to be seen is whether any reconciliation between these perspectives is possible.The ontology of interdependence between humans and the rest of nature does seem to be an important point of contact between ecocentrism and Engels's form of 'human welfare' ecology. Recognition of interdependence suggests that practical measures to enhance the environment should coincide with measures to improve human well-being. Even though there may remain a gulf between the two perspectives at the level of moral values, their policy prescriptions may be very close over many, if not all, issues.

But there may be some prospect of reconciliation at the level of fundamental values, too. Some of the human needs in relation to nature which are recognized by human welfare ecologists turn out to be very difficult to fit into the 'instrumental' relationship to nature which ecocentrics take as a defining characteristic of anthropocentrism. When people marvel at the beauty of some natural object, or wonder at the richness and diversity of living forms, it is true that these things are serving a purpose in their lives. However, the attitude to nature which makes these experiences possible is not an instrumental one. What is indispensibly involved in the experience is a respect for the object of contemplation by virtue of what it is. Consistency with the tradition of Marx and Engels would require us to think of value as conferred by humans in terms provided by their historically variable cultural traditions. But to say this is not to concede that humans are forbidden by their cultural traditions to value only such things as are useful. To value a thing by virtue of what it is may turn out to be little different from recognizing its 'inherent value'.

ENGELS AND THE CULTURAL POLITICS OF SCIENCE

The relationship of science and technology to human and ecological survival and well-being has become a central complex of issues in our present-day politics of nature. The optimistic view of this relation was pervasive in the nineteenth century, and was shared by Marx and Engels, but it has, from the early days of the scientific revolution, been shadowed by critics and sceptics who foresaw the potentially disastrous consequences which might flow from human attempts to change what they saw as the course of nature. As we have seen, Engels was acutely aware of the disastrous consequences for the industrial workers of the introduction of new labour process technologies, but he attributed those consequences to the prevailing social relations under which the technologies were introduced, not to the technologies themselves.

Today, green politics is deeply ambivalent about science. On the one hand, there is a tendency to attribute contemporary ecological problems to the spread of industrialism. This is itself seen as an expression of the modern Promethean project of domination of nature, while science and technology are both seen solely as core elements in that project. One influential strand of ecofeminism takes up a wider feminist critique of science as an expression of 'patriarchal' thinking so as to link this whole complex also with male dominance of culture and politics (see, for example, Mies and Shiva, 1993). Set against this, green social thought relies extensively on (its interpretation of) scientific ecology, both substantively and methodologically. Moreover, many of the environmental threats which are addressed by green social and political movements are only identifiable or demonstrable by means of scientific analysis. Some dangers, for example, from pesticide residues in food or from radioactive substances are not perceptible by unaided human sense organs, but are detectable with the use of scientific instruments. In the case of ozone depletion, again, increased exposure to ultraviolet light is not directly perceptible, but its effects on human health can be predicted on the basis of scientific theory and measured by epidemiological studies. Yet again, in the case of global climate change, effects are predicted on the basis of theoretically identified causal mechanisms combined with immensely complex computer models. The green case is heavily dependent on scientific knowledge, while the prevailing culture of green politics tends to be deeply sceptical about science, both for its claim to displace other forms of knowledge and for its complicity in the Promethean drive to dominate nature.

Green suspicion or hostility towards science is shared by other contemporary radical movements and with intellectual currents sustained by them. In the specifically human sciences, Foucault's 'genealogies' have provided ways of thinking of, for example, psychiatry, medicine, and penology as so many discursive apparatuses for the exercise of power over their subjects. In this Foucault and his followers come close to inverting the 'Enlightenment' view of the emancipatory character of knowledge.

So far as the natural sciences are concerned, we may also note what might be called a cultural politics of science. The popularization of scientific ideas with a wider public always entails some form of mediation between the 'internal' discourse of the scientific community and the prevailing forms of understanding available to 'lay' audiences. Any significant innovation, from Darwin's evolution by natural selection through relativity theory and chaos theory to molecular genetics, provokes a bitter struggle between contending cultural traditions. One remarkable continuity between Engels's day and our own is the way in which biological ideas in particular have been used to 'naturalize' and so legitimate politically contested social forms – male dominance, racial hierarchies, imperial power, private property, warfare, competition and the market, and so on. This too has tended to consolidate both political hostility and intellectual scepticism towards scientific knowledge-claims on the part of the contemporary left.

The cultural formation of the left in Germany in the 1840s and 1850s was entirely different. Anti-clericalism was the dominant priority, so that science, materialism in philosophy and radical politics tended to go together (see Benton, 1974 and 1979; Gregory, 1977). The physiologists Schwann and Du Bois Reymond developed research programmes based on materialist ontologies, abandoning reliance on teleology and 'vital forces'. These doctrines were generalized into politically radical materialist worldviews by mid-century popularizers such as Vogt, Moleschott and Büchner. This context was formative for Marx and Engels, and they took from it an attitude to science which can be summarized in the following five propositions:

(a) Science is the primary source of authoritative knowledge about the world. However, this does *not* mean that current science is 'absolutely' or 'ultimately' true. In *Anti-Dühring*, for example, Engels says: 'The theory of evolution itself is, however, still in a very early stage, and it therefore cannot be doubted that further research will greatly modify our present conceptions, including strictly Darwinian ones' (Engels, 1969b: 92).

(b) Methodologically and substantively there are no grounds for the separation of the human and the natural sciences. However, the terms on which the unity of the sciences is to be achieved are quite different from those advocated by positivists and other traditions of materialism – more on this later.

(c) Both social and natural sciences have an indispensible role to play in the historical emancipation of the human species. The adverse consequences of scientific and technical innovations for the working class during capitalist industrialization are to be understood as a product of the specifically capitalist domination of social and economic relations. Once these relations are transcended by a socialist revolution, the emancipatory potential of the developed 'forces of production' will be realized.

(d) Natural and social scientific knowledge is also emancipatory in that it overthrows the cognitive authority of religious, superstitious and secular ideologies which legitimate existing relations of domination, by representing them as ordained by either Nature or the Deity. ('At that time natural science also developed in the midst of the general revolution and was itself thoroughly revolutionary; it had to win in struggle its right of existence. Side by side with the great Italians from whom modern philosophy dates, it provided its martyrs for the stake and the prisons of the Inquisition . . .' (Engels, 1940: 3).)

(e) The sciences are human social practices with definite historical and cultural conditions of possibility. Not only this, but the content of scientific innovations may be dependent on the use of metaphors whose sources are in the wider culture. This is particularly evident in comments by both Marx and Engels on Darwin's 'discovery' of the competitive individualism of bourgeois society in his account of the mechanism of natural selection ('Darwin did not know what a bitter satire he wrote on mankind, and especially on his countrymen, when he showed that competition, the struggle for existence, which the economists celebrate as the highest historical achievement, is the normal state of the *animal kingdom*' (Engels, 1940: 19).)

To the contemporary eye, what is striking about this combination of views about science is that it straddles what is now widely taken to be the central issue which separates rival approaches to the history, philosophy and social studies of science. Engels, in particular, was unequivocally committed to a realist view of science, as making explanatory reference to an independently existing world. He was also a 'rationalist' in the sense that he recognized in scientific innovation progressive enhancement of human knowledge of this independent reality. But this realism and anti-relativism were combined with proposition (d), which clearly marks him out, in today's terms, as a 'social constructionist'. That scientific knowledges are, indeed, socially constructed and employ conceptual resources drawn from the wider culture would not have seemed to Engels at all inconsistent with a positive evaluation of them as knowledges of independently real objects.

This general view of science can be elicited from numerous writings from 1844 onwards, but it was not until the early 1870s that Engels was able to dispense with his business commitments and devote more time to the study of contemporary developments in science and philosophy. From this time onwards, a clear division of labour was established between Marx and Engels, and the latter took up the challenge of developing their joint approach to history and politics into a systematic world outlook, or 'philosophy'.

The first fruit of this phase of Engels's work, *Anti-Dühring*, was prefaced by a strong expression of his reluctance to engage in it. Engels fulminates against the 'systems of cosmogony, of natural philosophy in general, of politics, of economics, etc.' which have been 'springing up by the dozen overnight, like mushrooms' (1969b: 10). This proliferation of worldviews forces Engels to enter 'into realms where at best I can only claim to be a dilettante' because the fashion of system-building has taken off among socialists, too. In Engels's view, the newly won unity of the German workers' movement is threatened with doctrinal splits, and he has been called upon to subject Herr Dühring's system, in particular, to critical scrutiny. However, despite the wide range of issues this task forces him to address, Engels denies that he offers a rival 'system'. Rather, 'it is to be hoped that the reader will not fail to observe the connection inherent in the various views which I have advanced.'

Engels has, of course, been widely represented, by proponents and detractors alike, as just such a system-builder. The *Dialectics of Nature* is particularly open to being read in this way, as a 'philosophical' system in which Hegel's laws of the dialectic are held to apply to nature, human history and to the history of thought. This system, as Dialectical Materialism, became the 'official' philosophy of orthodox Marxism. As such it is of little but historical interest. However, if we try to locate Engels's later work on philosophy and science (as he himself signals we should) in the context of the specific intellectual and political disputes and alignments of his time, a more illuminating encounter with his ideas is possible.

As we have seen, the mid-century setting which was formative for Marx and Engels was characterized by a widely recognized affinity between science, materialism in philosophy and political radicalism. This is a measure of the success of what I have elsewhere (Benton, 1979 and 1982) referred to as 'mediating discourses' in appropriating some of the key scientific developments of the time as intellectual supports for radical movements of the left. The characteristic form of such popularizing discourses in Germany during this period was that of a 'philosophical' system which represented scientific ideas as elements within a wider theoretical ontology, epistemology and methodology of the sciences, and proceeded to draw normative and political conclusions about human nature and historical prospects. Such systems were very effective in popularizing scientific ideas, but also took the form of social movements, often with leading scientists and lay intellectuals at their head.

The mid-century materialisms which I mentioned above took this form, and they provided the set of cultural assumptions through which Darwinian evolutionism was enthusiastically received by the German left, including Engels and Marx. These forms of materialism also remained influential within the German Social Democratic Party after 1875, and were, apparently, often confused with the materialism of Marx and Engels. It was this form of materialism, in the particular version popularized by Dühring, which Engels linked with the eighteenth-century French materialists and criticized, variously, as 'vulgar', 'mechanical' or 'metaphysical' materialism. It was the requirement for this clarification which seems to have provoked the critique of Dühring.

But from the beginning of the 1860s Darwinian evolutionism became the centrepiece of scientific popularization and cultural conflict. Given their initial enthusiasm for Darwinian evolution, the subsequent struggles over the appropriation of evolutionism in Germany demanded recurrent attention from Marx and, especially, Engels. Evolutionism had such a commanding hold in Germany from the 1860s that almost every social and cultural conflict saw contenders on every side calling on some version or other of 'Darwinism' in their support.

There were two main sources for this diversity of rival readings of evolutionary biology. One was the presence of indeterminacies and unresolved disputes within the scientific discourse itself – questions concerning the mechanism of inheritance, the taxonomic level at which the 'struggle for existence' primarily operated, the existence or otherwise of macro-evolutionary trends or laws, and other issues. The other was the diversity of conceptual means and value-assumptions at work in the rival readings.

But amidst all the diversity it is possible to identify certain appropriations of the evolutionary corpus as dominant, and also to trace historical shifts in the patterns of use of evolutionary ideas. The career of the leading German evolutionist Ernst Haeckel is particularly instructive here. He was not only a scientist of great authority (even Engels, a stern critic of his social and philosophical pronouncements, always deferred to him on strictly biological matters), but also an immensely influential popularizer. Haeckel's popular writings in the 1860s and 1870s are in many ways continuous with the radical scientific materialism of the mid-century. An enthusiastic supporter of evolutionary doctrines, he unhesitatingly applied them to the understanding of human nature and history. Like most other German evolutionists at this time, Haeckel read Darwin's concept of natural selection through the lense of prior disputes in German evolutionism. On this reading, Darwin was understood as advocating a view of evolution in which the environment was of overwhelming importance in shaping organic change, independently of whether it did so by way of selection or by inducing adaptations which could then be inherited. This particular conceptual fudge opened the way to a *literal* and direct application of evolutionary biology to the understanding of human historical development since no significant distinction is drawn between genetic and sociocultural inheritance and change.

Armed with this loosely 'environmentalist' version of Darwinism, and an unqualified naturalistic extension of it to the human case, Haeckel was able to draw a series of social and political conclusions favourable to German liberalism. 'Progress' is written into human history with the certainty of a natural law. This progress is interpreted as a growing perfection of the human intellect and culture through intellectual and economic competition. The persistence of aristocratic privilege and the hereditary principle in social life stands in the way of progress thus conceived. But the liberalism espoused by Haeckel was of a timid and compromising kind even in this period, and there is also support for hierarchy and for authoritarian projects such as negative eugenics. In the early 1870s Haeckel supported Bismarck's *Kulturkampf* against the Catholic church with further reliance on the authority of Darwin and other scientific revolutionaries subjected to clerical abuse.

With the growth of an independent working class, and the unification of the working class parties in 1875, the centre of gravity of German liberalism shifted further to the right. Materialism and evolutionary ideas were now closely associated both with each other and with political radicalism. This association was confirmed by the promulgation of radical liberal versions of evolutionary social thought, such as that of F.A. Lange, which interpreted the capital/labour conflict in terms of the Darwinian 'struggle for existence'. Still more threatening to conservative opinion was the growing explicitly socialist appropriation of 'Darwinism'. August Bebel's *Die Frau und der Socialismus* was a hugely influential work of socialist feminist social Darwinism which went through fifty editions between 1879 and 1911. Like Haeckel, Bebel read Darwin as an 'environmentalist'. For human beings, the conditions of life which make for progressive change are social relations. The wide gulf now separating the social classes and the sexes would be overcome in a generation given the necessary social changes. Bebel takes great delight in telling the story of one Professor Bischoff, a prominent advocate of the view that women's allegedly inferior intellectual ability was a result of their smaller brains. On his death it was, apparently, discovered that his brain was somewhat lighter than that of the average woman!

Alarmed at the danger posed by this growing association between naturalistic evolutionism and radical politics, the scientific establishment retreated into two sharply opposed new postures in relation to evolutionism. This polarization was most famously exposed in the debate between Haeckel and another leading German biologist (and politician) Rudolph Virchow which took place at the 1877 Congress of German Natural Scientists and Physicians. Virchow was explicit about the political dangers of irresponsible promulgation of evolutionism: '. . . I trust it has not escaped your notice that socialism has already established a sympathetic relation to it' (quoted in Benton, 1982: 102). The subjective and speculative aspect of science, to which evolutionism so far belongs, is necessary to scientific progress, but should not be taught beyond the boundaries of the scientific community. Virchow emphasizes the empirical weakness of the theory in relation to specifically human descent, and advocates a focus on *contrasts* between the human and animal, as against too hasty an integration. Although this does not amount to a fully fledged anti-naturalistic dualism, it is interpreted as such by Haeckel. The latter insists on the necessity for freedom of thought and teaching, and in his turn accuses Virchow of political irresponsibility in associating the scientific theory of evolution with socialism. In fact, Haeckel's position is now to commend the evolutionary hypothesis as 'the best antidote to the fathomless absurdity of extravagant Socialist levelling' (cited in Benton,1982: 102). Whereas in the 1870s Haeckel had used arguments from the descent theory to justify egalitarian conclusions, he now uses a doctrine of evolutionary progress as specialization and differentiation to justify inegalitarian ones. Further, in a complete about-face, he now uses an orthodox Darwinian selectionist argument to justify the aristocratic principle:

> If this English hypothesis is to be compared to any definite political tendency as is, no doubt, possible – that tendency can only be aristocratic, certainly not democratic, and least of all socialist. (Haeckel, 1879: 92)

In the closing decades of the century this complex of reactionary and increasingly racist uses of evolutionary ideas became more and more pervasive. In Germany, Haeckel's own 'Monist' movement gave support to colonial aspirations, just as parallel social Darwinist doctrines did in Britain and elsewhere. In 1906 a Monist League, with Haeckel at its head, provided the movement with an organizational framework and political programme. It has been argued (by D. Gasman, 1971) that Haeckel's Monist movement was an important source of later Nazi ideology.

In the face of this increasingly reactionary character of social Darwinism, and its claim to the intellectual terrain of the human and social sciences, there were two broad forms of resistance. One, prefigured by Virchow's reluctance to accept the descent hypothesis in the human case, was alignment with the various currents of neo-Kantian and hermeneutic philosophy, which were mainly explicitly anti-naturalistic in taking human intentionality, subjective meaning and culture as distinctively human attributes. A qualitative gulf must separate the natural and cultural sciences.

The second form of resistance was to challenge reactionary social Darwinisms on their own ground. This was the strategy pursued by Engels. Darwin remains important for his dismissal of teleology in a whole domain of science, and for his demonstration of historicity in organic nature. Darwinism remains a source of scientific insights into human origins and nature. However, the various currents of social Darwinism, radical as well as reactionary ones, derive direct political conclusions from Darwinism on the basis of illegitimate philosophical arguments.

Engels's later writings contain powerful critiques of the general philosophical theories which formed the basis of both social Darwinisms and other forms of what we would now call biological reductionism (such as Bischoff's cranial sexism!). They also contain more detailed working out of these general philosophical arguments in relation to social Darwinism itself. First, Engels's critique of 'mechanical' or 'metaphysical' materialism: for Engels, this form of materialism was established in the eighteenth century as a philosophical (over-)generalization of the science of mechanics. It has subsequently been extended on the basis of nineteenth-century physiology and also philosophically inadequate interpretations of evolutionary theory. Its characteristic feature is its undifferentiated view of the unity of nature. Methodologically, all qualitative changes are to be explained in terms of quantitative ones. In Dühring's case: 'A single and uniform ladder of intermediate steps leads from the mechanics of pressure and impact to the linking together of sensations and ideas' (Engels, 1969b: 83).

Against this view of the undifferentiated unity of nature and the sciences, Engels argues for a view of nature as a hierarchically ordered and differentiated unity, with an associated view of the sciences as discrete but interconnected domains of knowledge. Motion, he says, is an inherent attribute of matter, and the different levels in the hierarchy of organization of matter are constituted by different levels of complexity of motion. This view of nature is often expressed by Engels in a dialectical vocabulary drawn from Engels's youthful engagement with Hegelian philosophy. Engels's use of this vocabulary is philosophically very questionable, but, perhaps more seriously, it opened the way to a codification and dogmatizing of Marxist philosophy as 'Dialectical Materialism'. It is therefore of considerable significance that Engels's position can be – and, indeed, was – stated without recourse to the Hegelian terminology. So, Engels's thesis that between the different orders of nature there is both continuity and qualitative change is sometimes expressed as an instance of the dialectical law of the 'transformation of quantity into quality and *vice versa*', but it is also presented in the notes to *Anti-Dühring* without this philosophical clothing:

> If I term physics the mechanics of molecules, chemistry the physics of atoms, and furthermore biology the chemistry of albumens,

> I wish thereby to express the passing of any one of these sciences into one of the others, hence both the connection, the continuity, and the distinction, the discrete separation.
>
> (Engels, 1969b: 442)

Put like this, Engels's position can be seen as a first approximation to a view of emergent properties consequent upon successive levels of organization of matter in motion. Such emergent properties require distinct concepts and methods of investigation and so provide the grounding in reality for the continued distinctions between the various sciences. However, the hierarchical relationships and continual interactions between the domains of nature also ground the interdependence of the different sciences, the necessary interconnections between them. Engels is thus able to oppose the reductionism of mechanical materialism without giving comfort to the rival dualist ontology of absolute separations between the living and the non-living, the animal and the human, the spiritual and the physical and so on.

Engels's second line of criticism of 'mechanical' materialism is closely related. The mechanical materialists recognize history in human affairs, but deny the historicity of nature. The Kant-Laplace hypothesis, geology and evolutionary theory in biology are all evidence of a growing recognition of historicity across the different domains of the natural sciences. However, it is not entirely clear what counts, for Engels, as 'historicity'. Sometimes this is presented in terms of unceasing flux in the world, of continual comings into being and passings away, but the reading of evolutionary theory, especially, strongly suggests history as progressive, directional change (the *Dialectics of Nature* presents yet another, cyclical, hypothesis for the history of the universe).

Though the teleological interpretation of organic evolution was extremely common in Engels's day, it would not be easy to defend now. However, quite independently of any such historical teleology, Engels can be seen as posing, especially in the historical sketch he gives in the Introduction to the *Dialectics of Nature*, the question of the emergence of qualitatively new structures and domains in nature as a specifically historical problem. Just as mechanical materialists cannot grasp the significance of the specificity of the different domains of nature considered analytically, neither can they comprehend the historical processes of emergence of, for example, living forms and, of course, the human species itself, and its various social forms of existence.

There remain, of course, many questions that could be asked about the status of Engels's own worldview. Is it any less flawed as an intellectual enterprise than its opponents'? Current intellectual fashion would be against the enterprise as such, independently of how well or badly Engels did it. Engels implies that he embarked on it only because the task was forced on him by the challenge of rival system-builders.

However, I think a stronger defence of Engels can be mounted. The cultural and political significance of scientific ideas was then, just as it is now, immense. To have refused to engage in the battle of ideas over how scientific innovations were to be understood by a wider public would have been to abandon this whole field to increasingly reactionary political forces.

Moreover, Engels's mode of argument is one which avoids a number of pitfalls. He does not, for example, build his worldview from supposedly self-evident or indubitable foundations. He offers a philosophical worldview which goes beyond the contents of the scientific orthodoxies of his day, but he is not a 'foundationalist'. The historically situated and provisional character of his position is repeatedly acknowledged. Engels's method is to generalize from the practices of scientists themselves in making interdisciplinary connections, and to make inferences from the historical patterns of development of the special sciences about the likely form of the relationship between their subject-matters. For Engels, the convergence of whole fields which had previously been developed separately is not intelligible unless we think of these different fields of theoretical discourse as so many different ways of apprehending a unitary natural world. However, the uneven historical development of the different disciplines and their continued discrete identities tells in favour of a view of the natural world as internally structured and differentiated.

So long as they recognize their openness to correction in the light of the further developments in the sciences and philosophical debate, such 'scientific metaphysics' are not only defensible, but, in my view, indispensible. The rival approaches to ecological politics which I discussed earlier in this chapter, for example, all recognize the need for some form of interdisciplinary collaboration. However, in the absence of any serious discussion of the philosophical basis for that collaboration, what results is either multi-disciplinary incoherence, or the reductionist domination of the agenda for research and policy by the most politically powerful disciplines – usually the 'hard' sciences, as in technocratic environmentalism. Engels's critique of 'mechanical' materialism has lost none of its topicality.

Finally, I have space for only a very brief discussion of Engels's contributions to the debate about the human significance of evolutionary theory. Some of the early comments of both Marx and Engels on Darwin's *Origin* suggest that they, like many others both on the right and the left, were disposed to read off from it a direct moral for human affairs. So far as Engels was concerned, his acceptance of the dominant German interpretation of Darwin's evolutionary mechanism as a loosely defined 'environmentalism' could also have led him (as it did lead Haeckel, Bebel and many others) into a reductionist fusion of organic and socio-cultural progressive development. However, his more sustained criticisms of the 'bourgeois Darwinians' are consistently anti-reductionist, while never renouncing Darwin's doctrine itself.

Engels expresses reservations about the 'absolute admissibility' of what he takes to be Darwin's extension of social concepts (Malthusian and Hobbesian) to apply to organic nature, but the primary object of his criticism is the reverse, properly social Darwinist, move. The social Darwinists directly apply concepts from evolutionary theory to provide 'eternal laws of human society'. Engels picks on the concept of a 'struggle for existence' to demonstrate the double error involved in this. First, he says:

> Let us accept for a moment the phrase 'struggle for existence' for argument's sake. The most that the animal can achieve is to *collect*; man *produces*, he prepares the means of life in the widest sense of the words, which, without him, nature would not have produced. This makes impossible any immediate transference of the laws of life in animal societies to human ones.
>
> (Engels, 1940: 209)

The distinction between collection and production marks Engels's recognition of this as the key feature of human evolution whose consequences require the invention of new theoretical concepts – a theory of specifically human as distinct from natural history. However, this does not commit Engels to a dualistic *opposition* between the two domains. This is signalled by his use of the phrase '*immediate* transference', and is evidenced by both Marx's and Engels's life-long commitment to a materialist view of history which puts the social forms of human need-meeting interaction with nature at its centre. That Engels's position was anti-reductionist but not dualist is also evidenced by his, admittedly highly qualified, willingness to explore the implications of trying to apply the Darwinian concept of 'struggle' to the human case:

> The struggle for existence – if, for the moment, this category be allowed – thus becomes a struggle for enjoyment, not just for the means of subsistence, but for the means of *development* – *socially produced* means of development – and in respect of this stage the categories of the animal kingdom are no longer applicable.
> (Engels [1875], 1991: 108)

So, under the new conditions which emerge with the transition from collection to production, the Darwinian struggle for existence is not *eliminated*, but rather *transformed* into a struggle for 'socially produced means of development'.

The second element in Engels's critique refers to the further qualitative breaks which occur on the basis of the initial establishment of production, each of which establishes a new relationship between human societies and their conditions of existence. So, whatever the 'laws' of human society are, they are not, *contra* the social Darwinists, either 'natural' or 'eternal'. In representing them as such the social Darwinists are not only seriously mistaken in theoretical terms, but they are also ideologists for capitalist society in representing its analogies with non-human nature as unalterable and ordained by nature itself. Evolutionary theory thus remains relevant, both methodologically and substantively, to the understanding of specifically human history, but the latter can by no means be *reduced* to the categories of the former. The critique of social Darwinism can, now, be seen as a more detailed special case of the broader critique of 'mechanical' or reductionist materialism.

It would not require too big a jump from this non-reductionist, but also anti-dualist, understanding of human history to apply Engels's insights to our contemporary disputes over humanity's place in nature. The concepts of both evolutionary biology and ecology apply to humans as a biological species. However, the specificities of human nature, and especially of human ecology, require a reworking of those concepts before they can shed any light on the human case. What Engels points to in his concept of social production as a distinctively human characteristic is the inapplicability (without qualification) of such ecological concepts as 'carrying capacity' to the human case. Elements and relations in the non-human world are constituted as so many conditions and materials for human activity only on the basis of historically variable patterns of social relationships, technical means, and socially produced knowledges and cultural forms. Each such social form is established as a specific way of relating to nature, and as such is subject to its own pattern of ecological limits and potentials. Ecological 'limits', whether deriving from shortage of raw materials, demographic change or pollution, cannot be validly specified independently of analysis of the particular forms of human social relations to their non-human conditions, means and media. Humans are, indeed, part of nature, and not set over and against it. They are, however, not an *undifferentiated* part of nature. They transform nature on the basis of their knowledge of its laws, but, also like Engels's 'conqueror of foreign people' (see p. 77 above), they are vulnerable to the unforeseen consequences of their actions.

Acknowledgements

The discussion of Engels's engagement with the scientific ideas of his time is a reworking of arguments first published in Benton (1979 and 1982). In those texts I acknowledged the influence of the work of G. Stedman Jones (1973), S. Timpanaro (1975), and F. Gregory (1977). I am happy to repeat the acknowledgement here. I would also like to thank Hilary and Steven Rose and Chris Arthur for providing me with the occasion to 'revisit' an earlier engagement with Engels's thought.

References

Beck, U. (1992) *Risk Society: Towards a New Modernity*, London: Sage.

Benton, E. (1974)'Vitalism in Nineteenth Century Scientific Thought', *Studies in History and Philosophy of Science*, Vol. 5, No. 1, pp. 17–48.

Benton, E. (1979) 'Natural Science and Cultural Struggle: Engels on Philosophy and the Natural Sciences', in J. Mepham and D.-H. Ruben (eds), *Issues in Marxist Philosophy*, Vol. 2. Brighton: Harvester.

Benton, E. (1982) 'Social Darwinism and Socialist Darwinism in Germany: 1860 to 1900', *Rivista di Filosofia*, No. 22–3, June, pp. 79–121.

Benton, E. (1989) 'Marxism and Natural Limits: An Ecological Critique and Reconstruction', *New Left Review*, 178: 51–86.
Benton, E. (1995) 'Biology and Social Theory in the Environmental Debate', in M. Redclift and T. Benton (eds), *Social Theory and the Global Environment*, London, etc.: Routledge.
Carver, T. (1981) *Engels*, Oxford: Oxford University Press.
Dobson, A. (1990) *Green Political Thought*, London: Unwin Hyman.
Eckersley, R. (1992) *Environmentalism and Political Theory: Toward an Ecocentric Approach*, London: University College Press.
Engels, F. (1940) *Dialectics of Nature*, London: Lawrence & Wishart.
Engels, F. [1845] (1969a) *The Condition of the Working Class in England*, London: Panther.
Engels, F. [1878] (1969b) *Anti-Dühring*, Moscow: Progress.
Engels, F. [1875] (1991) Engels to Lavrov, 12 [–17] Nov., in K. Marx and F. Engels, *Collected Works*, Vol. 45, London: Progress.
Gasman, D. (1977) *The Scientific Origins of National Socialism*, London: Macdonald and New York: American Elsevier.
Gregory, F. (1977) *Scientific Materialism in Nineteenth Century Germany*, Dordrecht and Boston: Reidel.
Haeckel, E. (1879) *Freedom in Science and Teaching*, New York: D. Appleton.
Mies, M. and Shiva, V. (1993) *Ecofeminism*, London and New Jersey: Zed.
Parsons, H.L. (ed.) (1997) *Marx and Engels on Ecology*, Westport, Conn., and London: Greenwood.
Red Green Study Group (1995) *What on Earth is to be Done?* 2 Hamilton Road, Manchester: RGSG.
Shiva, V. (ed.) (1991) *Biodiversity: Social and Ecological Perspectives*, London and New Jersey: Zed.
Stedman Jones, G. (1973) 'Engels and the End of Classical German Philosophy', *New Left Review*, 79: 17–36.
Timpanaro, S. (1975) *On Materialism*, London: New Left Books.
Yearley, S. (1991) *The Green Case*, London: Harper Collins.

5

The Condition of the Working Class in England: 150 Years On

Anne Dennehy

Engels collected his research material for *The Condition of the Working Class in England* between 1842 and 1844 while working in the family firm of Ermen and Engels. On returning to Barmen in the autumn of 1844 Engels wrote to Marx in November of the same year that he was 'buried up to my neck in newspapers and books from which I am compiling my book on the condition of the English proletarians' (*CW*, Vol. 4, p. 701). The book was first published in Germany in June 1845 and 'in socialist circles it was received with great approval' (ibid.). Reviews of the text not only commented on Engels's condemnation of the oppression he had witnessed in British capitalist society, they also referred to the 'feeling of hope and faith'(ibid.) Engels conveyed. For many workers, it was the first time they had been aware of the possibility of a working-class movement. However, the 'revolutionary conclusions' within the text were deplored by bourgeois critics – even though they acknowledged the accuracy of Engels's observations. The German economist Hildebrand argued that Engels's 'characterization of English bourgeois society' was 'true in detail but incorrect as a whole' (*CW*, Vol. 4, p. 702).

Engels's book was first published in English in New York in 1887 and in this edition Engels explains in an additional 'Afterword' how, with the decline of Chartism and the 'temporary preponderance of reformist tendencies in the English working-class movement' (ibid.), the social revolution he had anticipated in 1845 had not occurred. In 1892 Engels's text was published in England without the German and American prefaces; the 'Afterword' of the 1887 edition, however, was included. The second edition of the German publication was also published in 1892 with a new preface which was very similar to the English Preface of the same year. In 1844 Engels wrote to Marx that his intention had been to publish his address 'To the Working Classes of Great Britain' separately and send it to 'English party leaders, literary men and Members of Parliament' (*CW*, Vol. 4, p. 703). However, the 'Address' was included, in English, in both the 1845 and 1892 German editions but omitted from the American and English publications.

This volume, *Engels Today*, commemorates the 100th anniversary of Engels's death. But 1995 is doubly significant. It is now 150 years since the publication of Engels's classic text *The Condition of the Working Class in England*. Over the last 150 years there have, of course, been considerable technological and material advances. Consequently many have argued that this has rendered Marx and Engels's analysis of capitalist society obsolete. Dahrendorf, for example, argues that the social development of society over the last 100 years has refuted Marx's theory of class. He supports his argument by referring to the 'social rights of citizenship which . . . include old-age pensions, unemployment benefits, public health insurance, and legal aid, as well as a minimum wage and . . . a minimum standard of living' (Dahrendorf, 1965, pp. 62–3). Dahrendorf goes on to say that there can be little doubt that the 'social development of the past century has contributed greatly to changing the issues and diminishing the intensity of class conflict' (Dahrendorf, 1965, p. 61). Despite these many 'social developments' inequality of condition appears to be as evident today as it was 150 years ago. This becomes most apparent when looking at the same sources in 1994–95 as Engels used when witing in 1844–45, that is the 'newspapers and books' Engels refers to in his 1844 correspondence with Marx; the comparative contemporary sources are referred to below. These contemporary sources are not used in order to suggest that people are absolutely as badly off now as they were 150 years ago. What they do reveal, however, is that regardless of absolutes, there remains a growing divide between large sections of contemporary society which both perpetuates and exacerbates inequality. This continuing inequality in contemporary British society still appears to be due to the prevailing class structure and social relations which perpetuate systematic domination and exclusion. Engels's methods and explanations therefore are still relevant – particularly to work which emulates his own.

Dahrendorf refers to the reforms of the last 100 years and the improvements which these reforms have brought about for much of the population. However, most of these reforms have been a necessary response to the persistence of inequality which has become even more pronounced over the last fifteen years of Conservative government. Ian Gilmour, a Conservative MP from 1962 to 1992, has written that 'The Conservative Party has never sought to promote equality . . . on the other hand it has seldom gone out of its way to heighten inequality' (Gilmour, 1993, p. 128). Gilmour goes on to highlight the improvements brought about by social policy between the wars and the inception of the welfare state in postwar Britain. Conservative governments up to 1974, Gilmour argues, implemented social policy where market forces would lead to 'unacceptable social consequences' because 'the best way of protecting the social fabric was to improve the conditions of the least well-off' (Gilmour, 1993, p. 130). In contrast to this, Gilmour argues that during the Thatcher administration the condition of the least well off and the problem of poverty was no longer a priority. 'The New Right had long been hostile to the idea of relative poverty' (Gilmour, 1993, p. 135).

Townsend, in his definitive study of poverty in modern Britain, refers to relative poverty as a lack of 'the living conditions and amenities which are customary, or at least widely encouraged or approved in society' (Townsend, 1979, p. 31). Relative poverty over the past 15 years has affected an ever-increasing proportion of the population and this argument is supported by recent research findings published by a number of professional, charitable, independent and political organizations, for example by the British Medical Association, National Children's Homes and the Transport and General Workers Union, all of which are referred to below. Gilmour, who was part of the present administration until 1992, says that 'Relative poverty is real and does indeed exclude a growing number of people from sharing in the common life of the nation. Unfortunately, in Thatcherite Britain, absolute poverty was also a reality. Manifestly, it no longer exists on a Victorian scale, but it has not been eradicated' (Gilmour, 1993, p. 139). Engels, in his Preface to the First German Edition of *The Condition of the Working Class in England*, says that he preferred to use sources which originated from the bourgeoisie and cast 'their own words in their teeth' (Engels, 1987, p. 31) and it is perhaps appropriate to do the same 150 years on.

In our 'postmodern' era where many critics have adopted the post-Marxist sobriquet, it is argued that texts such as *The Condition of the Working Class in England* are no longer relevant in our 'classless' society. Geras challenges those who offer this argument, particularly when they refer to themselves as post-Marxists. This label, he suggests, only serves as a means of 'reminding us that Marxism is where they have come from' (Geras, 1987, p. 43). Geras interprets post-Marxism as 'an intellectual vacuum' (ibid.). This description may be applicable to those who choose to read *The Condition of the Working Class in England,* fail to consider how Engels's methods inform us historically and, therefore, dismiss the text as irrelevant to twentieth-century Britain. Such an interpretation of *The Condition of the Working Class in England* ignores the historical tendencies of the capitalist system and the structural constraints within it which reinforce inequality of condition in Britain today, both inequality according to class and the wider social relations which cross-cut those of class.

Geras interprets Marxism as emancipatory and 'against all forms of oppression, sexual, national, racial and religious, as well as economic' (Geras, 1987, p. 80) as does Wright who argues that non-class movements are significant and engage in 'class-like struggles' (Wright, 1994, p. 65). Wood (1986) suggests that, apart from their economic position, most people share a collective identity with others according to sex and ethnicity, for example. Wood goes on to refute the arguments of 'post-Marxists' such as Laclau and Mouffe (1985) who propose that class interests do not exist until they are expressed politically and subject to discursive construction. To deny the existence of inequality due to class, ethnicity or sex on the basis of Laclau and Mouffe's argument is to deny reality. The inequalities due to class, ethnicity and sex discussed, described and analysed by Engels in his 1845 text existed before he wrote and before they were the subject of political expression. On the same basis, the same inequalities exposed by Engels's methods today exist in contemporary society whether or not they are the subject of discursive construction by the working class.

Engels's 1845 text, and the research methods he used 150 years ago, expose the structural inequalities in capitalist society which informed his theory, for example inequalities which are manifest in the issues of poverty and the polarization of living standards between the richest and poorest. These social problems are as prevalent now as we approach the twenty-first century as they were in the nineteenth century. The persistence of the very same social inequalities exposed by using Engels's 1842–44 methodology supports the proposition that Engels's 1845 publication, his material analysis of society and his research methods which reject abstract theory are, in many respects, still relevant in 1990s Britain.

TOWARDS 'A KNOWLEDGE OF THE REALITIES OF LIFE'

Engels's text may be interpreted as a descriptive study (supported by empirical data) of the mental, physical and psychological condition of the working class in England, but Engels is telling the reader much more, as we shall see. Challoner and Henderson claim that Engels's text demonstrates a 'revolutionary bias' (1972, p. 183) and selectivity in his use of sources. What research or critical writing is without some form of bias? Most would argue none, not even that of Challoner and Henderson. Engels's conclusions and theoretical explanations may be described as 'revolutionary' but they are the result of his research methods – not a preconceived theory of revolution.

Engels did not have a theoretical analysis in which to seek the social conditions that would 'fit' his perspective. His early writings pre-date both his contact with 'radical' thinkers of the time and the formulation of socialist theories. Engels's life experience and observations as a young man, we shall see, illustrate how his theory was informed by 'reality', that is the reality of conditions as described by those who lived and experienced them. Engels's starting point therefore was *not* theoretical, but the raw empirical data of capitalist society. It is this data which informed his theory of class and social analysis which was later formulated in collaboration with Marx. It was 'real living man' (*CW*, Vol. 4, p. 93) that Engels observed and wrote about in England from 1842 to 1844, based on a 'knowledge of the realities of life' (Engels, 1987, p. 27). He developed not an abstract but a material analysis of life. Wilson suggests that Engels, by so doing, also performed a great service for Marx: 'Perhaps the most important service that Engels performed for Marx at this period was to fill in the blank face and figure of Marx's abstract proletarian and to place him in a real house and a real factory' (Wilson, 1967, p. 149).

During the period Engels was writing, he later says, 'International Socialism ... did not as yet exist. My book represents one of the phases of its embryonic development' (Engels, 1987, p. 38). However, it was not only socialism which was in a phase of embryonic development, historical materialism was yet to be formulated by Marx and Engels. Marx credits Engels with arriving at the 'same result as I, and when in the spring of 1845 he also settled in Brussels, we resolved to work out in common the opposition of our view to the ideological view of German Philosophy' (Marx, 1975, p. 5).

Here Marx is referring to Engels's conclusions in *The Condition of the Working Class in England* and one of their early collaborative works, *The German Ideology*, written in 1845–46.

The philosophy of the time, and German philosophy in particular, was greatly influenced by Hegel. But Marx and Engels moved on from the Hegelian idealist concept of history and introduced their materialist interpretation of history, that is social analysis based on the material reality of social conditions as applied by Engels in *The Condition of the Working Class in England* – not a Hegelian abstract method. In *The Holy Family* (1845) Marx and Engels argue that '*History* does nothing ... it wages no battles. It is *man*, real living man who does all that' (*CW*, Vol. 4, p. 93). They explain their concept of historical materialism in *The German Ideology* (1845), arguing that 'The premises from which we begin are not arbitrary ones ... but real premises from which abstraction can only be made in the imagination. They are the real individuals, their activity and the material conditions under which they live, both those which they find already existing and those produced by their activity' (*CW*, Vol. 5, p. 31).

Engels's aims and objectives in *The Condition of the Working Class in England*, though not couched in theoretical terms, can be seen as a decisive break with idealist and ideological analysis, and as a significant shift towards the perspective which we now know as historical materialism. Engels's text, therefore, is clearly a step forward in the process of formulating a material analysis of society based on 'a knowledge of the realities of life' (Engels, 1987, p. 27). His aims are clearly set out in his address 'To the Working Classes of Great Britain' where he argues that he had aimed for 'a faithful picture of your condition ... I wanted more than a mere *abstract* knowledge of my subject ... I wanted to observe you in your every day life ... thus I was induced to spend many a happy hour in obtaining a knowledge of the realities of life ... Having at the same time, ample opportunity to watch the middle class' (ibid.). Although Engels was just 24 years old when he wrote *The Condition of the Working Class in England* this was not his first observation of the disparate living conditions which prevailed at that time. In order to understand what motivated Engels to write so passionately about the English working class, it is necessary to consider his life and upbringing which show how his theory was derived from factual observation. Engels's early writings are indicative of his realization as a young man that reality contradicts 'ideas', that is 'ideas' which benefited those with most power in society and maintained the status quo, the use of religion, for example, as a form of social control, particularly as Calvinism played such a prominent role in Engels's upbringing.

THE 'BLACK SHEEP'

Engels was born into a wealthy Calvinist German family and, on the occasion of his birth, his father wrote to his brother-in-law, Karl Snethlage, saying that 'We thank and praise Him from the fullness of our hearts for this child' (*CW*, Vol. 2, p. 578). Engels's family home was in the Wupper valley and it was here that he first became aware of the living conditions of those who had the least resources in life, those who depended on the humanity of others to pay them a fair wage and treat them as they would wish to be treated themselves. Engels's response to the inequality he observed, and his early writings in particular, were not expected from a young man with his privileged background and antecedents. It was not surprising, therefore, when in 1842, the tone of Engels's father's correspondence had changed and he wrote to Snethlage that 'it is hard to bear having a son in the house who is like a black sheep in the flock' (*CW*, Vol. 2, p. 586).

It was the hypocrisy of the Wupper valley 'Pietists' which had led Engels to condemn, in particular, the very section of society which had raised and educated him; and it was this condemnation which induced his father to label him the 'black sheep'. The young Engels was scathing in his attack on industrialization, capitalism and the condition of those who lived in capitalist society. An excellent illustration of Engels's early writings are the *Letters from Wuppertal* which are based on his own observations. They were first published in the *Telegraph für Deutschland* in 1839.

Engels was 19 years old when he reviled the 'terrible poverty [which] prevails among the lower classes, particularly the factory workers in Wuppertal ... in Elberfeld alone, out of 2500 children of school age, 1200 are deprived of education and grow up in the factories – merely so that the manufacturers need not pay the adults ... twice the wage he pays a child' (*CW*, Vol. 2, p. 10). The reality of religious doctrine and practice contradicted the Christian ideals of religion and Engels could not reconcile himself to the pietists' justification for paying their workers the lowest wages of all. This, they argued, was both kind and correct because their actions allowed them to prevent their workers from spending their earnings on drink! During this early period of publication, Engels either signed his articles with an 'X' or used the pen-name F. Oswald. Obviously life for Engels and his family would have been extremely difficult if *Letters from Wuppertal* had been signed by the author. Despite this anonymity, Engels's parents soon became aware of their son's unconventional views. Family strife is well documented and accessible in the many biographies of Engels. However, it was after he left his immediate family surroundings that Engels's ideas became more clearly formed.

In 1841 Engels chose to complete a year of military service in Berlin and, as he was essentially a self-educated man, he also used this time to study philosophy at the university. Here he met the 'Young Hegelians' and became familiar with Feuerbach's *The Essence of Christianity*, through which Engels said 'The spell was broken; the "system" was exploded and cast aside . . . One must himself have experienced the liberating effect of this book to get an idea of it' (Engels, 1969, p. 17). Engels's year in Berlin, therefore, had a profound effect on his life and in 1842 his father wrote to Snethlage saying that 'now that all are preaching progress and that the old faith and the old mentality are consigned to the rubbish heap, how easily a young and spirited heart can be ensnared!' (*CW*, Vol. 2, p. 587).

During this same period Hess published *The European Triarchy*. Engels did not meet with Hess until 1842, but it is suggested by Carver (1991) and Hunley (1991) that it was Hess who converted Engels to communism. However, Carver does clarify the fact that at that time communism 'did not mean much more than community of goods, about which theorists of communism developed widely differing utopian schemes' (Carver, 1991, p. 96). It was not until 1848 that Marx and Engels formulated their theory of communism which condemned 'utopian schemes' that originated in a period when the proletariat was undeveloped. Engels was by now, in his father's words, 'ensnared' and his young, spirited mind committed to progress.

Engels's first inauspicious meeting with Marx in 1842 is well documented. Engels's tenacity, however, proved him to be an able, prolific writer and an intellectual who shared Marx's wish to understand and explain a world which was rife with inequality and antagonisms. Ironically, it was Engels's father who inadvertently gave his 'black sheep' the opportunity to write his best known work, which cemented his relationship with Marx. In October 1842 Engels's father wrote to his brother-in-law once again explaining that he was sending his son to England where he hoped 'to be able to give him a fair amount of work ... I shall watch over him unnoticed with the greatest care so that he does not take any dangerous step' (*CW*, Vol. 2, p. 586). The irony is that it was Engels's employment in a capitalist enterprise which led to his reaching wider theoretical conclusions based on the reality of his early observations in Germany and culminating with his 1842–44 research in England.

ENGELS'S 'DANGEROUS STEPS' IN ENGLAND

Engels was a prolific writer during his stay in England and during this period he regularly contributed to the *Rheinische Zeitung* where Marx was editor, and this went some way towards forming their early intellectual relationship. Engels's early critique of theory from reality may be interpreted as the development of a theory of praxis which placed him 'firmly in the world of human action'. This becomes more apparent when Engels's 1842–44 publications are considered in conjunction with *The Condition of the Working Class in England*. Engels's research data logically leads to conclusions and theoretical explanations which refer back to the reality of human action and working-class resistance to their condition. Engels studied the condition of the working class in the context of capitalist society and the conclusions he arrived at are based on his research data. In Engels's 1844 critique of Carlyle, he wrote that understanding did not come from 'the bare conclusions of which we are in such need but rather *study*; the conclusions are nothing without the reasoning that has led up to them' (*CW*, Vol. 3, p. 457). In Engels's 1845 text, his research data clarifies the reasoning that led to his conclusions regarding conditions in England and the condition of the working class in particular.

Throughout Engels's critique of Carlyle he argues that 'The condition of England is of immense importance for history and for all other countries; for as regards social matters England is of course far in advance of all other countries' (*CW*, Vol. 3, p. 468). Engels's argument regarding the significance of the condition of the English working class to other less advanced capitalist countries is referred to throughout *The Condition of the Working Class*, particularly in the

First German Preface. Conditions which existed in England were for Engels of great historical importance. But 'in order to redress the evil' of the inequality which reinforced the condition of the working class in England 'its cause must be discovered' (*CW*, Vol. 3, p. 461).

In his series of articles *The Condition of England* (1844), Engels clearly states that the subject of the history of the working class was too great to include as part of a social history. In *The Condition of the Working Class in England* he argues that the essential part of England 'the condition of the working class . . . soon made it necessary for me to investigate it separately' (Engels, 1987, p. 29). Engels's, 1842–44 articles, therefore, were written while he was also collecting material which was used in his publication of 1845. Engels's writing during this period brings together his thoughts on material and social relations, class structure and class conflict in capitalist society, and the need to discover the cause of social evil and the possibility of social change through popular movements. According to Engels, it is the workers who 'still have a future . . . It is from them that England's salvation will come' (*CW*, Vol. 3, p. 446).

'AUTHENTIC SOURCES' AND 'PERSONAL OBSERVATION'

It is in the Prefaces and Engels's address 'To the Working Classes of Great Britain' that he outlines the research methods which enabled him to 'observe you in your every day life . . . to witness your struggles against the social and political power of your oppressors' (Engels, 1987, p. 27). It was 'real living man' that Engels observed and wrote about in England from 1842–44 and his research methods enabled him to obtain a 'knowledge of the realities of life' (ibid.) from which he later formulated a material analysis of society. In order to achieve this knowledge, rather than relying on abstract theory, Engels used 'requisite authentic sources' and 'personal observation'. The latter was necessary because 'the various official and non-official documents' (ibid.) were not enough. They were too abstract, too distant from working-class reality and most documentation was produced by the middle classes – 'your opponents' (ibid.). It was perhaps happy coincidence that the Engels family had business interests in Manchester, because at that time 'only in England has the necessary material been as completely collected and put on record by official inquiries as is essential for any in the least exhaustive presentation of the subject' (Engels, 1987, p. 29).

Engels makes prodigious use of official reports and documents, such as the blue books, throughout his text. But these reports and commissions did nothing to change social inequality. They were simply 'rotting blue books' (Engels, 1987, p. 28) which were not 'readable' or available to those who were the subject of their investigation or anyone else who wanted a truthful depiction of the 'condition of the great majority of "free born" Britons' (ibid.). These reports were too abstract, too distant from working-class reality. They were, for example, often superficial and only touched the surface of social problems because it was not in the interest of those who produced these documents to look deeper into the structure of capitalist society in order to find the cause of inequality. Engels, however, did go deeper, and constructed real history based on real lives. As Marx and Engels argue in *The German Ideology* (1845) 'the first premise of all human history is ... the existence of living human individuals ... their activity and the material conditions under which they live' (*CW*, Vol. 5, p. 31).

The 'requisite authentic sources' referred to by Engels did not therefore consider or seek to reveal the structural constraints which reinforced the condition of the working class in, what was for many, a daily struggle to survive. Engels refers to 'The proletarian, who has nothing but his two hands, who consumes today what he earned yesterday ... has not the slightest guarantee for being able to earn the barest necessities of life' (Engels, 1987, pp. 143–4). Throughout his text, Engels utilizes another written source – the press. He refers to the social issues, correspondence and court proceedings recorded in *The Times*, *The Manchester Guardian* and radical Chartist publications such as *The Northern Star* – all of these publications were available to his critics. Engels challenges those who disagree with him to prove his inaccuracy 'and to prove it by data as authentic as mine' (Engels, 1987, p. 30) – a challenge which would still be valid today, for both Engels's period and the 1990s.

CHARTIST SOURCES AND WORKING-CLASS RESISTANCE

It is evident from Engels's 1842–44 publications, and his 1845 text, that he was an enthusiastic admirer of the Chartists. He frequently attended Chartist lectures at the Hall of Science in Manchester and often met Julian Harney (the editor of *The Northern Star*) when he travelled to Leeds. The work of the Chartists, especially those with whom Engels had personal contact, was particularly important in informing the political aspects of Engels's theory regarding working-class resistance to their condition and the need for class solidarity. In *The Condition of the Working Class in England*, Engels declares the absolute necessity of 'a knowledge of proletarian conditions . . . to provide solid ground for socialist theories' (Engels, 1987, p. 27). His observations therefore pre-date his and/or Marx's formulation of socialist theories. But Engels makes clear that before there is theory there must be facts which lead to theoretical conclusions, and these in turn lead to action – praxis – such as the political action of the Chartists and other working-class movements. The Chartists were an integral part of Engels's information network which complemented, and confirmed, his own observations.

Engels's use of the 'requisite authentic sources' was supplemented by his own social observations and those of his network of informants. These observations revealed the reality of the material conditions under which the working class in England lived. There are numerous biographies and texts which support the argument that Engels's network was of particular importance to his 1845 publication. It is, for example, well documented that soon after Engels arrived in Manchester he met and formed a close relationship with Mary Burns, an Irish factory hand who was, according to Wilson (1967), employed at Ermen and Engels. Mary was already passionate in her condemnation of the conditions endured by the industrial proletariat and the capitalist system which reinforced those conditions. It appears most probable that Mary was one of Engels's network of informants in Manchester. Engels's private correspondence for this period has been destroyed, but the writings of another German 'radical', George Weerth who lived in Bradford, have survived and are informative regarding the information Engels gleaned from others who had first-hand information regarding the reality of the condition of the working class in England. Whitfield (1988) refers to Engels's visits to Weerth who was employed as a clerk in Bradford.

Weerth's Bradford contacts enabled him to observe conditions which would not normally be accessible to nineteenth-century 'gentlemen' such as Weerth or Engels. Kemp-Ashraf suggests that 'Bradford plus Engels were the stimuli under which Weerth matured' (Kemp-Ashraf, 1971, p. 192). One particular 'stimulus' in Bradford, which seems likely to have been important to both Engels and Weerth, was the work of Dr John Little McMichan. Kemp-Ashraf describes McMichan as a 'most valuable source of first-hand information' (Kemp-Ashraf, 1971, p. 196) because McMichan took Weerth to see for himself the extent of poverty in workers' homes in Bradford. The irony was that McMichan and Weerth, despite being close friends, were political opposites. McMichan was a radical Tory!

ENGELS AND HIS CRITICS

It was Engels's research methods in *The Condition of the Working Class in England* which led to his conclusions regarding the structural inequalities which were, and are, inherent in the capitalist system. It was real life that Engels observed and the logical conclusions he arrives at, based on his observations, make it possible to challenge some of the critics of his 1845 text. Challoner and Henderson, for example, describe Engels's observations as vivid, 'probably accurate' but requiring 'modification' (Challoner and Henderson, 1972, p. 182). They suggest that Engels's use of language is misleading, particularly when he describes conditions in areas he did not visit himself. For example, Engels writes about the mining areas of Northumberland and Durham and says 'In this district we find again the lodging-houses and sleeping places with which we have already become acquainted in the towns' (Engels, 1987, p. 249). Engels writes in the third person and his text leads the reader through what may be described as a journey which follows the progress of capitalism through England – *not* a geographic journey.

Engels pre-empts critics in his early Prefaces and, at the same time, does indicate some selectivity in his choice of sources. 'I always preferred to present proof from *liberal* sources in order to defeat the liberal bourgeoisie by casting their own words in their teeth' (Engels, 1987, p. 31). These liberal sources could scarcely be described as 'revolutionary'. It was in the interests of the middle class, who originated these sources, to maintain the status quo. They were not produced in order to reveal the structural constraints which reinforced the social order and the consequent inequality which prevailed in capitalist society. These structural inequalities were revealed by Engels's observations of the reality of life and his research confirmed the observations of capitalist society he had made as a young man in the Wupper valley. His conclusions in 1845 led to a theoretical analysis which exposed the historical progression of structural inequalities inherent in capitalist society.

GLOBAL CAPITALISM

In the first place, these structures reinforced the social order and condition of the working class in England where, Engels argues, 'proletarian conditions exist in their classical form' (Engels, 1987, p. 29). However, Germany was also a capitalist country, albeit less advanced, and *The Condition of the Working Class in England* was a warning aimed by Engels at 'my fellow countrymen' (Engels, 1987, p. 27). In the Preface to the first German edition (1845), Engels reiterates his critique of abstract theory: 'We German theoreticians still know too little of the real world to be driven directly by the real conditions to reforms of this "bad reality" ' (Engels, 1987, p. 30). The reality of the miserable condition of the working class in England would eventually prevail in Germany because, Engels argues, Germany has 'the same social order which sooner or later must necessarily reach the same extremes as it has already attained across the North Sea' (ibid.). Communism, as defined by Carver above, already existed in Germany as did German socialism which was based on 'theoretical premises' *not* reality. But without an understanding of the historical tendencies of capitalist society and the true condition of the workers in England, the condition of German workers would inevitably become as extreme as they were in England and the historical tendencies of capitalism would, according to Engels, 'engender the same results' (ibid.).

Engels's address 'To the Working Classes of Great Britain' (1845) is a rallying cry. His 1845 text is, he says, unlike official documents such as the blue books. It is written in 'readable' prose and the conditions it describes would be familiar to any worker who read it. It addresses the English workers who were 'members of the great and universal family of Mankind, who know their interest and that of all the human race to be the same' (Engels, 1987, p. 28). These interests are class interests which are universal and any collective action by the working class would, Engels argues, be watched by other capitalist societies and Germany in particular. Engels's text may have been aimed at his fellow Germans, but capitalism soon crossed the Atlantic to America where the working class emerged from the same capitalist system, but became conscious of their position through 'class-like struggles'.

The Preface to the American Edition (written 1885, published 1887) is of particular interest when considering the development of working-class movements and class consciousness. As with the capitalist countries of Europe, changes in economic conditions, production and exchange would, according to Engels, inevitably lead to a 'working-class movement on a national scale' (Engels, 1973, p. 17). It was the emancipation of black slaves and the rise of manufacturing which raised the consciousness of the working class in America. This emancipation was a 'class-like struggle' which had the effect of transforming 'basic class relations' (Wright, 1994). The American working class came to realize that they formed a 'new and distinct class of American society . . . the lowest stratum' (Engels, 1973, p. 17). This in turn led to the formation of a political platform which spoke for the working class. Once again, Engels reiterates the need for solidarity: 'The labouring masses should feel . . . their solidarity as a class in opposition to all other classes . . . to embody it in the platform of the new Labour Party' (Engels, 1973, p. 18).

In his Preface to the English Edition (1892), Engels analyses and describes the historical development of the capitalist system and the working class in England over a period of approximately fifty years. The trade unions, for example, had become more acceptable to employers, but these employers, according to Engels, soon discovered in strikes 'a powerful means to serve their own ends' (Engels, 1987, pp. 35–6). Time lost through strikes and employment legislation, such as the Ten Hours Bill, meant that small manufacturers were unable to sustain the costs of lost production time. The large manufacturers were the beneficiaries of these changes, which became 'a means to accelerate the concentration of capital in the hands of the few' (ibid.).

For many years, England had enjoyed a 'manufacturing monopoly' but the nature of capitalism is such that it will always seek new markets and, as shown in the American Preface, global capitalism was creating a new social order in many other societies. It also created competition. Global capitalism, the continuing decennial crises and increased competition added to the 'stagnation, distress, excess of capital here, excess of unemployed work people there' (Engels, 1987, p. 44). It was this historical tendency of capitalism which led Engels to reason that 'there will be socialism again in England' (Engels, 1987, p. 45).

THE STRUCTURE OF CAPITALISM AND THE POSITION OF THE WORKING CLASS

In 1892, Engels wrote the Preface to the Second German Edition in which he says 'the English working-class movement has again made a good step forward' (Engels, 1973, p. 39). Engels was referring to the recent Parliamentary elections where three seats were won by 'workers' who stood 'openly as Socialists at that' (ibid.). Now, Engels argues, it was no longer an electoral competition between Conservative and Liberal. There was a third party to contend with and Engels was optimistic that 'the English workers' party will surely be sufficiently constituted to put an early end to the seesaw game of the two old parties which have been succeeding each other in power and thereby perpetuating bourgeois rule' (Engels, 1973, p. 40). Despite, or perhaps because of, the small victory of working-class politics, Engels's final Preface (to the Second German Edition) ends on a similar note to his opening lines in 1845. The only way forward for the working class was through collective opposition to their condition.

Between 1845 and 1892 there had been many developments in British capitalist society and in his English Preface, Engels refers the reader to Volume I of Marx's *Das Kapital* which 'contains a very ample description of the state of the British working class, as it was about 1865' (Engels, 1987, p. 37). Engels observes that 'The state of things described in this book belongs today, in many respects, to the past, as far as England is concerned' (Engels, 1987, p. 34). He goes on to say that steam and machinery 'dwindles into nothing compared with the immense mass of productions of the 20 years from 1850–70' (Engels, 1987, p. 41). However, Engels does not question the relevance or value of his 1845 text when he refers to the changes between 1845 and 1892. On the contrary, he explains these many changes in the context of the historical development of the capitalist system. For example, the condition of the working class in England continued to be a 'miserable' condition and the cause of this misery 'is to be sought . . . in the *capitalist* system itself' (Engels, 1987, p. 36).

In his 1845 Introduction Engels continues his theoretical analysis of capitalist society in England. During the Industrial Revolution, the proletariat was 'called into existence by the introduction of machinery' (Engels, 1987, p. 61). Industrial capitalist society created the conditions which were a prerequisite for the very existence of the working class. The working class in England were those who 'lived wholly upon wages, had no property whatever, not even the pretended property of a holding, and so became working-men, proletarians' (Engels, 1987, p. 53). With the introduction of machinery there was a change in social relations between workers. Engels refers to the once cooperative relation between spinner and weaver and the 'impossibility of vigorous competition of the workers among themselves' (Engels, 1987, p. 50). This cooperation ended with the introduction of mechanization. Workers had had an element of freedom and choice previously, therefore they 'did no more than they chose to do, and yet earned what they needed' (Engels, 1987, p. 51). However, Engels was not romanticizing some bygone ideal, for he describes pre-industrial workers as 'toiling machines in the service of the few aristocrats. The Industrial Revolution has simply carried this out to its logical end by making the workers machines pure and simple' (Engels, 1987, p. 52).

Industrialization also created a rapid growth in urban population which had a profound effect on working-class conditions. Communication was revolutionized, particularly through association in the workplace, and this led Engels to say that 'Now, for the first time ... the proletariat was in a position to undertake an independent movement' (Engels, 1987, p. 62). The collective action of an independent working-class movement, Engels argues, 'before too long a time goes by, a time almost within the power of man to predict, must break out into a revolution in comparison with which the French Revolution ... will prove to have been child's play' (Engels, 1987, p. 64).

Engels was writing during a period of rapid change and he addresses the issues of continuity and change through *The Condition of the Working Class in England.* The interaction of machinery and industrialization did not affect the whole of British society simultaneously; Engels therefore refers to a process of industrialization and proletarianization whereby relations of production and the capitalist system brought about a class society. In *Socialism: Utopian and Scientific* (1880), Engels explains this process as the economic development of society and the consequent changes in production and exchange which created social divisions, 'distinct classes and ... the struggles of these classes against one another' (Engels, 1993, p. 37).

In the Prefaces and Introduction to Engels's text, he discusses the physical organization of society – from agrarian to industrial. He analyses capitalist society and the interdependent relationships of living, human individuals, and these relationships are explained throughout in class terms. *The Condition of the Working Class in England* is a study of class relations, the antagonisms and inequalities which arise from class relations and working-class resistance to their condition as capitalist society develops. The multitude of social issues introduced in the Prefaces and Introduction continue throughout the body of the text, in particular the enduring nature of structural constraints which reinforce the flourishing prosperity at the top of the social pyramid and the poverty which endures at the lower strata. By using the 'requisite authentic sources' and observations available to us all in contemporary British society it is possible to evaluate the argument that *The Condition of the Working Class in England* is as relevant today as it was 150 years ago.

THE RELEVANCE OF ENGELS'S TEXT TO 1990S BRITAIN

On first reading Engels's graphic text describes Dickensian England in all its squal or and ascribes it to the exploitative, ambivalent relationship between the bourgeoisie and working class. But what has a class analysis like Engels's to tell us in our supposedly postmodern, 'classless' society? Over the last fifteen years the language of class has become even more unfashionable and the writings of Marx and Engels have, to a great extent, been discarded; but inequality of economic condition remains as deep as ever. As Engels argued when he commented on examples of the persistence of deprivation: 'the same economic necessity which produced them in the first place, produced them in the next place also' (Engels, 1979, p. 74). If we do discard the work of Marx and Engels, we ignore the humanitarian aims of texts such as *The Condition of the Working Class in England*. In his book Engels uses the term 'working class' to describe wage labourers who sell their labour power in order to buy the means of subsistence. Those who experience the same conditions when 'selling' labour power and buying their means of subsistence in society, therefore share the same structural class position. But who are the working class in contemporary British society?

In 1990s Britain there exists a broad range of workers who now share the common experience of insecurity, and in 1845 Engels argued that it was 'the insecurity of his [the worker's] position, the necessity of living upon wages from hand to mouth, that in short which makes a proletarian of him' (Engels, 1987, p. 143). By using Engels's 1842–44 research methods in the 1990s, it is possible to evaluate the relevance of his (and Marx's) concept of the working class today. There are numerous contemporary sources which refer to the number of workers who are experiencing insecurity and living, quite literally, from hand to mouth. In 1994 Hutton wrote an article 'Hand to mouth', which highlighted the precarious position of at least 50 per cent of households in Britain. If the wage earners in these households became ill, lost their jobs or were in debt, their average savings were less than £450 in 1991–92 when average earnings were approximately £250 per week (Hutton, 1994a).

Over the last fifteen years in particular, government legislation has led to the proletarianization of large sections of the population who previously enjoyed long-term, secure employment, with pensions and many other fringe benefits. But are these workers middle class or working class and where are the class boundaries? Marx argues that those who are employed as supervisors and managers are but 'a special kind of wage labour' (Marx, 1990, p. 450). He also states that 'middle and transitional levels always conceal boundaries' (Marx, 1991, p. 1025) – in our society these boundaries have become less concealed. When looking at conditions and struggles in the 1840s and 1990s there are many extraordinary similarities which lead back to Engels's period, his writing and analysis of society.

In *The Condition of the Working Class in England*, Engels describes more than class relations. He comments on wider social relations which cross-cut those of class, such as inequality due to ethnicity and sex. Wright argues that struggle cannot always be reduced to class and we should therefore consider, and include in any social analysis, the struggles of non-class movements which are based on ethnicity, sex or minority interests. These groups engage in 'class-like struggles, struggles that systematically transform basic class relations' (Wright, 1994, p. 65).

In the 1840s Engels condemned the sexual harassment of women in the workplace, the paucity of childcare available to women in economic employment, women's low pay and the exclusion of women and children from 'the great trade unions. They are the oganizations of those trades in which the labour of *grown-up men* predominates, or is alone applicable' (Engels, 1987, p. 42). The same problems persist today. According to Howard Davies, CBI director general, women have been 'entirely responsible for the growth in employment in Europe in the last two decades ... This trend has been particularly marked in the UK' (Davies, 1994). Despite this, or perhaps because of it, Davies also refers to the over-representation of women in low paid, part-time employment and 'the new poor' (ibid.).

Racial discrimination and the marginalization of ethnic minorities also persists 150 years on. Engels, in the 1840s, discusses in some detail the problems of immigration, discrimination and racism. He makes numerous references to the most prominent ethnic minority of his period – the Irish. They, Engels argues, endured the worst rates of pay, housing and working conditions. Similar conditions are experienced by many ethnic minority groups in Britain today. The ethnic minority groups of Engels's period were, as in contemporary society, among those most likely to experience poverty and marginalization. In the 1990s skilled ethnic minority women are more likely than less skilled white women to be unemployed or in low paid employment. Black women therefore experience a 'double bias' (Jury, 1994b), while black male and female entrepreneurs are less likely to be given financial backing and advice than their white counterparts (Woodcock, 1994).

An ever-increasing proportion of the British population now experiences insecurity and poverty through the casualization of the workforce, and so it was 100 years ago. Approximately fifty years after Engels's book was first published he wrote that there had been many improvements in the conditions experienced by the working class in England but 'to the great mass of working people, the state of misery and insecurity in which they live now is as low as ever' (Engels, 1987, p. 42).

REQUISITE AUTHENTIC SOURCES IN THE 1990s

> *... others who usually have full employment in the most depressed periods, now suffered greatly from want of work and reduction of wages.*
>
> (*The Condition of the Working Class in England*, 1845)

According to Elliott (1994) the scrapping of wages councils has led to ever-decreasing wages in order to match competitive pricing in certain industries. In the laundry industry, which employs mainly women, the demise of the laundry wages council removed 'protection for thousands of low-paid women workers' and has encouraged the more unscrupulous employers to compete by paying their workers 'rock-bottom rates'. An employer who has maintained the old laundry wages council rate for his employees commented: 'You don't create more wealth by paying less' (Elliott, 1994). The deputy general secretary of the Union of Shop, Distributive and Allied Workers (USDAW) refers to one worker, a shop assistant earning £3.70 an hour, who lost her job after 23 years. The rate of pay she was offered when interviewed for another post after the wages council had been scrapped was £1 an hour (ibid.). As Hutton (1994) argues: 'There is no more bashing of trade unions or lifting of labour market regulations to be done. Britain has no regulations and ranks bottom with the US in the international league table of labour standards' (Hutton, 1994b).

The Employment Acts of 1980, 1982 and 1988 introduced, among other things, the necessity for a secret ballot before strike action is taken, restrictions on picketing at the workplace, the end of closed shops being able to insist that employees join a trade union, and secondary strike action became illegal. If these regulations are not adhered to then unions risk sequestration of their funds, whereas in Engels's period, one of the most important roles of the trades unions was to act if 'one or more employers refuse to pay the wage specified by the union, a deputation is sent or a petition forwarded . . . if this proves unavailing, the union commands the employees to stop work, and all hands go home' (Engels, 1987, p. 226).

The spectre of insecurity is haunting Britain.
(Gray, 1994)

There are also those in society who function on the periphery of the labour market. These are the unskilled (usually unrepresented) workers whose skills are obsolete and those whose only experience of employment is on a casual, tenuous basis. Casual workers are often on the lowest rates of pay, their only 'security' is on a weekly, sometimes daily basis. Survival for many therefore has now become dependent on a constant transition between low paid, exploitative casual employment and the dole. Labour MP Alan Milburn has highlighted the growing trend among the low paid which 'forces a desperate one million to take second jobs' (Milburn, 1994). Engels, in 1845, referred to the workers who were forced by low pay to take more than one job and he quotes a weaver who describes his working life thus: 'My poverty forces me to it . . . Last Monday I got up at two in the morning and worked to near midnight; the other days from six in the morning to between eleven and twelve at night' (Engels, 1987, p. 204). Hutton suggests that 'we are returning to a nineteenth-century income distribution and pattern of work' (Hutton, 1994c).

But insecurity can affect even those with an education. There is no longer secure employment for lecturers and teachers. In November 1994, Meikle warned of 'hundreds of college lecturers facing redundancy' if they do not accept more demanding, short-term contracts (Meikle, 1994b). Teachers, bank employees and those who work in the medical services and media – to name but a few – are all experiencing greater insecurity and higher rates of unemployment as employment legislation is reviewed. Durham (1994) refers to a television film director who has not had 'a real job' since moving to London in the early 1990s. 'There are no jobs in television any more: only contracts, the odd day, the occasional week.' A secure job with promotions and a pension are, Durham (1994) argues, 'long past', while a spokesperson for BECTU (the broadcasting union) has said that in the 1990s it would be hard to find someone who has a 'continuing contract'. Employees in broadcasting are 'very afraid of managers who have the power to renew contracts. It breeds insecurity' (Donegan, 1994). It is this insecurity, Engels argues, which makes a worker into a proletarian.

But what of the unemployed? According to Engels, the condition of the unemployed 150 years ago was one of 'want of work, poverty and starvation' (Engels, 1987, p. 115). For the long-term unemployed in contemporary society it may be argued that the circumstances are much the same.

> *To what extent want and suffering prevail among those unemployed . . . I need not describe. The poor rates are insufficient, vastly insufficient.*
>
> (*The Condition of the Working Class in England*, 1845)

> *Britain joins Third World as Oxfam moves to help nation's poor.*
>
> (Meikle, 1994a)

Galbraith (1994) argues that , in the twentieth century, the unemployed who receive benefits in 'the fortunate lands' are subject to 'repetitive comment on the moral damage that comes from public support to the poor'. From 1996, those who are unemployed for more than six months will have to fulfil certain requirements if they wish to continue receiving 'public support'. For example, jobless persons will be required to 'take steps to improve their employability by attending courses or improving their appearance'. If they fail to do so they risk losing their benefit, as do those who refuse to accept 'reasonable direction by benefits staff' (Brindle, 1994b).

In 1994, the Joseph Rowntree Foundation reported that the 1986 Social Security Act had 'heightened the income differences between the unemployed and other claimants by making benefits to the unemployed less generous' (Joseph Rowntree, 1994). The government of 1834 also sought to reduce the 'generosity' of benefits paid to the unemployed. In 1834, the New Poor Law was introduced to replace the Old Poor Law of 1601. This, Engels states, was due to the belief that 'relief fosters laziness and increase of "surplus population"' (Engels, 1987, p. 283). The New Poor Law was introduced to replace the old because it was believed that the latter was 'ruining the nation' (ibid.). The Report of the Poor Law Commissioners said that the Old Poor Law was 'a national provision for discouraging the honest and industrious, and protecting the lazy, vicious and improvident . . . and ruin[ing] the taxpayers. Moreover, in the provision of aliment, it sets a premium upon illegitimate children' (ibid.). The same arguments can be heard today.

> *Malthus himself drew this conclusion, that charities and poor rates are . . . nonsense . . . they serve only to maintain and increase the surplus population.*
>
> (*The Condition of the Working Class in England*, 1845)

> *Behave well – or lose the dole.*
>
> (Bevins, 1994)

In 1992, at the Conservative Party Conference, Peter Lilley (Social Security Secretary) announced that he had 'a little list of young ladies who get pregnant just to jump the housing list' (Durham, 1994). In 1993, 160 years after the introduction of the New Poor Law, David Hunt, then Employment Secretary, stated: 'We want people to help themselves to work – not help themselves to taxpayers money to which they are not entitled' (ibid.). Some months later, Alan Duncan (Conservative MP and member of the Social Security Select Committee) argued: 'The social security system is losing widespread popular support, because it does not appear to meet the deserving, er, poor' (ibid.).

Were Engels able to comment on the social security reforms of the last two decades, his observations would be the same as they were on the New Poor Law 160 years ago. The same political rhetoric prevails today and those who promulgate social policy, be it the Poor Law Commissioners of 1833–34 or the Social Security Committee of the 1980s–90s, appear to believe that relief from poverty fosters laziness and a disincentive to work.

Engels refers to the consequences of insecurity, unemployment and poverty throughout his text. These conditions led to diseases of mind, body and spirit which, he argues, led to an increase in suicide, a breakdown in social order when the hungry were driven to steal food, and a multiplicity of slum diseases. Engels makes numerous references to the work of the Victorian physician Dr James Kay and many other reports from the Royal College of Physicians. He would, of course, have been able to complement these reports with observations made by Weerth and McMichan in Bradford. Much was written during Engels's period on the diseases of poverty which were prevalent at that time, and the increased morbidity and mortality of the poorest in society.

> *Their enfeebled constitutions are unable to resist disease . . . hence they age prematurely, and die early. On this point the mortality statistics supply unquestionable testimony.*
>
> (*The Condition of the Working Class in England*, 1845)

> *Poverty blamed for the first decline in longevity for 50 years. Study shows poor are dying younger.*
>
> (Jury, 1994a)

It is alarming to note that similar debates and discussions are still to be found in the *British Medical Journal* (BMJ) today, for example Delamothe's proposition that 'the poor pay for their poverty with their lives' (Delamothe, 1992) and Wilkinson's argument that 'poverty kills' (Wilkinson, 1992). It has become apparent over the last 15 years – from the publication of the Black Report in 1980 to the numerous reports of the 1990s – that those who are marginalized in society pay a high price for their inequality. In 1993, Sir Douglas Black, who chaired the 1980 inquiry, attacked the government for 'the attempted destruction of the health service' and called for a return to the values of the welfare state (Black, 1993). Wilkinson (1994) argues that 'the poor pay the price of increased social inequality with their health' and that since the 1980s, this inequality has become more marked. For example, mortality rates for the poorest in society are four times greater than those experienced by the more affluent. A further indication is the increased infant mortality rates in areas deemed deprived. In 1993 Davey-Smith and Egger reported that the socio-economic differentials in wealth and health were 'the legacy of the Thatcher years'.

It is difficult to avoid the specific details of Thatcherism when considering conditions in contemporary British society. There have, of course, been many changes and improvements in social conditions since Engels's period but the majority of these improvements originate from the postwar settlement which introduced a universal provision of welfare rather than the selective relief of poverty. The welfare state was based on the principle of 'Never Again' and removed the stigma of the Poor Law (Hennessy, 1993). In 1995, however, we read 'Lilley "returning to Poor Law" with benefits shift' (Brindle and White, 1995). The BMJ, Joseph Rowntree Foundation, National Children's Home, broad sheet press et al. cannot all be guilty of a hyperbolic interpretation of government policies over the last 15 years.

Government policies of the 1980s and 1990s in particular have ignored the structural constraints which have a profound effect on health status. The government has endorsed the World Health Organization's project of 'Health for All' by the year 2000 and the aim of this project is to bring about equity in health. However, as the medical journals indicate, this has not happened. The government's only action to achieve 'Health for All' has been to direct didactic missives to the poorest in society. Hence, the health divide has become even more polarized, and structural constraints, which compound the position of the poorest in society, remain.

Children who are half starved, just when they most need ample and nutritious food – must inevitably become weak, scrofulous and rachitic.

(*The Condition of the Working Class in England*, 1845)

Basic benefit will not buy children a workhouse diet.

(Brindle, 1994a)

The healthy eating objectives released by the Department of Health, and aimed at the whole population, are impossible to achieve for a large section of society. Work insecurity, unemployment, homelessness, low pay and a paucity of local amenities all constrain choice in food consumption. Engels drew attention to the need for a healthy diet and the effect of poor nutrition on health status. He argues that even if workers knew that 'the diet which is the root of all evil' (Engels, 1987, p. 132) was the cause of illness they were usually powerless to improve their condition. Engels asks: 'How could they obtain a more suitable regimen so long as they cannot adopt a different way of living?' (ibid.).

In 1994, research carried out by the charity Barnardos found that it is cheaper to buy food in Kensington that it is to subsist living on an estate with a paucity of amenities in the North of England. This situation has been exacerbated by deregulation of the bus service which ghettoizes poverty and puts amenities, such as food markets, out of the reach of those without private transport (Wainwright, 1994). In 1993, on an 'overspill' estate in Manchester, The Children's Society started providing Christmas dinners for £1.40 to meet the needs of many residents on the estate who could afford little else. Most households do aspire to eat a healthier, more nutritious diet. However, if they are unable to afford the electricity to cook jacket potatoes for 40 minutes, or perhaps they cannot afford a loan from the social fund to even buy a cooker, then take-away chips are hot food. In 1994, it was reported that 'welfare claimants who apply for loans to acquire necessities such as beds and cookers are being turned away at a rate of almost 100 000 per week' (McSmith, 1994). There are therefore a large number of citizens who cannot, as Engels argues, adopt a 'more suitable regimen'.

In 1991, National Children's Home (NCH) issued 354 questionnaires to families who use their centres. The questions they asked related to nutrition, hunger, income and poverty. The responses showed that when a family's weekly budget ran out it was usually the mother who went hungry. However, sometimes there was insufficient for the children, or the food was unsuitable for a child and refused. Consequently, in one month 50 per cent of the children (all aged under five years) went without food. The parents who were interviewed were well aware of the foods which were absent from their diet – fresh fruit and vegetables, in particular, which are costly on a low budget. The results of their study showed that 41 per cent of the children had a 'Poor Diet', 24 per cent had a 'Very Poor Diet' and none of the children in the survey had a 'Nutritionally Healthy Diet' (NCH, 1991). The foods which were lacking are those which protect against numerous diseases, particularly carcinogenic disease, osteoporosis in women, heart disease and mid-life onset diabetes (Barasi and Mottram, 1990; Leather, 1992; Fox and Cameron, 1989). As Engels observed in 1845:

> If the week's wages are used up before the end of the week, it often enough happens that in the closing days the family gets only as much food, if any, as is barely sufficient to keep off starvation. Of course, such a way of living unavoidably engenders a multitude of diseases and when these appear . . . then misery reaches its height, and then the brutality with which society abandons its members, just when their need is greatest, comes out fully into the light of day.
>
> (Engels, 1987, p. 108)

When diseases due to poor nutritional status manifest themselves in adults who have been malnourished children, the socio-economic differentials in wealth and health manifest themselves as well.

> *Live you shall, but live as an awful warning to all those who might have inducements to become 'superfluous'.*
>
> (*The Condition of the Working Class in England*, 1845)

> *Portillo lays into yobbos and feckless.*
>
> (Wintour, 1994b)

Lowry (1991) argues that the blame-the-victim syndrome is the worst disease we have in Britain. The prevailing medical and sociological evidence reveals the futility of the cult of individualism and the denigration of collective responsibility. It also shows how government rhetoric regarding the ideals we should aspire to discriminates against many in contemporary society. As Engels commented 150 years ago, 'the poverty of the proletarian is intensified to the point of actual lack of the barest necessaries of life, to want and hunger' (Engels, 1987, p. 143). Food and the rudiments of good health are as much a part of the 'barest necessaries' of life now as they were 150 years ago and history appears to have repeated itself regarding the want experienced by those who have least in society. In 1852 Marx remarked that history may repeat itself – the first time as tragedy, the second as farce. During Engels's period, Victorian 'values' of self-help and Malthusian tracts which argued that the lower classes were necessary so that those above them may fear to fall were, for a large section of the population, a 'tragedy'. What is farcical now is that this present government condones the political rhetoric of self-help.

Samuel Smiles, the author of *Self-Help*, argues that help 'from without is often enfeebling in its effect but help from within is invariably invigorating' (Smiles, 1986, p. 10). Keith Joseph wrote the Foreword to the 1986 edition of Smiles's book in which he suggests that the welfare state in Britain has become counter-productive and removed the incentive to work and save. This book, according to Joseph, is 'a book for our times: the purveyor of a message that we, government and governed, employer and employee, in work and out of work, need to take to heart and keep in mind' (Joseph, 1986, p. 16). In the 1990s very few of those in need are being enfeebled by help from without. However, low benefit levels have had an enfeebling effect which has led to an increase in poverty, homelessness and the increased visibility of beggars on the streets of Britain.

> *In London 50 000 human beings get up every morning, not knowing where they are to lay their heads at night.*
>
> (*The Condition of the Working Class in England*, 1845)

> *. . . the Government has ended support for its own Rough Sleepers Initiative after only 18 months.*
>
> (Johnson, 1994)

The 1994 Budget lowered the level of housing benefit available to claimants and those seeking help with interest payments on their mortgage. The Child Poverty Action Group found it ironic that help was being withdrawn by the government who had positively encouraged home ownership. This, housing charities argued, would lead to 'an increase in the number of homeless families' (Hunter, 1994). Throughout his 1845 text Engels refers to the problem of homelessness and those who were reduced to begging in order to survive. He describes a family who 'takes up its position in a busy street, and without uttering a word, lets the mere sight of its helplessness plead for it' and those who sing 'a pleading song in the streets' (Engels, 1987, p. 120). He quotes from a letter written by 'A Lady' to the *Manchester Guardian* in which she complains that, despite her numerous contributions to charities and payment of rates, she is still pestered by the 'swarms of beggars' who 'try to awaken the pity of the passers-by in a most shameless and annoying manner by exposing their tattered clothing, sickly aspect, and disgusting wounds and deformities' (Engels, 1987, p. 277).

In 1994, John Major could easily have been responding to the 'Lady' of Engels's period when he argued that he voiced the feelings of 'many millions of people in this country' by declaring that begging was 'unnecessary and offensive'. He went on to refer to Britain's adequate social security safety net which forestalled any need to beg (Harrison, Dodd and Durham, 1994). According to Young (1994), with this statement 'Major's mask drops into the gutter'. Young goes on to say: 'While some achieve beggary, nobody can doubt the great majority have beggary thrust upon them . . . the rightist agenda rolls, welfare spending high upon it. Turn the hoses of moral infamy on the homeless.' It was estimated in 1994 that 145 000 households a year are now declared homeless. However, this does not tell us how many individuals there are within each household in order to estimate the true number of homeless persons. The new housing regulations introduced in 1994 have also made it more difficult for homeless persons to be officially 'labelled' as homeless, for example: 'Families will be forced to sleep in doorways in order to be recognized as homeless' (Wintour, 1994a).

THE RELEVANCE OF ENGELS'S MATERIAL ANALYSIS TO CONTEMPORARY SOCIETY

In Britain today it is estimated that at least one in three children live their lives in poverty, low income households are often unable to afford the equivalent of the poor house diet of the last century and the 'poorest families' income fell 14 per cent under Thatcher' (Brindle, 1993). The Duke of Edinburgh has suggested that absolute poverty no longer exists. But how absolute does poverty have to be if citizens cannot afford basic necessities? That is, shelter, sustenance, the right to work, and dignity when our health or skills fail us. Real poverty and relative deprivation are as widespread now as they were 150 years ago. The spectre of uncertainty, insecurity and inequality, the social evils exposed by Engels's research methods in the nineteenth century, still prevail today. As Donnison (1994) argues: 'It is not poverty but inequality that damages our health.' A reassessment of *The Condition of the Working Class in England,* as we celebrate the 150th anniversary of its publication, is a worthwhile project in the context of the failure of capitalist economic development to deliver a more equitable society as we approach the twenty-first century.

The use of Engels's 'requisite sources' in 1990s Britain supports the argument that Engels's text, research methods and material analysis of society are still valid today. In the 1990s, as in 1845, a material analysis of society reveals conditions which are the 'necessary consequences of the historical development of England' (Engels, 1987, p. 292). Engels's research criticizes the superficiality of documents which are abstract and theoretical; the same criticisms are appropriate today. Consider, for example, the healthy-eating campaigns of the 1990s which are theoretically correct but not achievable in practice for a large section of the population. Engels's method reveals the structures in society which create and recreate want because 'the same economic necessity which produced them in the first place, produces them in the next place also' (Engels, 1979, p. 74).

Engels argued in 1845 that 'a knowledge of proletarian conditions is absolutely necessary to provide solid ground for socialist theories' (Engels, 1987, p. 27). Perhaps the same is needed in 1990s Britain. The Transport and General Workers Union (T&G) recently published their response to the reality of socio-economic differentials in wealth, health and welfare. Their findings argue that:

> This report has demonstrated the growing breadth and depth of poverty, insecurity and inequality in British society in recent years. At the same time, the forms of social protection built up after the war have been systematically eroded, in a step by step process to re-form social provision to mirror and entrench the fragmentation and stratification in our contemporary society ... What is clear is that nothing less than social reconstruction will do to attack these social evils and bring about a real social security in the changed world at the end of the twentieth century.
>
> (T&G, 1994, p. 132)

Engels's political theory therefore is still relevant today, and by using his research methods to inform socialist theory it may be possible to create a more equitable society for a majority of citizens as we approach the twenty-first century.

The utilization of Engels's research methods in the 1990s supports the proposition that a material analysis of society is still useful as a means of exposing the structural inequalities in advanced, capitalist society and refuting the superficiality of abstract notions which do not consider reality.

References

Barasi, M. and Motram, R. (1990) *Human Nutrition,* Edward Arnold.
Bevins, A. (1994) 'Behave well – or lose the dole', *The Observer,* 4.12.94.
Black, D. (1992) 'Black returns to fray in defence of NHS', *The Guardian,* 17.12.93.
Brindle, D. (1993) 'Poorest families' income fell 14 per cent under Thatcher', *The Guardian,* 1.7.93.
Brindle, D. (1994a) 'Basic benefit will not buy children a workhouse diet', *The Guardian,* 1.2.94.
Brindle, D. (1994b) 'New benefit rules to put pressure on jobless', *The Guardian,* 2.8.94.
Brindle, D. and White, M. (1995) 'Lilley "returning to Poor Law" with benefits shift', *The Guardian,* 10.1.95.
Carver, T. (1991) *Friedrich Engels. His Life and Thought,* Macmillan.
Challoner, W.H. and Henderson, W.O. (1972) 'Friedrich Engels and the England of the "Hungry Forties" ', in Hartwell et al. (eds), *The Long Debate on Poverty,* Institute of Economic Affairs.
Dahrendorf, R. (1965) *Class and Class Conflict in Industrial Society,* Routledge & Kegan Paul.
Davey Smith, G. and Egger, M. (1993) 'Socioeconomic differentials in wealth and health', *British Medical Journal,* Vol. 307, 1993, pp. 1085–6.
Davies, H. (1994) 'Women set the agenda for nineties job market', *The Observer,* 13.3.94.
Delamothe, T. (1992) 'Poor Britain Losing Out', *British Medical Journal,* Vol. 305, 1992, pp. 263–4.
Donegan, L. (1994) 'Lecturer given lesson on jobs', *The Guardian,* 3.8.94.
Donnison, D. (1994) 'Riches to die for', *The Guardian,* 27.7.94.
Durham, M. (1993) 'Benefits of Tory morality', *The Observer,* 14.11.93.
Elliott, L. (1994) 'Think tank's mixed message for Government', *The Guardian,* 8.6.94.
Engels, F. (1969) *Ludwig Feuerbach and the End of Classical German Philosophy,* Progress Publishers.
Engels, F. (1973) 'The Labour Movement in America. Preface to the American Edition', in *The Condition of the Working Class in England.* Progress Publishers.
Engels, F. (1973) 'The Preface to the Second German Edition' in *The Condition of the Working Class in England,* Progress Publishers.
Engels, F. (1975) 'Letters from Wuppertal' (1839), in *Collected Works,* Vol. 2, Lawrence & Wishart.

Engels, F. (1975) 'The Condition of England. Past and Present by Carlyle' (1843), in *Collected Works*, Vol. 3, Lawrence & Wishart.
Engels, F. (1979) *The Housing Question*, Progress Publishers.
Engels, F. (1987) *The Condition of the Working Class in England*, Penguin Classics.
Engels, F. (1993) *Socialism: Utopian and Scientific*, Bookmarks.
Fox, B. and Cameron, A. (1990) *Food Science, Nutrition and Health*, Edward Arnold.
Galbraith, J.K. (1994) 'Towards a new world deal', *The Guardian*, 26.1.94.
Geras, N. (1987) 'Post Marxism' *New Left Review*, No. 163, pp. 40–82.
Gilmour, I. (1993) *Dancing with Dogma. Britain under Thatcherism*, Pocket Books.
Gray, J. (1994) 'On the edge of the abyss', *The Guardian*, 18.7.94.
Harrison, D., Dodd, V. and Durham, M. (1994) 'Major chases votes in new attack on beggars', *The Observer*, 29.5.94.
Hennessy, P. (1993) *Never Again*, Vintage.
Hunley, J.D. (1991) *Friedrich Engels. A Reinterpretation*, Yale University Press.
Hunter, T. (1994) 'Disaster as safety net is withdrawn', *The Guardian*, 30.11.94.
Hutton, W. (1994a) 'Hand to mouth', *The Guardian*, 29.9.94.
Hutton, W. (1994b) 'Victorian values all too evident in income pattern', *The Guardian*, 3.6.94.
Hutton, W. (1994c) 'An end to the rule of fish market economics', *The Guardian*, 25.7.94.
Joseph, K. (1986) 'Foreword', in Smiles, S., *Self-Help*, Penguin.
Joseph Rowntree Foundation (1994) *The Effects of the 1986 Social Security Act on Family Incomes*, Social Policy Research Findings No. 54.
Jury, L. (1994a) 'Study shows poor are dying younger', *The Guardian*, 29.4.94.
Jury, L. (1994b) 'Ethnic women suffer double bias', *The Guardian*, 2.6.94.
Kemp-Ashraf, P.M. (1971) 'George Weerth in Bradford', in Kuczynski, I. and P. (eds), *A Young Revolutionary in 19th Century England. Selected writings of George Weerth*, Seven Seas Books, Berlin.
Laclau, E. and Mouffe, C. (1987) *Hegemony and Socialist Strategy – Towards a Radical Democratic Politics*, Verso.
Leather, S. (1992) 'Less money, Less choice. Poverty and Diet in the UK today', in National Consumer Council, *Your Food: Whose Choice?*, HMSO.
Lowry, S. (1991) *Housing and Health*, British Medical Journal Publication.
McSmith, A. (1994) 'Poor fall through final safety net', *The Observer*, 27.11.94.
Marx, K. (1975) *A Contribution to the Critique of Political Economy* (1859), in Tucker, R., (1975) *The Marx–Engels Reader*, Norton.
Marx, K. (1990) *Capital*, Vol. 1, Penguin Classics.
Marx, K. (1991) *Capital*, Vol. 3, Penguin Classics.
Marx, K. and Engels, F. (1975) 'Friedrich Engels Senior to Karl Snethlage, 1 December, 1820', in *Collected Works*, Vol. 2, Lawrence & Wishart.
Marx, K. and Engels, F. (1975) 'Friedrich Engels Senior to Karl Snethlage, 5 October, 1842', in *Collected Works*, Vol. 2, Lawrence & Wishart.
Marx, K. and Engels, F. (1975) *The Holy Family* (1845), in *Collected Works*, Vol. 4, Lawrence & Wishart.
Marx, K. and Engels, F. (1976) *The German Ideology* (1845–46), in *Collected Works*, Vol. 5, Lawrence & Wishart.

Meikle, J. (1994a) 'Britain joins Third World as Oxfam moves to help nation's poor', *The Guardian*, 2.8.94.
Meikle, J. (1994b) 'Hundreds of college lecturers facing redundancy', *The Guardian*, 30.11.94.
Milburn, A. (1994) 'Low pay forces desperate one million to take second jobs', *The Guardian*, 24.10.94.
National Children's Home (1991) *NCH Poverty and Nutrition Survey*, NCH Publication.
Simmons, M. (1994) 'Closures to make more homeless', *The Guardian*, 30.5.94.
Smiles, S. (1986) *Self-Help*, Penguin.
Townsend, P. (1979) *Poverty in the United Kingdom. A Survey of Household Resources and Standards of Living*, Penguin.
Transport & General Workers Union (1994) *In Place of Fear*, T&G Publication.
Wainwright, M. (1993) 'Christmas dinner for £1.40 tells a winter's tale', *The Guardian*, 17.12.93.
Wainwright, M. (1994) 'Estate families feel squeeze of London-plus costs', *The Guardian*, 31.5.94.
Whitfield, R. (1988) *Frederick Engels in Manchester*, Working Class Movement Library, Manchester.
Wilkinson, R.G. (1992) 'Income distribution and life expectancy', *British Medical Journal*, Vol. 304, 1992, pp. 165–8.
Wilkinson, R.G. (1994) 'Divided we fall. The poor pay the price of increased social inequality with their health', *British Medical Journal*, Vol. 308, 1994, pp. 1113–14.
Wilson, E. (1967) *To the Finland Station*, Fontana.
Wintour, P. (1994a) 'Families must sleep rough to be seen as homeless', *The Guardian*, 21.1.94.
Wintour, P. (1994b) 'Portillo lays into yobbos and feckless', *The Guardian*, 23.4.94.
Wood, E.M. (1986) *The Retreat from Class. A New 'True' Socialism*, Verso.
Woodcock, C. (1994) 'When the bankers say: "If you're black – keep back" ', *The Guardian*, 18.4.94.
Wright, E.O. (1994) *Interrogating Inequality*, Verso.
Young, H. (1994) 'Major's mask drops into the gutter', *The Guardian*, 31.5.94.

6

Engels's *Origin*: Legacy, Burden and Vision

Lise Vogel

INTRODUCTION

Friedrich Engels's *The Origin of the Family, Private Property and the State* has functioned as an authoritative theoretical text for two quite different social movements: the socialist movement on the one hand, and the modern women's movement on the other. Since the end of the nineteenth century, socialists have taken the book as the definitive Marxist pronouncement on women and the family. Confronting capitalist exploitation and, often, feudal social relations as well, socialist parties and movements have valued the *Origin* for its critique of marriage as an oppressive economic institution, its interest in women's participation in social production, and its vision of freely-chosen sexual relations in a collectively organized society.

In the late 1960s and early 1970s, feminists also turned to the *Origin*, but with different concerns. Where socialists focused on the text's implications for bettering marital and family life, modern feminists were more interested in its theorization of woman's position. Thus what drew them to the *Origin* were Engels's materialist account of patriarchy, his discussion of the evolution of female subordination, and his vision of women's liberation as only possible in a radically transformed social order.

Radical feminists recuperated the *Origin* above all for the making of a theory and history of patriarchy. Kate Millett, for example, emphasized the *Origin*'s analysis of marriage, reading Engels as an important contributor to radical feminism's critique of sexuality and male power.[1] Shulamith Firestone relied more directly on Engels's materialism. In her account, the *Origin* correctly targeted the sex division of labour and the private family as central to women's oppression. Radical feminists had simply to 'take the class analysis one step further to its roots in the biological division of the sexes'.[2]

Extremely influential, these authors both constructed Engels as a founding father of radical feminism.

Socialist feminists produced a different reading of the *Origin*. Like radical feminists they appreciated the text as an important, if somewhat problematic, contribution towards the development of a materialist understanding of patriarchy. But they paid more attention to the analysis it offered of the mechanisms of women's oppression. In Engels's linking of family forms to modes of production and the state they sought both theoretical guidance and a precedent for their efforts to conceptualize the personal as political. The achievement of the *Origin* was that it revealed 'women's oppression as a problem of history, rather than of biology, a problem which it should be the concern of historical materialism to analyse and revolutionary politics to solve'.[3]

In this essay I look again at Engels's *Origin* and what late twentieth-century feminists have made of it. In my interpretation the text provides an unsteady point of departure for theorizing about women's liberation. Despite its significant contributions, it is a hastily assembled and contradictory work. To the extent that both the socialist tradition and modern feminists have relied on the *Origin* for theoretical insight, their efforts have been, I argue, confounded by its ambiguities.

SOURCES

Engels wrote the *Origin* between March and May of 1884, one year after the death of his colleague and mentor Karl Marx. The circumstances of Engels's startlingly rapid production of the book are mysterious. Writing to the German socialist Karl Kautsky on 16 February 1884, he described Marx's enthusiasm for the anthropological writings of the day, adding: 'If I had the time I would work up the material with Marx's notes, . . . but I cannot even think of it.' Yet by late March Engels was already at work on the *Origin* and by the end of April close to finishing.[4] The full explanation of the reasons for his change in plan, which is especially striking in view of the fact that he was already immersed in the editing of Marx's unfinished volumes of *Capital*, must await further research. It is likely that the context was political. In 1879, the German socialist leader August Bebel had published *Woman in the Past, Present and Future*, which appeared in a revised and expanded version late in

1883. Tremendously popular from the start, Bebel's *Woman* bore the influence of emerging tendencies toward reformism within the socialist movement.[5] Engels's decision to write the *Origin* surely reflected a recognition of the weaknesses in Bebel's work. The socialist movement's interest in women's emancipation required a more adequate foundation, and the *Origin* represented Engels's attempt to provide one. The book constituted an implicit polemic within the movement.

The *Origin* is thus a document produced at a particular historical conjuncture. Best understood as a palimpsest, it amalgamates texts by three men with disparate projects. The earliest is that by Lewis H. Morgan, *Ancient Society*, published in 1877 – an enquiry of strictly anthropological intent.[6] Morgan's book forms the basis for the second text, a set of extracts embedded among other notes from Marx's reading in contemporary ethnography; whether Marx had an ultimate purpose for these 'Ethnological Notebooks' is unknown.[7] Third is Engels's hurried effort, no doubt politically motivated, to use both sources in order to produce a guide for the socialist movement – the *Origin*. Morgan's *Ancient Society* is thus complexly filtered as it makes its way into the *Origin* – first by Marx in the 'Ethnological Notebooks' and then again by Engels as he rereads Morgan in the light of Marx's notes. To grasp the meaning of the *Origin* it is therefore necessary to examine the assumptions and incoherences of *Ancient Society* as well as the way Marx excerpted Morgan's text in his 'Notebooks'.

In *Ancient Society*, Morgan sought to demonstrate the parallel evolution of four 'characteristics' of human society: inventions and discoveries, government, family and property. Ranging across a vast array of ethnographic data, the book is divided into sections corresponding to the four characteristics. In the first, Morgan sketches three stages in the evolution of human inventions and discoveries. At the most primitive level of social organization, peoples in the stage of 'savagery' gather wild plants, fish and hunt. The second period, 'barbarism', is characterized by food production, first horticulture and later agriculture. Finally, in the period of 'civilization', societies use advanced agricultural methods and keep written records. Morgan divides such societies into two broad types, ancient and modern. With this sequence of stages, Morgan rests human history on a materialist foundation, but one whose nature is technological, not social.

Morgan devotes nearly two-thirds of *Ancient Society* to the second characteristic, government, tracing the evolution of social organization from early kin-based governance to the state. The social organization of the most primitive peoples is based simply on broadly defined 'classes' of persons permitted to marry one another. As the circle of possible marriage partners narrows, the 'gens', or clan, develops. In a 'gentile' society, an individual belongs to the clan of either mother or father, not to both. Living in northern New York State, Morgan believed he had observed the most developed form of gentile organization among the matrilineal Iroquois, a confederacy of tribes that included thousands of members governed through personal ties rather than formal political institutions. Eventually, clan organization gives way, pressed by technological advances in productivity. Property attains a dominant role and government can no longer rest on personal relations. Morgan sketches the early evolution of the state, which organizes people, now distributed in property classes, on a territorial basis.

Even before the emergence of developed political organization, a critical change occurs within the clan system. At a certain point, matrilineal clan organization succumbs to the principle of patrilineality. The impetus is the development of property. According to Morgan, descent through the female line was the original form of clan organization. As soon as property in cattle and land arises, however, two facts, entirely self-evident in Morgan's view, doom matrilineality. First, men naturally become the owners of the property. Second, they develop a natural wish to transmit it to their own children. Hence accumulation of property has the consequence that in the middle stages of barbarism, the patrilineal clan becomes the basic unit of the gentile social system.

A discussion of the third characteristic of human society, the family, follows, making up roughly one-quarter of *Ancient Society*. Morgan describes the evolution of five family forms, differentiated by progressive restriction of permissible marriage partners. He conjectures the first two as types of group marriage, 'consanguine' and 'punaluan', implying an even earlier stage of promiscuous intercourse. The third form, the 'pairing' family, is associated with clan-based societies. Single pairs marry and live in communal kin-based households; the marriage bond may be dissolved at will. Lineage ties remain primary to each partner, for the clan is the basic social unit. Morgan notes the collective security the pairing family system provides to individuals, as well as its egalitarianism when compared with subsequent family forms.

The last two family forms reflect the influence of the development of property. The 'patriarchal' family organizes a group of persons – slave, servant, free – under a male head who exercises supreme authority. The 'monogamian' family consists of a single couple which, with its children, composes an independent household. Morgan conceptualizes both family types as institutions whose primary purpose is to hold property and transmit it to offspring. To ensure the children's paternity, strict fidelity is required of women. Paternal power is more or less absolute, and only death can break the marriage bond. The patriarchal and monogamian families are forms more appropriate for political society and they appear in the last stages of barbarism and continue into the period of civilization.

Morgan argues that the patriarchal and monogamian families represent a social advance, for they permit a heightened individuality of persons. At the same time, he recognizes that in practice such individuality was available only to men. Women as well as children were generally subordinated to the paternal power of the family head. By contrast, the pairing family of clan society provided women with a certain level of equality and power, particularly before the transition to patrilineal descent. So long as children remained in their mother's clan, the pairing family was embedded in the matrilineal clan household, and Morgan thought it likely that the woman rather than the man functioned as the family's centre. With the shift to descent in the male line, the pairing family became part of the patrilineal clan household and the woman was more isolated from her gentile kin. Because she was still a member of her own clan she nevertheless retained a measure of independent social standing. The advent of paternal power in the patriarchal and monogamian families opens the way to a profound degradation of women's position. Here, the cruel subordination of women and children belies Morgan's optimistic notions of evolutionary development.

Ancient Society closes with a brief consideration of the fourth characteristic, property. Morgan distinguishes three stages in the development of property, generally corresponding to the three major evolutionary periods. Among the most primitive peoples, those at the level of savagery, property scarcely exists. Lands are held in common, as is housing, and Morgan speculates that the germ of property lies in a developing right to inherit personal articles. Property in land, houses and livestock emerges in the stage of barbarism. The rules of inheritance at first conform to clan organization: property reverts to the clan of the deceased, not to his or her spouse. Eventually, individual ownership through the monogamian family prevails, with property inherited by the deceased owner's children. The period of civilization has arrived.

In conclusion, Morgan offers the observation that in his own time property has become an 'unmanageable power'. Society is heading towards destruction, the logical outcome of a social organization in which 'property is the end and aim.' Still, Morgan holds out hope for society's reconstruction on 'the next higher plane', where it will appear to be 'a revival, in a higher form, of the liberty, equality and fraternity' of ancient clan society.[8]

In *Ancient Society*, Morgan solved the puzzle of clan organization and analysed the sequence of social institutions in evolutionary terms. The book became the foundation for all subsequent research on the history of early human societies, despite its many factual and interpretive errors. These shortcomings, as well as Morgan's substantial contributions, have been much discussed.[9] Here, the emphasis will be on Morgan's assumptions about the mechanisms and motivations of social change.

Morgan describes four 'characteristics' evolving in parallel along the path from savagery through barbarism to civilization. Each sequence constitutes 'a natural as well as necessary sequence of progress', but *Ancient Society* does not identify the impetus for the forward motion. The book's extremely repetitive organization likewise suggests an inability to establish a clear relationship among the four kinds of phenomenon. A theory of social development lies implicit nonetheless in Morgan's work. Frequently observing that 'the experience of mankind has run in nearly uniform channels', Morgan proposes that the placement of the major markers in these channels is determined by the evolution of the arts of subsistence – that is, by the types of inventions and discoveries used to acquire or produce the means of subsistence. Human progress ultimately rests on technological advances in the mode of material life.[10]

But what motivates technological progress? Morgan points to the critical role played by property. The need to transmit property to heirs underlies the shift from matrilineal to patrilineal clan organization. The rise of new 'complicated wants', growing out of an accelerated accumulation of property, brings about the dissolution of clan organization and its replacement by political society. For Morgan, property consists simply of things, the objects of subsistence, with no particular location within a network of social relations. Once the idea of property appears, it grows automatically, extending itself in both magnitude and complexity while nurturing a sequence of stages in the arts of subsistence: 'Commencing at zero in savagery, the passion for the possession of property, as the representative of accumulated subsistence, has now become dominant over the human mind in civilized races.' That is, a passion in the minds of men – greed – leads naturally to the evolution of property and, consequently, to technological advances and social development in general.[11]

Morgan's book captured the attention of many, among them Marx. In the 'Ethnological Notebooks', published only in the twentieth century, Marx made copious extracts. Perhaps the most interesting feature of these notes is the way Marx revised the structure of *Ancient Society*, altering both the sequence of presentation and the relative weight of the sections.[12] Morgan had begun with the evolution of the arts of subsistence and then surveyed the parallel development of government, family and property. Marx moved Morgan's long section on government to the end and altered the relative amount of space given to each part. He reduced by half the already short discussion of the arts of subsistence and by a third the section on the family. At the same time he extended, proportionately, the space given by Morgan to the consideration of property and government. In sum, Marx's notes rearrange Morgan's material as follows: arts of subsistence (reduced); family (reduced); property (expanded); government (slightly expanded). Through this reorganization Marx perhaps sought to put Morgan's findings in an intellectually more coherent order.

THE *ORIGIN* AS A PALIMPSEST TEXT

To the extent that Engels incorporated the material in *Ancient Society* into his *Origin of the Family, Private Property and the State*, he adopted the order of Marx's excerpts in the 'Ethnological Notebooks' – making, however, several important structural changes. He did not devote a separate chapter to the subject of property. He greatly enlarged the relative importance of the chapter on the family, giving it almost as much space as he assigned to the chapters on the state. And he shifted the focus to the transition between barbarism and civilization. In this way, Engels converted Morgan's four 'lines of human progress' into three sections, which make up the bulk of the *Origin*.

Substantively, Engels followed Morgan quite closely. He pruned the wealth of ethnographic evidence, even replacing it where his own reading offered more relevant data. He emphasized the points that most tellingly exposed the revised explanatory framework he was seeking to establish. And he employed a more readable, even engagingly chatty, literary style. In general, the *Origin* seems to be a shorter, more focused and more accessible version of *Ancient Society*. A closer examination of the ways in which Engels's presentation of the material differs from Morgan's reveals both the contribution and the limitations of the *Origin*.

In a short opening, chapter 1, 'Stages in Prehistoric Culture', Engels succinctly recapitulates Morgan's account of the evolution of three stages in the arts of subsistence. Emphasizing the richness of Morgan's material, Engels also acknowledges a certain inadequacy in his own discussion, for not until the last chapter will he recast Morgan's work in the light of Marx's understanding of social development. 'My sketch [is] flat and feeble compared with the picture to be unrolled at the end of our travels.'[13] As it turns out, the *Origin* remains far closer to *Ancient Society* than Engels intended.

Chapter 2, 'The Family', constituting about one-third of the *Origin*, presents a reworked and augmented version of Morgan's sequence of family types. Engels underscores the importance of Morgan's discoveries and takes the opportunity to situate Morgan's work in the context of eighteenth- and nineteenth-century speculations concerning primate evolution, early human social behaviour and the possibility of a primitive state of promiscuous sexual intercourse. Concluding these half-dozen pages with the observation that bourgeois moral standards cannot be used to interpret primitive societies, he comments on Morgan's discussion of the two hypothetical forms of group marriage.[14] Like Morgan, he believes that natural selection, through the innate mechanisms of jealousy and incest taboos, triggered the succession of family types. In addition, the logic behind the change Marx had made in Morgan's sequence of presentation now becomes clear, for Engels is able to explain the origin of the clan system in the course of his description of the punaluan family.

Having disposed of group marriage and the genesis of the clan, Engels turns to the pairing and patriarchal families. Here he merges the material Morgan had covered in his chapter on property into his discussion. Along with Morgan, Bachofen and others, Engels assumes that supremacy of women characterized early human societies, but he argues that it rested on the material foundation of a natural sex division of labour within the primitive communistic household. Only if 'new, social forces' caused that natural material foundation to take a different form could women lose their position of independence.[15] And this occurred when society began to produce a sizeable surplus, making it possible for wealth to amass and eventually pass into the private possession of families. Like Morgan, Engels sees the development of productivity as an automatically evolving process, but he makes a distinction, however vaguely, between wealth as a given accumulation of things and private property as a social relation.

Once wealth is held privately, its accumulation becomes a central social issue. 'Mother right', that is descent in the female line and, along with it, the supremacy of women in the communal household, now constitutes a barrier to social development. Earlier, the supposedly natural division of labour between women and men placed women in charge of the household while men had the task of providing food. In a society at a low level of productivity, therefore, women possessed the household goods and men the instruments necessary to hunt, fish, cultivate plants and the like. With increasing productivity and the development of private property in land, cattle and slaves, this historical accident, as it were, has the grim consequence that men, the former possessors of the instruments of gathering and producing food, now own the wealth. Mother right makes it impossible, however, for men to transmit the newly evolved private property to their children. 'Mother right, therefore, had to be overthrown, and overthrown it was.'[16]

Engels regards the shift to the patrilineal clan system as crucial in its impact on society and on women's position. It marks the establishment of a set of social relations conducive to the further evolution not only of private property but of full-scale class society. More dramatically, 'the overthrow of mother right was the *world historic defeat of the female sex*. The man took command in the home also; the woman was degraded and reduced to servitude; she became the slave of his lust and a mere instrument for the production of children.'[17] The patriarchal family, with its incorporation of slaves and servants under the supreme authority of the male head, now emerges as a form intermediate between the pairing family and monogamy. Engels offers specific historical examples of this transition stage, emphasizing the relationship between land tenure and social structure, as well as the brutality of the patriarch toward women in the household.

In discussing the monogamous family, Engels again follows Morgan while simultaneously incorporating a clearer analysis of property relations and focusing on the question of woman's position. The monogamous family appears toward the end of the second stage in the development of the arts of subsistence – that is, at the threshold of civilization – and represents a perfected form for the transmission of private property from father to children. Engels emphasizes the origin of the monogamous family in economic conditions and its function as a property-holding institution. 'It was the first form of the family to be based not on natural but on economic conditions – on the victory of private property over primitive, natural communal property.'[18] Although Engels never states it unambiguously, the implication is that the form of the monogamous, as well as the patriarchal, family constitutes a product of the rise of class society.

Engels has no illusions about the position of women in the monogamous family. Monogamy is a standard enforced on the woman only, and exists solely to guarantee the paternity of the offspring, not for any reasons of love or affection. Men are free to live by a different standard. At the same time, the phenomenon of the neglected wife begets its own consequences. Thus, side by side with the institution of so-called monogamous marriage flourishes all manner of adultery and prostitution. Furthermore, 'monogamous marriage comes on the scene as the subjugation of the one sex by the other; it announces a struggle between the sexes unknown throughout the whole previous prehistoric period.' In Engels's formulation, this struggle between the sexes appears simultaneously with class relations. 'The first class opposition that appears in history coincides with the development of the antagonism between man and woman in monogamous marriage, and the first class oppression coincides with that of the female sex by the male.' Contrary to a common misinterpretation of these remarks, Engels does not assert that the sex struggle antedates class conflict. Neither, however, does he clearly argue that it is rooted in the emergence of class society. He simply treats the two developments as parallel, skirting the difficult problems of historical origins and theoretical relationships.[19]

With the basic character of monogamous marriage established, Engels turns briefly to a number of topics not addressed by Morgan. To start, he presents a quick history of the monogamous family's development in the period of civilization, with emphasis on the extent to which it fostered 'individual sex love'. According to Engels, love-based marriages were impossible prior to the great 'moral advance' constituted by the monogamous family. Moreover, in all ruling classes, even after the rise of the monogamous family, expedience rather than love governed the choice of marriage partner. After a brief glance at the medieval ruling-class family, Engels focuses on marriage in capitalist society. Among the bourgeoisie, marriage is a matter of convenience, generally arranged by parents to further property interests. By contrast, the proletariat has the opportunity to truly experience 'modern individual sex love'. Among the proletariat, 'all the foundations of typical monogamy are cleared away. Here there is no property, for the preservation and inheritance of which monogamy and male supremacy were established; hence there is no incentive to make this male supremacy effective . . . Here quite other personal and social conditions decide.' Moreover, Engels believes that with the increasing employment of women in wage labour, and women's accompanying independence, no basis survives for any kind of male supremacy in the working-class household, 'except, perhaps, for something of the brutality toward women that has spread since the introduction of monogamy'.[20]

Most of Engels's discussion of women's situation in capitalist society is framed in terms of the gap between formal and substantive equality.[21] He begins with an analogy between the marriage contract and the labour contract. Both are freely entered into, juridically speaking, thereby making the partners equal on paper. This formal equality disguises, in the case of the labour contract, the differences in class position between the worker and the employer. The marriage contract involves a similar mystification since, in the case of a propertied family, parents actually determine the choice of children's marriage partners. In fact, the legal equality of the partners in a marriage is in sharp contrast with their actual inequality. Once the patriarchal and monogamous families develop, the wife's labour within the household becomes a private service. As Engels puts it, 'the wife became the head servant, excluded from all participation in social production.' Her work loses the public or socially necessary place it had held in earlier societies. Both excluded and, later, economically dependent, she therefore becomes subordinate. Only with large-scale capitalist industry, and only for the proletarian woman, does the possibility appear for re-entry into production. Yet this opportunity has a contradictory character so long as capitalist relations endure. If the proletarian wife 'carries out her duties in the private service of her family, she remains excluded from public production and unable to earn; and if she wants to take part in public production and earn independently, she cannot carry out family duties.'[22]

Engels's conclusions regarding the conditions for ending women's subordination, summarized in a few paragraphs, generally converge with the equally brief remarks on the subject made by Marx in *Capital*.[23] Like Marx, Engels underscores the progressive role that participation in the collective labour process can potentially play and its crucial importance as a condition for human liberation. But where Marx had embedded his comments in an analysis of the historical impact of capitalist large-scale industry, Engels places his observations in the context of a discussion of legal inequality. He again draws an analogy between workers and women, arguing that both groups must have political rights if they are to understand the character of their respective struggles.

> The democratic republic does not do away with the opposition of [the proletariat and the capitalist class]; on the contrary, it provides the clear field on which the fight can be fought out. And in the same way, the peculiar character of the supremacy of the husband over the wife in the modern family, the necessity of creating real social equality between them and the way to do it, will only be seen in the clear light of day when both possess legally complete equality of rights.[24]

The discussion of women's oppression in Engels's chapter on the family marks a significant advance over *Ancient Society*. From the perspective of late twentieth-century feminism, however, the account is problematic in many ways. Engels does not delineate the relationship between women's position and the emergence of class, or, perhaps, capitalist society. With respect to precapitalist class societies, he fails to specify the nature of women's subordination in different classes. For capitalism, he misses the significance of the working-class household as an essential social unit, not for the holding of property but for the reproduction of the working class itself. Thus he cannot see that a material basis for male supremacy is constituted within the proletarian household. Throughout the text he assumes that it is natural for 'family duties' to be the exclusive province of women. And he underestimates the range of ideological and psychological factors that provide a continuing foundation for male supremacy in the working-class family. Finally, Engels's emphasis on the strategic importance of democratic rights leaves open the question of the relationship between socialist revolution, women's liberation and the struggle for equal rights. The result is ambiguous, potentially suggesting that the socialist programme for women's liberation consists of two discrete objectives: equal rights with men in the still-capitalist short term, and full liberation on the basis of a higher form of the family in the far distant revolutionary millennium.

Engels closes the chapter on the family with a long look to the future.[25] These pages sketch a society in which the means of production have been converted into social property and marriage is no longer tied to economic inequality. True monogamy, that is monogamy for the man as well as the woman, is now possible. Men and women come together on the basis of 'individual sex love' and part when 'affection definitely comes to an end or is supplanted by a new passionate love'. Engels's focus on the emotional and sexual content of relations within the family reflected a common view that they represented the essence of the so-called woman question. Only at one point in this section does he dwell on the more everyday implications of the future abolition of the family's economic functions, observing that with the means of production held in common, 'the single family ceases to be the economic unit of society. Private housekeeping is transformed into a social industry. The care and education of the children becomes a public affair.'[26] These brief hints of programmatic guidance do not differ, in substance, from nineteenth-century communitarian proposals. Engels's chapter on the family in the *Origin* remains an unintegrated mix of Morgan's dry materialism and a radical view of sexual liberation – seasoned with genuine insights into the nature of property and social relations, and liberally sprinkled with Engels's warmth and wit.

In chapters 3–8 of the *Origin*, corresponding to the section on government in Morgan's *Ancient Society*, Engels examines the nature of clan society and traces the rise of the state. As in chapter 2 on the family, he follows Morgan's general line of argument, while at the same time incorporating the material on property. In Engels's words, the changes 'in form' between the institutions of the gentile constitution and those of the state 'have been outlined by Morgan, but their economic content and cause must largely be added by myself'.[27] The resulting discussion suffers from problems similar to those already observed in Engels's account of the family. Moreover, it becomes more obvious in these chapters that Engels identifies private property and the market exchange of commodities as the pivotal social developments in history. Nowhere, however, does he clearly discuss these phenomena in terms of the social relations that constitute the mode of production in which they originate.

In these chapters, a critique of property overwhelms the critique of class relations. Property not exploitation – the appropriation of the surplus labour of the producing class by another class – becomes the implicit object of class struggle. From the point of view of Marx's analysis of social reproduction, however, both private property and commodity exchange only represent specific manifestations of particular types of class society. In such societies, a given set of relations of exploitation always dominates, constituting the basis for specific social relations and forms of private property, the market, the state and so forth. The difference between this formulation and that in the *Origin* is not simply a matter of style or manner of exposition. Rather, it indicates that Engels's arguments generally remain within the framework of a utopian socialist critique of property.[28] Furthermore, Engels has confused the circumstance that the products of labour are exchanged in a society, with the presence of capitalist, or at least class, relations of production.

In the *Origin*'s closing chapter 9, 'Barbarism and Civilization', Engels examines the 'general economic conditions' behind the developments presented in previous chapters. He restates his account of social evolution in the period of the decline of clan society and the emergence of civilization, this time pointing out a series of major milestones. In the middle stages of barbarism, the separation of pastoral tribes from the mass of other peoples marks the 'first great social division of labour'. These tribes tame animals and develop agriculture; as a result they soon find themselves with products that make regular exchange possible. Inevitably and automatically, the increasing exchange leads to higher productivity, more wealth and a society in which the harnessing of surplus labour becomes feasible. Hence, slavery appears. 'From the first great social division of labour arose the first great cleavage of society into two classes: masters and slaves, exploiters and exploited.' Engels reminds the reader that the change in the division of labour also has consequences for relations between the sexes in the family. Because the pre-existing division of labour had supposedly assigned the task of procuring subsistence to men, men became the holders of the new wealth, and women found themselves subordinated and confined to private domestic labour. A 'second great division of labour' occurs at the close of the period of barbarism, when handicraft separates from agriculture. On this basis, a new cleavage of society into classes develops, the opposition between rich and poor. Inequalities of property among individual male heads of families now lead to the break up of the communal household, and the pairing marriage dissolves into the monogamous single family, even more oppressive to women. Finally, a third division of labour emerges in the period of civilization: a class of merchants arises, parasites whose nefarious activities lead to periodic trade crises. In the meantime, the rise of class cleavages has necessitated replacement of the gentile constitution with a third force, powerful but apparently above the class struggle – namely the state.[29]

In sum, the final chapter of the *Origin* argues that civilization results from the continual evolution of the division of labour, which in turn gives rise to exchange, commodity production, class cleavages, the subordination of women, the single family as the economic unit of society, and the state. Once again, Engels simply lists phenomena without locating them in social relations and the workings of a dominant mode of production. Moreover, he awards the leading role to the technical division of labour in the labour process – what Morgan had considered under the rubric 'arts of subsistence'. The development of class cleavages simply follows automatically, once a certain level of material productivity is reached. The emphasis on technological progress in this chapter constitutes a new element, tending somewhat to replace the focus in earlier chapters on the rise of private property as the prime mover of social change. At the same time, Engels, like Morgan, often invokes innate human greed and competitiveness to explain historical development.[30] All in all, the scattered analysis of social development presented in this final chapter represents some of the least coherent reasoning in the *Origin*.

Engels's concluding comments on the emancipation of women exhibit similar contradictions. He emphasizes, yet again, the crushing impact of the 'first great social division of labour' on women's position, and then leaps to the supposedly self-evident conclusion that the entry of women into social production is emancipatory. As in the chapter on the family, Engels assumes that domestic labour is purely women's work, does not locate his statements about women with respect to a specific class society, and blurs the relationship between women's eventual liberation in communist society and immediate strategic goals.

PRODUCTION AND REPRODUCTION

Engels made one argument in the *Origin* that the socialist movement later refused to endorse but which became central to modern feminist discourse. In a frequently cited passage in the preface, he spoke of two types of production proceeding in parallel:

> The determining factor in history is, in the final instance, the production and reproduction of immediate life. This, again, is of a twofold character: on the one side, the production of the means of existence, of food, clothing and shelter and the tools necessary for that production; on the other side, the production of human beings themselves, the propagation of the species. The social organization under which the people of a particular historical epoch and a particular country live is determined by both kinds of production: by the stage of development of labour on the one hand and of the family on the other.[31]

In these sentences Engels gives equal emphasis to procreation and to the production of things. It is difficult to believe, however, that he meant what this passage seems to imply: an equal theoretical weighting of human reproduction and social production. Throughout the *Origin*, as elsewhere, Engels describes developments in production as fundamentally causal. For the nineteenth-century socialist movement of which he was a leader, class struggle in the workplace was the key to revolutionary social transformation.

The passage actually reflects the *Origin*'s perilous relationship to yet another text – the 'German Ideology', written with Marx in 1846. The dependence of the *Origin* on the unpublished 'German Ideology' is obvious although rarely noted. Engels drew quite heavily on the forgotten manuscript of his and Marx's youth, which he had just rediscovered among Marx's papers.[32] The paralleling of the production of means of subsistence to the production of human beings in the preface, for example, recalls the earlier manuscript's discussion of the dual essence of social reproduction: 'The production of life, both of one's own in labour and of fresh life in procreation, ... appears as a twofold relation: on the one hand as a natural, on the other as a social relation.'[33] More generally, both texts make a sharp distinction between natural and social phenomena, emphasizing the purely biological or animal-like character of procreation. Furthermore, the 'German Ideology' assigns, as does the *Origin*, a central motivating role in social development to the continual evolution of the division of labour. According to the 'German Ideology', society develops in stages, beginning from the simplest forms, in which the only division of labour is natural and rooted in the sexual act. With the growth of the division of labour, social relations distinguish themselves from natural ones, and the 'family relation' becomes subordinate. Both the 'German Ideology' and the *Origin* refer to the development, at this point in history, of a relationship of latent slavery within the family, representing 'the first form of property'.[34] Finally, both texts put forth an equivocal image of the family as a germ or nucleus within which larger social contradictions originate or are reflected, and which itself constitutes the fundamental building block of society.[35]

The many convergences with the 'German Ideology' suggest that the older manuscript entered as a fourth text into the making of the palimpsest that is the *Origin*. Less visible than Morgan's *Ancient Society* or Marx's reading notes, the 'German Ideology' nonetheless plays a constitutive role. Its incorporation also has the effect of importing into the *Origin* many of the weaknesses of the earlier manuscript. In particular, the positing of two separate systems of production of material life implies a very primitive distinction between natural and social phenomena.[36] The revival of the dichotomy epitomizes the theoretical instability found throughout the *Origin*.

Socialists and feminists have differed in their evaluation of Engels's assertions concerning the twofold character of social reproduction. Reading the *Origin* as a seamless canonical text, socialists found the claims in its preface 'very remarkable', indeed 'almost incomprehensible'. What disturbed them was the implication that the family could be understood as an autonomous centre of social development. Soviet commentators eventually settled on the view that Engels was mistaken, and that the statement can at most refer to the very earliest period of human history, when people were supposedly so much a part of nature that social relations of production could not be said to exist.[37]

The implication that family and class constitute independent but interacting systems was precisely what caught the interest of feminist theorists in the 1970s. Their citation of the *Origin*'s preface in article after article had several purposes. It emphasized the material essence of the social processes for which women hold major responsibility. It implied that the production of human beings constitutes a process that has not only an autonomous character but a theoretical importance equal to that of the production of the means of existence. It suggested the importance of placing the problem of women's oppression in the context of a history of overall social reproduction. For socialist feminists, it also affirmed their commitment to the socialist tradition and suggested that Marx and Engels had more to say about the question of women than the later socialist movement was able to hear.

In short, this much-quoted passage from the *Origin*'s preface seemed to offer authoritative backing for feminists' focus, in the 1970s, on the family, sex divisions of labour and unpaid domestic work. As well, it appeared to validate their efforts to theorize a human reproduction process comparable to, but separate from, commodity production. Feminists posited the existence of a family or housework or domestic mode of (re)production alongside the capitalist or industrial mode of production, a sex/gender system alongside the class system, or, to put it at its simplest, patriarchy alongside capitalism. Engels thus became the conveyor of official revolutionary approval for the dualism of much of 1970s feminist theory, and particularly for that of socialist feminism.

During the 1980s, feminist theorizing turned, for a number of reasons, to questions for which Engels's *Origin* had little relevance. In the US, feminist thought moved into the academy and new generations of feminists no longer identified with an activist, much less socialist, feminism. Meanwhile, social theory repositioned Marxism as one of many emancipatory grand narratives, all now presumed irrelevant in the postmodern world order. In a changed political climate the *Origin* was retired to the status of an outdated text for an archaic social movement. Socialist feminism survived more as an outlook and an orientation than as a substantive focus.[38]

For those who still explicitly ponder the relationship of socialism and feminism, Engels remains a significant figure. Feminists often disparage the weaknesses of his theoretical contribution, the limitations of his vision of women's liberation, and the way in which he put his feminist principles into practice in his own life. But, as Jane Humphries wisely notes, Engels has become a target of criticism 'precisely because of his, by contemporary if not modern standards, sensitivity to feminist issues'.[39] His work endures as an important touchstone for socialist-feminist politics and theory.

Many socialist feminists continue to use a dual-systems conceptualization, viewing patriarchy and capitalism, reproduction and production, sex and class, as distinct but 'inextricably interrelated' structures that together shape women's lives. From this point of view, the theoretical task remains that of integrating an analysis of women with one of class. Engels's affirmation of the twofold nature of social reproduction is thus still key, constituting, for example, 'the major unifying theme' of the papers presented at a 1984 conference commemorating the centenary of the *Origin*.[40] Socialist feminists rise to defend the formulation and extend what they believe to be its kernel of truth. Jane Humphries maintains a literal interpretation, arguing that Engels indeed intended to parallel reproductive and productive activity as 'analytically equivalent'; in her view, his failing was not to have fully pursued his own insight. Martha Gimenez suggests the *Origin*'s preface makes better sense when interpreted as utilizing a dialectical rather than a dualistic mode of analysis. Juliet Matthaei comments approvingly on an effort to conceptualize 'the household as a mode of reproduction (*à la* Engels's view of a society as a mode of production and reproduction)'. Ann Ferguson presents her theory of sex/affective production as an authentic development of a multisystems approach first posited by Marx and Engels in the 'German Ideology' and then reprised in the preface to Engels's *Origin*.[41]

Why do socialist feminists hold on to dual-systems discourse, despite numerous trenchant critiques of it as a methodological and epistemological procedure?[42] For many, I suspect, dual-systems thinking is still preferable to the only two options that appear to be available. To give up the emphasis on an independent sphere of reproduction would mean, they assume, subordination within a Marxist theory stubbornly resistant to the substantive incorporation of gender and other dimensions of diversity. Yet to conceptualize women's oppression solely in terms of patriarchy would require a renunciation of the vision of the just society as simultaneously feminist and socialist. Socialist feminists fear a unified theoretical framework would put class before gender, race/ethnicity and other categorical specificities. But they also hesitate to abandon the Marxist tradition altogether, with its concern for those at the bottom of hierarchies and its hopes for individual fulfilment in the context of community. Few dare name, much less address, the daunting task that might resolve the dilemma: to radically transform Marxism itself. Yet, as Jean Gardiner observes, socialist feminists were, in the 1970s, among the first to intuit the coming crisis of Marxism and to delineate the limitations of Marxist political economy. The feminist critique of Marxist theory remains to be carried through.[43]

CONCLUSION

Engels's stated purpose in publishing the *Origin* was 'to present the results of Morgan's researches in the light of the conclusions of [Marx's] materialist examination of history, and thus to make clear their full significance'.[44] Engels's treatment of the material fell short, however, of this goal, for he only partially transformed Morgan's crude materialism. The *Origin* is marred throughout by Engels's failure to deploy a coherent account of social development. Instead, he relies on several theoretical frameworks in addition to his understanding of Marx's work: the technological determinism implicit in Morgan's *Ancient Society*, his main source of data; the 'German Ideology's' early version of historical materialism; and a generally utopian critique of property and view of the socialist future. While the *Origin* manages, in places, to rise above this eclecticism, its conceptual instability was to have serious consequences. The *Origin* constitutes an erratic text whose ambiguous theoretical and political formulations nevertheless became an integral part of the socialist – and, more recently, the feminist – undertaking.

This evaluation of the *Origin*, written one hundred years after Engels's death, may seem inappropriately harsh. It is, however, strictly a critique of the book as a theoretical text. Nothing said here can tarnish the *Origin*'s bright legacy of hope for freedom, equality and love in a socialist society. As we move through difficult times into the twenty-first century, we can still call upon Engels for a vision of how that collectivist future might liberate us from and for each other:

> But what will there be new? That will be answered when a new generation has grown up: a generation of men who never in their lives have known what it is to buy a woman's surrender with money or any other social instrument of power; a generation of women who have never known what it is to give themselves to a man from any other considerations than real love or to refuse to give themselves to their lover from fear of the economic consequences. When these people are in the world, they will care precious little what anybody today thinks they ought to do; they will make their own practice and their corresponding public opinion about the practice of each individual – and that will be the end of it.[45]

Notes

1. Kate Millett, *Sexual Politics* (New York: Doubleday, 1970).
2. Shulamith Firestone, *The Dialectic of Sex: The Case for Feminist Revolution* (New York: Morrow, 1970), p. 12.
3. Rosalind Delmar, 'Looking Again at Engels's *Origin of the Family, Private Property and the State*', in *The Rights and Wrongs of Women*, eds Juliet Mitchell and Ann Oakley (Harmondsworth: Penguin Books, 1976), pp. 271–87, esp. 287.
4. Engels to Kautsky, 16 February and 26 April 1884, in Karl Marx and Frederick Engels, *Selected Correspondence*, 2nd edn (Moscow: Progress Publishers, 1965), pp. 368, 372. See also Lawrence Krader (ed.), *The Ethnological Notebooks of Karl Marx* (Assen, Netherlands: Van Gorcum, 1972), pp. 388–90.
5. For Bebel's *Woman*, see Lise Vogel, *Marxism and the Oppression of Women: Toward a Unitary Theory* (New Brunswick, NJ: Rutgers University Press, 1983), pp. 96–103, and Anne Lopes and Gary Roth, 'Marxism's Feminism: Bebel and Zetkin in Opposition', *Rethinking Marxism*, Vol. 6 (Fall 1993), pp. 66–78.
6. Lewis Morgan, *Ancient Society* (New York: Holt, 1877).
7. Krader, *Ethnological Notebooks*.
8. Morgan, *Ancient Society*, pp. 561–2.
9. See, for example, the introductions by Eleanor Leacock in Lewis Morgan, *Ancient Society* (Cleveland: World Publishing Co., 1963).
10. Morgan, *Ancient Society*, pp. vii, 3, 8.
11. Ibid., p. vii.
12. Krader, *Ethnological Notebooks*, p. 11 and p. 365, n. 21. See also U. Santamaria, 'Review Article: The Ethnological Notebooks of Karl Marx, ed. by L. Krader', *Critique of Anthropology*, Nos 4–5 (Autumn 1975), pp. 156–64.
13. Engels, *The Origin of the Family, Private Property and the State* (New York: International Publishers, 1972), p. 93.
14. Ibid., pp. 101–10.
15. Ibid., p. 117.
16. Ibid., pp. 119–20.
17. Ibid., pp. 120–1.
18. Ibid., p. 128.
19. Ibid., pp. 128, 129.
20. Ibid., pp. 132, 135.
21. Ibid., pp. 135–8.
22. Ibid., p. 137.
23. Karl Marx, *Capital*, Vol. 1 (Moscow: Progress Publishers, n.d.), p. 460.
24. Engels, *Origin*, p. 137.
25. Ibid., pp. 138–46.
26. Ibid., pp. 145, 139.
27. Ibid., p. 171.
28. Cf. Marx's comments about Proudhon in a letter to J.D. Schweitzer, 24 January 1865, in Marx and Engels, *Selected Correspondence*, p. 153.
29. Engels, *Origin*, pp. 218–25.

30. Ibid., pp. 223, 224, 235; see also pp. 119, 161.
31. Ibid., pp. 71–2.
32. Karl Marx and Friedrich Engels, *Werke* (Berlin: Dietz Verlag, 1956–), Vol. 36, pp. 33–4; see also pp. 39, 41 and 54, and Engels, *Origin*, p. 129. On the textual similarity, see also H. Kent Geiger, *The Family in Soviet Russia* (Cambridge, Mass.: Harvard University Press, 1968), pp. 30–2.
33. Karl Marx and Frederick Engels, *Collected Works* (New York: International Publishers, 1975–), Vol. 5, p. 43.
34. Marx and Engels, *Collected Works*, Vol. 5, pp. 33, 46; Engels, *Origin*, pp. 121, 134, 137.
35. Marx and Engels, *Collected Works*, Vol. 5, p. 46; Engels, *Origin*, pp. 121–2, 129, 131, 137.
36. For discussion of how Marx and Engels address the role of biology in women's oppression, see Janet Sayers, *Biological Politics: Feminist and Anti-Feminist Perspectives* (London: Tavistock Publications, 1982), pp. 181–203; Vogel, *Marxism and the Oppression of Women*, pp. 60–2.
37. On socialist and Soviet understanding of the *Origin*, see Geiger, *Family in Soviet Russia*, pp. 31–2; Bernhard Stern, 'Engels on the Family', *Science & Society*, Vol. 12 (1948), pp. 42–64; Janet Sayers, Mary Evans and Nanneke Redclift (eds), *Engels Revisited: New Feminist Essays* (London: Tavistock Publications, 1987), pp. 1–3.
38. For discussion of the evolution of the US women's movement, socialist feminism and feminist thought over the past three decades, see Karen V. Hansen and Ilene J. Philipson, 'Women, Class, and the Feminist Imagination: An Introduction', in *Women, Class, and the Feminist Imagination: A Socialist-Feminist Reader*, eds Karen V. Hansen and Ilene J. Philipson (Philadelphia: Temple University Press, 1990), pp. 3–40; Sandra Morgen, 'Conceptualizing and Changing Consciousness: Socialist-Feminist Perspectives', in *Women, Class and the Feminist Imagination*, pp. 277–91; Lise Vogel, introductions to the essays in *Woman Questions: Essays for a Materialist Feminism* (London: Pluto, and New York: Routledge, 1995). Note that many who started out in the US women's movement as socialist-feminist activists became important participants in the development of women's studies and feminist scholarship during the later 1970s and 1980s.
39. Jane Humphries, 'The Origin of the Family: Born Out of Scarcity not Wealth', in Sayers, Evans and Redclift, *Engels Revisited*, pp. 11–36, esp. p. 12.
40. Sayers, Evans and Redclift, *Engels Revisited*, p. 9.
41. Humphries, 'Origin of the Family', p. 15; Martha Gimenez, 'Marxist and Non-Marxist Elements in Engels's Views on the Oppression of Women', in Sayers, Evans and Redclift, *Engels Revisited*, pp. 37–56; Julie Matthaei, 'Surplus Labor, the Household, and Gender Oppression', in Harriet Fraad, Stephen Resnick and Richard Wolff (eds), *Bringing It All Back Home: Class, Gender and Power in the Modern Household* (London: Pluto, 1994), pp. 42–9, esp. p. 43; Ann Ferguson, *Sexual Democracy: Women, Oppression, and Revolution* (Boulder, Col.: Westview, 1991), pp. 71 and p. 93, n. 6.

42. For discussion and critique of dual systems theorizing see, among others: Veronica Beechey, 'On Patriarchy', *Feminist Review*, No. 3 (1979), pp. 66–82; Iris Young, 'Beyond the Unhappy Marriage: A Critique of the Dual Systems Theory', in *Women and Revolution: A Discussion of the Unhappy Marriage of Marxism and Feminism*, ed. Lydia Sargent (Boston: South End Press, 1981), pp. 43–69; Hansen and Philipson, 'Women, Class, and the Feminist Imagination', pp. 16–25; Elizabeth V. Spelman, *Inessential Woman: Problems of Exclusion in Feminist Thought* (Boston: Beacon Press, 1988); Vogel, *Woman Questions*.
43. Jean Gardiner, 'Domestic Labour Revisited: A Feminist Critique of Marxist Economics', paper presented at the CSE Conference, Leeds, England, July 1994.
44. Engels, *Origin*, p. 71.
45. Ibid., p. 145.

7

Engels and Materialism

Sean Sayers

Engels was a Marxist. He describes himself as a proponent of ideas whose 'leading basic principles' were due to Marx;[1] and it is in relation to Marx that his work is usually regarded by others too. But that is not how I am going to discuss him here.[2] On this, the centenary of his death, it is appropriate to consider Engels as a thinker in his own right.

I shall focus on the subject of philosophical materialism. This is a topic which occupied a great deal of Engels's attention in the later years of his life,[3] but about which Marx wrote little.[4] Engels's ideas on it are original and important, and of considerable current philosophical interest. In this paper I will describe these ideas and try to bring out their significance by placing them in the context of related contemporary work.

In general terms, materialism holds that everything that exists or happens is material and can be described and understood in purely naturalistic terms, without recourse to the notions of a divine creator or an immaterial human mind. This philosophy is fundamental to the scientific approach. However, as Engels stresses, it is important to distinguish this general philosophical outlook from the specific forms in which it is put forward by particular thinkers at particular periods. Both in Engels's time and still today, materialism often tends to be put forward as a narrow, mechanistic and reductionist philosophy. Engels calls this form of materialism 'mechanical' materialism. Nowadays it goes under the title of 'physicalism'. Then and now, quite standardly, it is treated as if it were the only form of materialism. As Engels shows, it is not so. The central purpose of his work in this area is to develop a non-mechanistic, non-reductive form of philosophical materialism.

Philosophical materialism

Engels gives a clear and useful general account of what the philosophy of materialism involves. He defines it in relation to 'the great basic question' of modern philosophy: 'the relation of thinking and being'.[5] Materialism holds that the material, natural world is 'primary'. More strictly defined, it is a form of ontological monism: everything that exists is material in character. 'The material, sensuously perceptible world to which we ourselves belong is the only reality; ... our consciousness and thinking, however supra-sensuous they may seem, are the product of a material, bodily organ, the brain. Matter is not a product of mind, but mind is itself merely the highest product of matter.'[6]

However, Engels is less clear when it comes to the classification of non-materialist philosophies. All too often he lumps them all together under the heading of 'idealism'. Many other Marxists have followed him in this. Important distinctions are thus obliterated. Idealism, more accurately defined, is the opposite of materialism: it is the view that everything is ultimately ideal or mental in character. As such it is also a form of monism. Idealism in this sense is a major influence in classical German philosophy, but it has little support among contemporary philosophers, at least of the analytic variety. More influential are various forms of dualism, which try to acknowledge the validity of the scientific account of the natural world, while at the same time insisting upon the irreducible reality of human and mental phenomena.

Engels characterizes the materialism of the eighteenth century as 'mechanistic'. In this, he is following Kant and Hegel. This philosophy was based upon the ideas of the natural sciences of its day, and particularly on mechanics and physics because, Engels argues, only these 'had then come to any definite close'.[7] It is sometimes argued that the physical sciences have developed since that time and that such materialism is no longer influential. That is questionable. It lives on in contemporary philosophy as 'physicalism'.

According to physicalism, the material world is (more or less) as it is described by modern physics and quantum mechanics. It is true that quantum theory involves statistical rather than mechanical laws. Nevertheless, in its exclusive reliance on mechanics and physics and in its reductionism, physicalism is the modern heir of the mechanistic materialism of the eighteenth century.

As an ontological doctrine, physicalism holds that all things are composed of fundamental physical particles and fields of force, whose behaviour is determined by the basic laws of physics and quantum mechanics. Complex entities and phenomena, such as chemical substances, biological organisms, human actions and states of consciousness, are all ultimately composed (in very complex ways, still not well understood) of such particles and forces.

This ontology, it is argued, implies that all phenomena can be described and understood in purely physical terms. The 'special sciences' (chemistry, geology, biology, the social sciences and psychology, etc.) can in principle be reduced to physics and mechanics. In practice, it is readily conceded, such reductions would be immensely complicated. They are not now feasible, and perhaps they never will be.[8] In principle, however, all empirical knowledge can be reduced to the terms of physics. Other sciences have no independent validity, no irreducible content; they contain nothing that cannot be stated in purely physical terms.[9]

Many philosophers reject reductionism of this sort, Engels among them.[10] Contemporary philosophical criticism of physicalism is focused in the main on its reductive account of human thought and activity. Donald Davidson's work has been particularly influential. He maintains that human belief and action are intentional in character, and intentionality, he insists, is a 'holistic' phenomenon. A particular belief or intention can be identified and described as such only by reference to a context of other intentional events (beliefs and actions), and ultimately to a web of meaningful social practices, to which a purely physicalist account is blind. Moreover, such identification involves assessing the belief or action according to norms and principles of 'coherence, rationality and consistency',[11] which the physicalist picture excludes. To describe and explain human thought and intentional activity as such, Davidson argues, we need to adopt a distinctive 'mental' or 'psychological' standpoint which uses concepts and theories which are irreducible to those of physics and mechanics.

These arguments are correct, I believe, and there is every reason to believe that Engels would also have endorsed them. However, since materialism is quite standardly identified with physicalist reductionism, the rejection of the latter is often taken to imply a rejection of materialism *tout court* and to point instead towards either dualism or out-and-out idealism. Neither of these alternatives is attractive, and neither is adopted by Engels. Engels argues for a non-mechanistic and non-physicalist form of materialism, which avoids reductionism on the one hand, and idealism and dualism on the other.

Davidson's 'anomalous monism'

Davidson also argues for a non-reductive form of materialism, but it is very different to that of Engels. For Davidson wants to combine a non-reductive account of the mental with a physicalist ontology of the sort that Engels criticizes. There are great problems with Davidson's position, as I will now briefly argue.

Davidson calls his philosophy 'anomalous monism'. This involves a physicalist ontology, in that it holds that all events, including mental ones, 'simply *are* (in the sense of *are identical with*) physical events'.[12] And yet Davidson wants to avoid the reductionism which is usually thought to follow from this. Like Kant, he insists that we can also see human thought and action as intentional and rational. This 'psychological' standpoint cannot be captured in purely physical terms. For as we have just seen, Davidson insists that descriptions of mental events are not reducible to the terms of physics. How can these positions be reconciled?

Although every particular human belief or action is identical with some particular physical state or event, Davidson argues, mental events as such (as kinds or types) have no general counterparts at the physical level. In the current jargon, there is a 'token' not a 'type' identity between the mental and the physical. For, according to Davidson, there are no psycho-physical laws linking descriptions in mental terms with descriptions at the purely physical level. Nor, he insists, are mental events determined by 'strict quantitative laws' of the sort that operate in physics; they are subject only to 'irreducibly statistical correlations'.[13] Mental events 'resist capture in the nomonological net of physical theory';[14] they are 'anomalous'.

As a physicalist, Davidson maintains that every particular mental event is identical with some particular physical event. However, in using mental concepts we are describing it in a way which has no precise equivalent at the purely physical level. 'Events are mental only as described.'[15] Thus mental concepts give us a way of 'describing' or 'interpreting' events which carries no implications of the existence of a separate realm of mental entities. As Davidson puts it: 'The mental is not an ontological but a conceptual category.'[16]

The attraction of this approach is that it seems to 'make room'[17] for an irreducible mental standpoint, while at the same time affirming physicalism and thus sidestepping the troubling ontological implications of dualism. As Evnine says: 'Davidson effected a kind of liberation when he showed how one could be a materialist without having to posit unlikely identities between kinds of mental events and kinds of physical events.'[18]

Unfortunately, this liberation is illusory. Davidson's approach does not ultimately escape the problems of traditional, ontological dualism; it merely shifts them elsewhere. The view that 'events are mental only as described' has the effect of making the mental into a mere 'standpoint' or way of 'describing' things. The result is what one might call a form of 'standpoint' dualism. Mental properties are no longer located in the object being described; they are shifted into the 'subjective' sphere: into the standpoint, into the description and/or the describer. Here the old problems of the relation of the mental and physical simply arise again. How is such a thing as a 'description' or a subjective 'standpoint' possible in a material world? How is it embodied? How does it arise? These problems are relocated by Davidson's philosophy, but they are not resolved. In Davidson's account, the mental seems to hover above the material world, neither reducible to it nor autonomous from it: hence the charge of 'epiphenomenalism' which is brought against it by philosophers like Kim.[19]

Nor can these problems be resolved within the framework of Davidson's philosophy. By refusing to 'ontologize' the mind, he does not avoid ontology altogether. On the contrary, his ontology is quite explicitly physicalist. His sole concern is to ensure that this ontology does not rule out the possibility of a distinct and irreducible mental standpoint; but physicalism is left quite unquestioned and uncriticized as an account of the world in its material aspect. This is characteristic of dualism, which typically tries to combine a physicalist account of the material world with the recognition of an irreducible mental sphere.

Philosophies of nature

A more far-reaching criticism of physicalism is required in order to develop a satisfactory non-reductive materialism. To understand how this is possible it is essential to see that physicalism gives an unsatisfactory and reductive account not only of human activity but also of purely material phenomena. This is where Engels comes in.[20] He explicitly recognizes this and attempts to develop a materialist but non-physicalist philosophy of nature.

The contrast with the approach of contemporary philosophers like Davidson is striking. Modern discussion of materialism takes place in a field which has come to be identified as 'philosophy of mind'. The assumption commonly made in this field is that the Cartesian, Enlightenment concept of mind (the 'ghost in the machine') is the main obstacle to a satisfactory understanding of the mind–body relation. Engels's approach is quite different. Of course, as a materialist, Engels rejects the Cartesian notion of the mind as an immaterial entity. With Marx, he gives a social and historical account of human thought and activity. At the same time, however, he criticizes mechanistic materialism – the physicalism of his day – not just for its reductive philosophy of mind, but also as a philosophy of nature.

Philosophy of nature is now generally taken to involve the attempt to propound a speculative theory of nature a priori. Accordingly, it is dismissed as a suspect and discredited field of philosophy, particularly by contemporary analytic philosophy of mind, which prides itself on the scientific and empirical basis of its outlook. No doubt some philosophies of nature take this form, as Engels is well aware: he criticizes Hegel's system for involving an a priori scheme of this sort.[21] However, philosophy of nature may take other forms as well.

For Engels, the task of the philosophy of nature is to summarize and generalize, in theoretical and philosophical terms, the basic features of the natural world as disclosed by the natural sciences. In this sense, philosophy of nature is not a peculiar aberration of German idealism: it is an essential part of every general metaphysical theory. Even those contemporary philosophers who dismiss the very idea of a philosophy of nature and claim to base their views purely on those of the natural sciences have such a philosophy, if only unconsciously. For physicalism is a philosophy of nature in just this sense.

Like the mechanical materialism of the Enlightenment, modern physicalism claims to be based on modern science, particularly physics and quantum mechanics. It trades on the authority and prestige of these theories. In fact, it is quite different from them. Physics and mechanics are particular branches of natural science. As such, they must ultimately be assessed and criticized in scientific terms, not purely philosophically. Physics describes and explains the material world in its physical aspect. This is the most fundamental and universal aspect, for everything material has a physical aspect. Nevertheless, the physical aspect is only one aspect of the material world, and there are others. But physicalism regards the physical aspect as the sole aspect; it generalizes this aspect into a universal 'worldview'. It treats physics as sufficient on its own to give a complete and comprehensive account of the world. In short, physicalism is a metaphysical theory. As such it can certainly be criticized philosophically.

Eighteenth-century materialism was physicalistic and mechanistic, Engels argues, because physics and mechanics were the only sciences which had reached maturity at that time. Developments since then have extended scientific understanding into fields such as chemistry, cosmology, geology and biology. No doubt physics and mechanics are still the most fully developed and precise sciences, but the physicalist view that other sciences have no independent validity is no longer tenable. In his philosophy, Engels takes explicit account of the development of the non-physical sciences and attempts to describe the transformations of the concept of nature to which they have led.[22] Modern physicalism, with its reductionist approach, denies them a priori. Increasingly it functions as a narrow and blinkered dogmatism, particularly in the human and social sciences, where it attempts to legislate in a fashion which is just as a priori and just as sterile as the most extravagantly idealist and speculative philosophies of nature.[23]

TOWARDS A NON-PHYSICALIST MATERIALISM

Not that the physicalist account either of nature or of human activity is entirely mistaken; rather it is partial and one-sided. Modern physics tells us that all material entities are ultimately composed of fundamental physical particles and fields of force. All material things are physical in nature. That is the truth in physicalism. It does not follow, however, that all material phenomena are fully describable or explicable in terms of physics. For all actual and particular material entities and events are parts of processes which go beyond those described by physics. They may be seen in other contexts and explained in different terms.

This point is perhaps clearest in the case of biological and chemical phenomena. Of course, all biological entities (such as cells, organisms and their parts) are made up of chemical constituents in the form of atoms and molecules, and these in turn are composed of more fundamental physical particles. Nevertheless, the concepts describing biological entities and the laws governing their behaviour are distinct from, and irreducible to, the concepts and laws of physics. This is not just because such descriptions and explanations would be too complex. Rather it is because the properties identified by biological concepts have no counterparts at the purely physical level. Biological phenomena cannot be comprehended as such in purely physical terms.

A biological organism is not a mere collection of chemical or physical constituents; it is an entity with its own specific form and properties. Its parts, as parts, cannot adequately be understood as merely externally related to each other and to the organism as a whole. 'The limbs and organs . . . of an organic body are not merely parts of it: it is only in their unity that they are what they are, and they are unquestionably affected by that unity, as they also in turn affect it.'[24] They can be comprehended only in the context of the whole, 'holistically'.

Similarly, the behaviour of an organism can be explained only in terms of laws governing the organism as a whole. For these laws make essential reference to the life processes of the organism as a whole: to its 'interest' in its own preservation and in the preservation of its species. Such laws postulate ends towards which the behaviour of the organism is oriented. They thus involve 'norms' – or at least they describe the material process of goal-directedness which is the essential material basis of norm-governed behaviour. As Dennett says:

> When an entity arrives on the scene capable of behaviour that staves off, however primitively, its own dissolution and decomposition, it brings into the world its 'good'. That is to say, it creates a point of view from which the world's events can be roughly partitioned into the favourable, the unfavourable and the neutral. As the creature thus comes to have interests, the world and its events begin creating reasons for it, whether or not the creature can fully recognize them. The first reasons preexisted their own recognition.[25]

This is not to suggest that living things are animated by an immaterial 'vital force' or anything like that. Biological organisms are purely natural, material entities. In some cases the underlying physical and chemical mechanisms and processes that govern their behaviour are beginning to be understood. Yet this does not mean that biological phenomena as such can be described and explained in terms of mere physics or chemistry, or that such reduction will ever be possible. For biology involves a different and higher level of understanding.

For example, insulin is a biological product; it is a hormone which is secreted in the pancreas. The chemical composition of insulin is now known, and it can even be synthesized artificially. Some of its chemical effects in the body are understood. But this does not mean that the biology of insulin has been or can be reduced to chemistry. To describe and understand insulin in biological terms involves much more than a knowledge of its chemical composition and properties. It involves understanding its role as a hormone and its function in the body as a whole. Chemistry can provide an account of the mechanisms underlying this role, but this role itself can be comprehended only with a different level of concepts and principles which are constitutive of biology as a distinct science.

Moreover, biological laws are not 'strict laws', but rather what Davidson calls 'statistical generalizations'. They hold only within limits: only in 'normal conditions' and 'for the most part'. In short, the same considerations that Davidson uses to argue for the irreducibility of the mental to the physical can also be used to argue for the irreducibility of biological explanations to merely physical ones. Yet this does not warrant the conclusion that biological events are 'anomalous' in Davidson's sense.[26] No doubt, biological phenomena are 'anomalous' *relative to* the laws of physics and chemistry, in that they are not reducible to such laws. However, such anomalousness is only relative. Biological phenomena are governed by a distinct level of biological laws.

Ontological Implications

Similar arguments apply to other areas of science as well. In general, different ways of describing and understanding the material world are embodied in the different 'special sciences', such as physics, chemistry, biology, etc.[27] These different theories involve different explanatory levels which are irreducible to each other. What does this imply about the material nature of the entities described?

As we have seen, Davidson gives a non-realist account of the mental standpoint. Whether that is true of mental descriptions we shall see presently. First, however, I want to argue that it is not true in the case of biology.[28] For it is not the case that biological concepts embody only a different subjective 'standpoint': a different way of 'describing' or 'interpreting' things, which has no objective or 'ontological' implications. The concepts and principles which the biologist uses are not simply a – or the – biological 'way of seeing things'. On the contrary, they describe real, objective and material features of the world.

Of course, a living organism is composed of physical and chemical constituents, and nothing more. Nevertheless, it is not a mere collection of such constituents, nor even of anatomical and physiological parts. It is these parts unified, organized and acting as a whole. This unity and organization are not only features of our descriptions: they are properties of the thing itself; they are constitutive of it as a biological organism. Nor are the laws governing its behaviour simply a function of our theories; they are operative in the organism itself as *its* laws. There are real – objective and material – differences between a living thing and a merely physical or chemical entity which it is the aim of biology to describe. This is the realist and materialist view.[29]

Again, it must be stressed, this is not to suggest that living things involve a transcendent 'organic unity' or that they are animated by any non-natural 'vital principle'. Biological forms and laws do not transcend those of physics and chemistry; they do not supplant or replace them. On the contrary, in a living thing the laws of the lower – physical and chemical – levels continue to operate. On this basis, however, new structures and forms develop. New – biological – principles come into effect, and physical and chemical laws, although they continue to operate, in Hegel's words, 'cease to be final and decisive, and sink, as it were, to a subservient position.'[30] Physical processes are subsumed within a higher form. Engels echoes Hegel's line of thought when he says that in organic processes, the laws of physics are 'pushed into the background by other higher laws'.[31] These new 'higher' laws have an objective existence and real effects, not by acting independently of physical laws, nor by replacing them, but rather by giving a new and higher form of organization to the physical and chemical phenomena. The biological level arises within, and exists on the basis of, the physical and chemical levels, not outside or apart from them.

Process in nature

In this way, biological concepts and principles are neither reducible to those of chemistry or physics, nor are they entirely autonomous or transcendent. These different levels are relatively autonomous:[32] they are not only distinct but also united; there is continuity as well as difference between them. The clearest demonstration of this is provided by the fact – and modern science takes it for a fact – that biological phenomena *emerge* from merely chemical and physical – i.e. non-biological – conditions, by purely natural processes.

Evolution of higher and more complex forms from lower and simpler ones is not peculiar to biological evolution, it is a fundamental feature of material existence more generally. It is exhibited at a simpler level in the evolution of the universe as a whole – in the formation, development and ultimate death of galaxies, stars and planetary systems – described and explained by cosmology. Likewise, geology describes the development of the material features of the planet. These phenomena are material processes which have their basis in certain physical and chemical mechanisms. Nevertheless, such processes cannot be reduced to chemistry, physics or mechanics. And this is not just for the reasons given so far: that the concepts and principles of these sciences are irreducible to purely physicalist terms. It is a specific limitation of mechanistic, physicalist materialism, Engels argues, that it is unable 'to comprehend the universe as a process, as matter undergoing uninterrupted historical development'.[33] For such materialism involves the reductionist view that all natural processes can be entirely explained in terms of a few simple and eternal laws of physics and mechanics. This view excludes a priori the very idea of the emergence, development or evolution of new forms and new laws within the material world. Physicalism thus gives an unsatisfactory account of the material world even in its *physical* aspect.

This is not to deny that cosmology, geology, biology and other scientific theories which study processes of natural development postulate purely physical and chemical mechanisms as the basis for the evolutionary processes they describe. Indeed, it is essential to their being scientific theories that they do so, in that these theories are thus given a naturalistic and materialistic basis, and non-materialist explanations in terms of 'rational purpose' or 'divine providence' in natural history are excluded. However, it is impossible to understand cosmological, geological or biological evolution in terms of purely physical processes alone. The underlying physical mechanism is merely a postulated basis for evolutionary processes, the explanation of which, in all these fields, relies on concepts and principles specific to these sciences.

HUMAN ACTIVITY AND THOUGHT

We are now in a better position to consider the nature of the mental and its relation to the physical. For similar arguments apply in this area too; and when this is understood, there is less temptation to privilege the mental and portray it as in some special way (absolutely) autonomous.

Human beings are, of course, biological organisms. They are made up entirely of physical, chemical, biological constituents. Nevertheless, human thought and activity cannot be described or understood as such in purely biological, let alone chemical or physical, terms; a distinct and independent set of concepts and principles, a new and different approach or 'standpoint', is needed for this task. Engels is at one with writers like Kant and Davidson on this. As Davidson argues, this is not simply because of the complexity of mental phenomena. Rather, it is because the description of mental activity as such involves reference to a wider context of meaningful human activity, and it involves appeal to norms of coherence and rationality which are beyond the scope of physical theory.

Davidson's term for the discipline which describes and explains human intentional activity is 'psychology', and when he contemplates the idea of a material basis for mental phenomena he thinks in terms of neurobiology. These are common tendencies in current analytic philosophy of mind. However, his own account of the mental diverges significantly from the individualistic perspectives of both psychology and neurobiology. With his appeal to the notion of a context of meaningful practices, Davidson's own account suggests that 'social theory' and/or 'history' would be more appropriate terms. The mental is not just a psychological or neurobiological but also a social and historical phenomenon. And the wider context of practices, and the principles of rationality and coherence to which his account appeals, are essentially social in character. Marx and Engels, it hardly needs adding, are the main authors of this theoretical insight in its modern form.

As we have seen, Davidson gives a non-realist, non-ontological, account of the mental standpoint. Descriptions of human thought and activity are merely different forms of interpretation, with no objective ('ontological') implications. I have criticized these views as they apply to biology, and the same criticisms apply here too. The concepts and principles we use to describe and understand human thought and activity refer to real and objective features of human life. The context of intentional activities to which we must refer when we characterize a phenomenon in mental terms is not a function of our interpretation only. The 'holism' of the mental is not a feature merely of the concepts and categories with which we describe it; it has an objective, material existence. It is constituted by the social practices and institutions within which we necessarily operate as human agents.

Likewise, the normative principles of rationality and coherence that we must use to assess human actions are not only our subjective creations. They are embodied in social institutions and practices, and particularly those of language. These provide the context in which alone human beings can develop the ability to reflect on what they are doing and act in a self-consciously intentional and rational fashion.

No doubt, a human being is a biological organism, and society is a collection of such organisms. Nevertheless, it is impossible to understand human thought and activity in purely biological terms. For, in society, those biological organisms are united and function according to social and not merely biological principles. Their behaviour can be understood only in the context of the social institutions and practices in which they are embedded. Moreover, these social relations have a real, objective, material existence; they are not merely a function of our descriptions.[34] Of course, society is as it is on the basis of human anatomy and physiology. It is also the case, however, that human anatomy and physiology are as they are because they have developed and function within a social context.[35] Although human thought is an activity of the brain, it cannot be explained in narrowly neurophysiological terms. For the brain's activity is determined not just by neurophysiological laws, but also by its historical, social and psychological context. To understand the activity of the brain, as the organ of thought, it must also be seen in its social and psychological context, to which the concepts and principles of neurophysiology are blind.

The emergence of the mental

According to Davidson, mental phenomena are not governed by 'strict quantitative laws', they are 'anomalous'. Similar arguments apply to biological phenomena, as we have seen. This vitiates Davidson's attempt to draw a sharp distinction between the mental and material standpoints on this basis. As with biology, moreover, the mental is 'anomalous' only relatively. It is 'anomalous' in the sense that it cannot be described and explained as such in merely biological terms. However, it is governed by a new and different – historical, social and psychological – level of forms and laws. These new forms and laws do not transcend or supplant those of biology. Biological laws continue to operate in all of human life, even in the highest mental activities. However, with historical development, higher – social and psychological – forms of organization come into operation, to which biological laws are subsumed and subordinated.[36]

Davidson has a further argument for the view that there are fundamental differences between human intentional activity and other natural processes. Human behaviour is not just law-like, he maintains, it is intentionally so. In Kant's terms, human beings can act not just 'according to' principles, but 'from' them.[37] This distinction captures a fundamental difference between the laws of biology and those governing human thought and activity, which Engels also recognizes.

> With man we enter *history*. Animals also have a history, that of their descent and gradual evolution to their present position. This history, however, is made for them, and in so far as they themselves take part in it, this occurs without their knowledge and desire. On the other hand, the more that human beings become removed from animals in the narrower sense of that word, the more they make their history themselves, consciously, the less becomes the influence of unforeseen effects and uncontrolled forces on this history.[38]

However, this distinction is not an absolute one, and one must beware of treating it as if it were. Human activity is not absolutely 'anomalous' or 'autonomous'. The ability to act from principle, in a reflective and self-conscious manner, as Engels stresses, emerges gradually and by degrees out of simpler, non-conscious capacities and law-like forms of behaviour. As such, this ability is only *relatively* autonomous from the natural conditions and social practices from which it develops and on which it is based. It is not a merely biological ability, but nor is it an ability that entirely separates us from the material world and transcends its processes. It is an ability which emerges and develops, gradually and by degrees, in the course of biological and historical evolution.

The ability to act reflectively is particularly connected with the capacity to use language. The latter is normally present in adult human beings but not in other animals. It has a material and biological basis. Only in this respect does it make sense to talk of a 'language instinct'.[39] Even so the term is misleading. The ability to use language is not instinctive or innate; it grows and develops. The new-born child is only potentially a language user.[40] For this ability to be actualized, it must be elicited and developed from without, socially. The ability to act reflectively and rationally is one which presupposes a basis of biological capacities, but which can develop and be realized, both in the species and the individual, only in a social context.

Human beings are not 'by nature' self-conscious or rational, they become so – partially and to a degree – through the course of their development. Self-consciousness and rationality are essentially social phenomena. They are a product not only of biological processes, but also of human social activity and historical development. These developments result in the emergence of self-consciousness and rationality from natural conditions by natural processes. They involve the development of new and higher, social and historical, laws and principles in human life. These are not absolutely 'anomalous' or 'autonomous'. They do not supplant the laws and principles of biology, which continue to operate in every aspect of human life. Just as with the relation of biology to chemistry previously discussed, however, and within the limits that biology determines, these new social forms and principles develop and become operative, and the lower, biological principles become secondary and subservient.

Evolutionary processes of this sort are incomprehensible within the framework of Davidson's 'standpoint' dualism: not just because he attempts to give a 'non-ontological' (i.e. non-materialist) account of the mental, which makes it impossible to understand how mental phenomena could have emerged from material conditions or be embodied by them, but also because the physicalism it involves is incapable of comprehending natural evolution and development. Indeed, these are two correlative aspects of such dualism. By trying to 'make room' for mental phenomena, by separating them off into their own logically autonomous space, such dualism makes a mystery of how they could have emerged and developed in the material world. However, the non-physicalist form of materialism for which I have been arguing shows there is no need to 'make room' for consciousness, intentionality and rationality in this way. They have evolved naturally from material conditions. They have made room *for themselves* by emerging and coming into operation *on the basis of* our biology, and *within* the parameters and limits it imposes.

The dialectic of nature

There is no room for the ideas of natural evolution and development in the physicalist picture of nature. As Engels argues, this is a relic of the Enlightenment period, even if it is still the predominant philosophy of nature among analytic philosophers.[41] With scientific advances in numerous fields since the Enlightenment, however, ideas of evolution and development have come to form an integral part of the modern picture of nature. It is these ideas to which Engels is referring when he talks of a 'dialectic of nature'. So far, I have tried to explain and defend them without mentioning this term because I am well aware of the scepticism and hostility it invariably provokes. I am not going to try to deal systematically with objections to it here.[42] However, a couple of points may help to mitigate some of them.

As Engels stresses, the dialectical view of nature derives from the attempt to learn general lessons from the natural sciences as they have developed since the Enlightenment. It does not, or should not, claim to explain evolution and development in nature: that is the job of the natural sciences. Its purpose, rather, is to provide a philosophical framework within which it is possible to *think* the idea that nature evolves and develops through stages and levels, whereas materialism in its physicalist and reductionist forms excludes this thought and makes it impossible.

Engels draws his basic ideas about dialectic from Hegel, who also argues that nature is dialectical. However, as Engels points out, Hegel does not ultimately succeed in transcending the unhistorical view of nature which prevails in Enlightenment philosophy. In nature, Hegel believed, the relation between the different levels that he identifies – 'mechanism', 'chemism' and 'teleology' – is only logical or conceptual: there is no concrete, temporal evolution of natural forms in his philosophy.[43] In stressing that modern science posits such evolution, and by comprehending this in dialectical terms, Engels goes beyond Hegel and makes a contribution to philosophy of originality and importance in its own right.[44]

But this is not the way in which the idea of a materialist dialectic is usually seen by academic commentators on his thought. It is almost invariably dismissed as a confused borrowing from Hegel. Dialectic, we are told, is a logical and rational process; it applies only to human thought and activity. The very idea of a dialectic in nature involves attributing human intentional and rational processes to mere things. Far from being the expression of a materialist philosophy, it is an extreme form of idealism.

According to Colletti, for example, 'in order to be a form of materialism, "dialectical materialism" must affirm the heterogeneity of thought and being.'[45] Such views are exceedingly common.[46] Nevertheless they are mistaken. Colletti here insists that thought is distinct from matter, and claims that this is materialism. But the mere distinguishing of thought from matter – the keeping of them apart in this way – is dualism, not materialism. Materialism, by contrast, asserts that there is no thought independent of matter. It insists on the *unity* of thought and matter: it is a form of monism, a form of identity theory.

So too, it is true, is idealism, which is also a form of monism. Idealism and materialism agree in rejecting dualism and in asserting the unity of the mental and the physical. Beyond that, however, these two philosophies are opposites. For, according to materialism, all phenomena are material and not ideal. Intentionality, reason and other mental phenomena are ultimately embodied materially. Natural processes are at the basis of our rational capacities. Human thought and activity emerge and develop, by natural processes, out of simpler natural conditions. Mind is matter organized and acting in a particular way; it does not transcend the material world. No appeal to ideal or transcendent principles is required to describe and explain it. These are Engels's views. His aim in putting forward the idea of a dialectic in nature is not to idealize nature, but rather to naturalize the mental and to develop a form of materialism which is consonant with modern science.[47]

Notes

1. F. Engels, *Ludwig Feuerbach and the End of Classical German Philosophy, Selected Works in Two Volumes,* Vol. 2, Foreign Languages Publishing House, Moscow, 1962, p. 386n.
2. For my views on Engels as a Marxist, see Richard Norman and Sean Sayers, *Hegel, Marx and Dialectic: A Debate,* Harvester Press, Brighton, 1980 (reprinted Gregg Revivals, London, 1994), Ch. 4.

3. See especially *Ludwig Feuerbach,* and *Dialectics of Nature,* trans. Clemens Dutt, Progress Publishers, Moscow, 1964; also *Anti-Dühring,* Foreign Languages Publishing House, Moscow, 1962, Part I, Chs I–VIII.
4. In his later years at least; materialism is a central theme in *The Holy Family* (1844) and *The German Ideology* (1845), both 'early' works written jointly with Engels.
5. *Ludwig Feuerbach,* p. 369.
6. Ibid., pp. 372–3.
7. Ibid., p. 373.
8. 'Chemistry, for example, reduces to quantum mechanics, but actually constructing the quantum mechanical explanations of chemical phenomena is generally beyond human capabilities.' Richard Warner, 'Introduction: The Mind–Body Debate', in R. Warner and T. Szubka (eds), *The Mind–Body Problem: A Guide to the Current Debate,* Blackwell, Oxford, 1994, p. 2.
9. See, for example, Paul M. Churchland and Patricia S. Churchland, 'Intertheoretic Reduction: A Neuroscientist's Field Guide', in Warner and Szubka (eds), *The Mind–Body Problem,* pp. 41–54.
10. *Ludwig Feuerbach,* pp. 373f.
11. Donald Davidson, 'Psychology as Philosophy', *Essays on Actions and Events,* Clarendon Press, Oxford, 1980, p. 233.
12. Davidson, 'The Material Mind', *Essays,* op. cit., p. 248.
13. Davidson, 'Psychology as Philosophy', p. 230; cf. 'Mental Events', *Essays,* op. cit., p. 216.
14. Davidson, 'Mental Events', p. 207.
15. Ibid., p. 215.
16. Quoted by Simon Evnine, *Donald Davidson,* Polity Press, Cambridge, 1991, p. 63.
17. Cf. Kant, *Critique of Pure Reason,* trans. Norman Kemp-Smith, Macmillan, London, 1933, Preface to Second Edition, p. 29 (Bxxx).
18. Evnine, *Donald Davidson,* p. 63.
19. Jaegwon Kim, 'The Myth of Nonreductive Materialism', in Warner and Szubka (eds), *The Mind–Body Problem,* pp. 242–60; see also Anthony Skillen, 'Mind and Body: A Problem that Refuses Dissolution', *Mind,* Vol. 93 (1984), pp. 214–26. Davidson sometimes appeals to the notion of 'supervenience' to describe this relation ('The Material Mind', p. 253), but this term merely labels this relationship, without clarifying it.
20. As in many other areas of philosophy, Engels here draws heavily on Hegel. 'Mechanism ... is ... a shallow and superficial mode of observation, one that cannot carry us through in connection with Nature and still less in connection with the world of Mind', G.W.F. Hegel, *Logic,* trans. W. Wallace, Clarendon Press, Oxford, 3rd edn, 1975, §196z.
21. At the same time, Engels recognizes the mass of empirical data and the encyclopedic knowledge of the natural sciences of his day which Hegel incorporates in his system: *Ludwig Feuerbach,* pp. 364–5.
22. This is the major purpose of much of *Dialectics of Nature.*
23. Physicalism has a greater practical impact in the human and social

sciences than in the physical sciences. See S. Sayers, *Reality and Reason: Dialectic and the Theory of Knowledge*, Blackwell, Oxford, 1985, pp. 149–50.

24. Hegel, *Logic*, §135z; cf. §216z. See also, S. Sayers, 'Marxism and the Dialectical Method: A Critique of G.A. Cohen', *Radical Philosophy* 36 (Spring 1984), pp. 4–13 (reprinted in Sean Sayers and Peter Osborne (eds), *Socialism, Feminism and Philosophy: A Radical Philosophy Reader*, Routledge, London, 1990).
25. Daniel C. Dennett, *Consciousness Explained*, Penguin, Harmondsworth, 1993, pp. 173–4.
26. Cf. J. Searle, *Minds, Brains and Science: the 1984 Reith Lectures*, Penguin, Harmondsworth, 1989, p. 74. Davidson himself is non-committal: 'I do not want to say that analogous remarks may not hold for some other sciences, for example, biology. But I do not know how to show that the concepts of biology are nomonologically irreducible to the concepts of physics. What sets apart certain psychological concepts – their intentionality – does not apply to the concepts of biology': 'Psychology as Philosophy', p. 241. I discuss this argument below.
27. Though physics is universally applicable, it is also a 'special' science on the view that I am defending, in that it describes only one aspect of material phenomena.
28. Davidson does not suggest this (see note 26 above). Kant, however, does. He argues that we cannot comprehend organic forms in mechanical, causal terms, yet nor must we have resort to explanation in terms of a 'vital principle'. The judgement of organic organization is purely 'reflective', not 'constitutive', and implies nothing about the object described, *The Critique of Judgement*, trans. J.C. Meredith, Clarendon Press, Oxford, 1952, Part II, §14.
29. This is also the view usually taken in the natural sciences where, as Hegel says, 'objective reality is attributed to laws, forces are immanent, and matter is [looked upon as] the true nature of the thing itself ... Genera, too ... are not just a grouping of similarities, an abstraction made by us; they not only have common features but they are the object's own inner essence ... Physics looks upon these universals as its triumph': *Philosophy of Nature*, trans. A.V. Miller, Clarendon Press, Oxford, 1975, §246z. See Sayers, *Reality and Reason*, Ch. 2, for a fuller discussion of such realism.
30. Hegel, *Logic*, §195z.
31. *Ludwig Feuerbach*, p. 373.
32. Engels uses this term to describe the relation of base and superstructure in Marx's social theory. See Engels, 'Letters on Historical Materialism', in Marx and Engels, *Selected Works in Two Volumes*, Vol. 2, pp. 486ff FLPH, Moscow, 1962; and Sayers, *Hegel, Marx and Dialectic: A Debate*, pp. 90–4.
33. *Ludwig Feuerbach*, p. 374.
34. Language is a 'spatial and temporal phenomenon ... not ... some non-spatial, non-temporal phantasm': Wittgenstein, *Philosophical Investigations*, Blackwell, Oxford, 2nd edn, 1958, I.108.

35. This is the theme of Engels, 'The Part Played by Labour in the Transition from Ape to Man', *Dialectics of Nature*. Despite its Lamarckianism this piece gives an illuminating and suggestive sketch of the way in which biological and social development interact and reciprocally determine each other.
36. As Hegel notes with reference to the phenomenon of illness, 'in Nature, when the higher or organic functions are in any way checked or disturbed in their normal efficiency, the otherwise subordinate aspect of mechanism is immediately seen to take the upper hand': *Logic*, §195z. Even illness, however, cannot be understood in purely physical or biological terms, for it is not a merely physical or biological process: there is a human dimension to it as well. Thus there are different ways of responding to and 'living with' illness, both on the patient's part and on the part of others in relation to the patient. A doctor must be sensitive to this and respond to illness, not just as a physical process, but also as a human event.
37. Davidson, 'Mental Events', p. 216, cf. Kant, *Groundwork of the Metaphysic of Morals*. Similarly, Hegel distinguishes between natural processes, in which reason is present only 'in itself', from human social activity which is rational both 'in and for itself'.
38. *Dialectics of Nature*, p. 35.
39. Steven Pinker, *The Language Instinct: The New Science of Language and Mind*, Penguin, Harmondsworth, 1995.
40. 'The child is still in the grip of natural life, has only natural impulses, is not actually but only potentially or notionally a rational being': Hegel, *Philosophy of Mind*, trans. W. Wallace and A.V. Miller, Clarendon Press, Oxford, 1971, §385z.
41. And not just among reductionist materialists but equally among dualists, of both the Cartesian and Davidsonian varieties. A more muted form of physicalism is present in much contemporary continental philosophy as well, but this is not my topic here.
42. But see Sayers, *Hegel, Marx and Dialectic*, Chs 1, 4.
43. *Ludwig Feuerbach*, pp. 387ff.
44. I am here leaving aside the contentious issue of Marx's contribution to the creation of this materialist form of dialectic.
45. L. Colletti, *Marxism and Hegel*, Verso, London, 1973, p. 104.
46. See, for example, G. Lukács, 'What is Orthodox Marxism?', *History and Class Consciousness*, Merlin Press, London, 1971; J.-P. Sartre, 'Materialism and Revolution', *Literary and Philosophical Essays*, Hutchinson, London, 1968; A. Schmidt, *The Concept of Nature in Marx*, Verso, London, 1971; Norman, *Hegel, Marx and Dialectic*, Chs 2, 3, 5.
47. I am grateful to Colin Radford, Robin Taylor and, particularly, Simon Glendinning for comments on earlier drafts of this essay.

8

Engels as Interpreter of Marx's Economics

Christopher J. Arthur

INTRODUCTION

It is a little known fact that Frederick Engels was the original pioneer in the territory Karl Marx later made his own, namely the critique of political economy. Prior even to Engels's empirically-based study of the condition of the English working class in 1844 was his article *Outlines of a Critique of Political Economy*, written in 1843. This came into Marx's hands in his capacity as editor of the *Deutsch-Französische Jahrbücher* in which it was duly published.[1] Marx studied it again when he himself turned to the subject in 1844, and in his own publications he continually praised it. However, when Marx indicated that he intended to write a big work on economics, Engels seems to have happily resigned the matter to him, for he had many other interests. But as Marx's literary executor Engels had not only to bring out the remaining volumes of *Capital* but to explain and defend the theory in debate.

This paper is concerned with Engels's work on Marx's critique of political economy. As is the case in general, Engels was originally taken as a reliable guide to Marx's work in this area; but the claim has been made that Engels's views as a commentator and popularizer are to be rejected, and that, in the editorial work Engels did on Marx's *Capital*, he abused (consciously or unconsciously) the trust Marx placed in him as the literary executor of the Marxian legacy. While the main interest of the paper lies in its consideration of Engels's interpretation of Marx's method, I shall first consider the charges pertaining to his work as Marx's literary executor.

Before considering such charges it is worth noting that the habit of taking Marx and Engels as one person is so deeply ingrained from earlier times[2] that traces of it survived in places until very recently. As a prime example of this tradition let us take the well-known textbook by M.C. Howard and J.E. King on *The political economy of Marx,* which appeared in 1975. Treating of what they assume is Marx's 'logical-historical method', they give passages as if they quote from Marx (e.g. 'in history . . . development as a whole proceeds from the most simple to the most complex relations') when the passages in question are really the work of Engels![3] They are from a review Engels wrote in 1859 of Marx's *Contribution to the Critique of Political Economy.* (I deal with it extensively below.)

Howard and King also calmly say that Marx begins *Capital* with a model he terms 'simple commodity production'.[4] No source is given for this – which is not surprising for the simple reason no such term occurs in *Capital,* Volume I. Their previous footnote is supposed to give relevant passages from the whole three volumes but not one exhibits the term, none are from chapter 1, and furthermore, again without acknowledgement, the last is from an appendix by *Engels*!

However, Howard and King were simply reproducing what they had read in R.L. Meek. In all his work Meek was absolutely unselfconscious about treating Marx and Engels as one person. Throughout, he quoted freely from Engels when purporting to give Marx's views. In his 1967 essay on 'Karl Marx's Economic Method', he used both the 1859 review (in order to allege Marx's method is 'logical-historical') and Engels's Preface to *Capital,* Volume III (in order to allege Marx had a model 'he called "simple" commodity production', and to claim Marx described the capitalistically produced commodity as a 'secondary form').[5] As late as 1973 Meek was still working in the same way:

> I still think I was right in laying special emphasis on Marx's 'logical-historical method': indeed, if anything I think I underestimated the extent to which Marx's economic work was guided by it . . . Marx's *logical* transition in *Capital* (from the commodity relation as such to the 'capitalistically modified' form of this relation) is presented by him as the 'mirror-image' of a *historical* transition (from 'simple' to 'capitalist' commodity production) . . .[6]

The 'by him' in this remark is simply false, because all the quoted material is not from Marx but from Engels. (The mysteries of 'the logical-historical method' and of 'simple commodity production' – in truth inventions of Engels's – will be treated below.)

After disposing of some strictly textual questions, my paper will conclude with a discussion of the substantive issue of Marxian method, of what Engels made of it, and what it should be.

ENGELS AND *CAPITAL*

In the literature the writer who exhibits the most obsessive hatred for Engels is Norman Levine, an attitude signalled well enough in the title of his first book *The Tragic Deception: Marx Contra Engels*. However, his most extraordinary achievement was to read into Engels's reviews of *Capital* the exact opposite of what is stated there. This occurs in his 1984 book *Dialogue Within the Dialectic*.[7]

Endeavouring to show that Engels tried to turn Marx into some kind of natural scientist, Levine claims one such review states that political economy is 'now universally valid': in fact the review said it was considered 'hitherto just as abstract and universally valid a science as mathematics', a concept to which 'Marx put an end'.[8] Levine goes on to claim that the review attributes to Marx the discovery of 'laws' of social development. The review does nothing of the sort, but rather points out that after Marx's work it will 'no longer be possible ... to apply laws which are valid for modern industry' to earlier epochs.[9] Levine claims the same review says that for Marx the laws in question *do* apply, and, where they do not, 'this contradiction did not show that the laws of wage-labor were wrong but rather that "the old conditions were heretical".' However, Engels here characterized not Marx's view but views he *contrasted* to Marx's.[10]

Turning to another review, Levine says that 'Engels applauded Marx for taking "economic laws for eternal truths".' But the review in question says that Marx's 'sense of history ... forbids the author to take the laws of economics for eternal truths'.[11]

Levine is clearly suffering from an Engels phobia. But the most tragicomic case of his determination to show Engels always in the wrong comes when he quotes *correctly*. He gives a long passage, from a review Engels placed in the *Stuttgarter Beobachter*,[12] to show that Engels falsified Marx by talking about 'science', 'laws' and 'abolition [of capitalism]'. There is only one thing wrong with this 'evidence' – the whole passage was *copied by Engels from Marx*, as may be seen by comparing it with the letter Marx wrote to Engels instructing him how to compose this very review![13]

It is a pity Levine shows himself to be such an unreliable commentator,[14] for he is one of the few to have investigated in detail Engels's editing work on Volumes II and III of *Capital*.[15] There may well be discoveries to be made about this, but we must await the publication of the manuscripts in the *Marx-Engels Gesamtausgabe* (hereafter MEGA) to see.[16] However, it has to be said that one of Levine's complaints is very odd. Since Marx had planned to bring out the next two 'books' of *Capital* in one volume, he argues that Engels wilfully disregarded this wish, and in the process of producing two more volumes gave us a bloated text.[17] Yet everything we know about Marx's writing shows that promised 'brochures' turn into books, and books into many volumes; there is little doubt that if Marx had been able to carry forward his work we would have been lucky to escape with merely *two* more volumes of *Capital*!

Let us turn now to Engels's work on *Capital*, Volume I, which includes the English translation for whose content and text he took 'ultimate responsibility' and on which he spent considerable time.[18] Since the editions and translations of Volume I have been available for a long while, the anti-Engels faction has not been silent in this area. But alas! – they trip up.

The key thing here is the existence of the French edition, virtually written by Marx himself, since he went over every word as Roy submitted it to him, section by section, correcting it, freely editing his own text, and inserting many new passages to the point where he felt able to add a note at the end informing the reader that the French edition 'possessed a scientific value independent of the original and must be consulted even by readers familiar with German'.[19] Given this, the strategy of comparing the English edition supervised by Engels with the German original, in order to detect interference by him, is defective. The fact is that changes made by Engels generally follow changes Marx had *already* made in the French.

Of great importance in this connection are Marx's letters to N. Danielson, his Russian translator, for example: 'In regard to the second edition of *Capital* . . . I wish that the *division into chapters* – and the same goes for the subdivisions – be made according to the French edition.'[20] No doubt he gave Engels the same instructions.

Given this, it is odd that Ben Fowkes in his modern translation published by Penguin should attribute the English chapter divisions to 'Engels's arrangement'[21] without mentioning why this was done. Also A. Oakley, following Fowkes, complains that 'Engels chose to rearrange' the chapter and part divisions of *Capital*, for the English ones do not follow the German.[22] Quite so. They do not. They follow the French![23] From the second edition on, the German has 25 chapters in seven parts. The French, and later the English, has 33 chapters in eight parts.

Still more astonishing, given his erudition, is that Hal Draper failed to say this in his monumental *Marx-Engels Cyclopedia*. In Volume II, *The Marx-Engels Register*, he says that Engels renumbered the chapters for the English edition, but he does not say why; nor does he mention the matter of renumbering when dealing with the French edition.[24]

Raya Dunayevskaya, in spite of calling attention to the importance of the French edition, became confused herself when (probably misled by Fowkes) she charged Engels with creating 'a new Part Eight' for the section on 'so-called Primitive Accumulation'; this was a mistake in her view 'for that section ... should have been inseparable from [that on] the Accumulation of Capital'.[25] But – alas! – the culprit was Marx, who himself introduced '*Huitième section. L'accumulation primitive*'! Engels was simply copying his master in preparing the English with the same divisions.

More alarming to students than the chapter renumbering may be the fact that the very title was changed in Engels's English edition. The German book was *Das Kapital: Kritik der politischen Oekonomie* and the first volume was *Der Produktionsprocess des Kapitals*. The English version put out by Engels in 1887 was called *Capital: A Critical Analysis of Capitalist Production* with the first part called *Capitalist Production*.[26]

It seems to me that these are very different, in that the emphasis in the German seems to be on how capital produces itself as a value form (with a promise of how it circulates to come), whereas the English sounds rather more pedestrian: there is production in general but here we look specifically at its capitalist form. However, whether there is anything in such reflections or not, Engels was not the originator of a deviation from the German. For Marx's French edition was called simply *Le Capital* with the first volume called *Développement de la Production Capitaliste*. The English version was a cross between the two earlier ones.[27]

In general the lesson is that no assessment of Engels's work as editor of Marx's Volume I can be made without close examination of the French edition. It seems certain that Marx instructed him to use this as a guide for other translations, for he wrote to Danielson: 'I was obliged to rewrite whole passages in French to make them accessible for the French public. Later it will be so much easier to translate from the French into English.'[28] But then he had doubts about the French, complaining to Danielson in 1878 that he was 'sometimes obliged – principally in the first chapter – to "*aplatir*" the matter in its French version'.[29] A few days later, probably with this in mind, he decided that 'the first two sections ("Commodities and Money" and "The Transformation of Money into Capital") are to be translated exclusively from the German text'.[30] The French is a great help in other matters too: for instance, when translating from the German, the French can be consulted for guidance.[31]

At all events, it should be noted that Engels did not feel it incumbent on him to annotate his editions as carefully as we might demand today. For example, the explicit reference to Hegel in note 21 of his English edition does not occur in any German or French edition, and was therefore inserted by Engels without particular notice.[32]

An omission, which has acquired importance because of the central place given to the term '*Träger*' in structuralist interpretations of *Capital*,[33] occurs in chapter 2. After Marx said that 'the characters who appear on the economic stage are but the personifications of the economical relations that exist between them',[34] he added: 'it is as bearers [*Träger*] of these economic relations that they come into contact with each other'.[35] Engels missed this out, but in doing so he was simply following the French.[36] (What is odd, however, is that in neither of the respective *Apparat* volumes to the French and English MEGA editions is the omission noted![37])

But sometimes the Engels edition unaccountably omits something. For example, the sentence 'What is the case with the forces of nature, holds for science too' is left out of the chapter on machinery after the reference to 'the elasticity of steam'.[38] (Oddly, the Fowkes translation which claims to restore 'whole sentences omitted by Engels'[39] does not restore this one[40] even though it is there in the *Werke* edition from which the translation was made.[41])

Engels's Prefaces to the Third and Fourth German editions indicate his reliance on notes left by Marx on what was to be incorporated from the French. Engels's additions were not consistent, however. The sentence 'The religious world is but the reflex of the real world' added to the English from the French[42] he failed to put in these German editions.

An example where a mere word may make all the difference to the reading of a passage occurs in the case of the controversial topic of skilled labour. Bernstein claimed to have found a passage in *Capital* in which it appeared that Marx had directly derived the higher value produced in a given time by skilled labour from the higher value of that sort of labour power. The sentence quoted was: *'Ist der Wert dieser Kraft höher, so äussert sie sich aber auch in höherer Arbeit und vergegenständlicht sich daher, in denselben Zeiträumen, in verhältnissmässig höheren Werten.'*[43]

Hilferding, in his polemic of 1904 against Böhm-Bawerk, digressed from his main theme in order to point out that the sentence does not say what Bernstein claimed it does. (It is in truth compatible with the Marxian axiom that the value of a product cannot come from the 'value of labour'.) He argued further that, for it to do so, *'aber'* would have to be changed to *'daher'*.[44] Bernstein was using the second edition, Hilferding the third; but, as Hilferding's translators point out in a note, in the fourth edition, edited by Engels, *'aber' is* replaced by *'daher'*![45]

As Hilferding pointed out, the issue under discussion is valorization, so Marx's purpose in raising the topic of skilled labour is to argue that it makes no difference to the basic process. Even if the skilled labourer receives a higher wage, surplus value is still obtained because he produces more value in a given time. Given this, it is clear that *'aber'* is needed to emphasize this point. I would translate: 'Albeit of higher value, this power manifests itself, however [*aber*], in labour of a higher sort, [which] objectifies itself therefore . . . in proportionately higher values.' Substituting *'daher'* ('therefore') considerably weakens the force of the sentence, and could indeed lead to a Bernsteinian reading, as Hilferding thought. In fact, Engels is doubly at fault; for he let pass a sloppy translation of this sentence in the English edition: 'This power being of a higher value, its consumption is labour of a higher class, labour that creates in equal times proportionately higher values . . .'[46] – *'aber'* has simply disappeared!

More research could be done on such questions, but I now turn to the more substantial question of Engels's views on the nature of Marx's method.

HOW ENGELS REVIEWED MARX

The first occasion on which Engels endeavoured to interpret Marx's work to the public was in a review which later became enormously influential. For the idea that the way to understand Marx's method was as a modification of Hegel's dialectical logic entered the public domain[47] with Engels's review of Marx's 1859 *Contribution to the Critique of Political Economy*, appearing in two instalments in *Das*

Volk.[48] More specifically, Engels claimed that Hegel had shown Marx how logic and history went hand in hand, both proceeding from simple relations to more complex ones. This 'logical-historical method'[49] became so firmly established within Marxism that when R.L. Meek was challenged on the question in 1975 he reacted first by pointing out that he had inherited this view from a long tradition of interpretation, and cited Engels's review at length as the *locus classicus* for it.[50]

The challenge in question had its own authoritative text, namely Marx's unpublished 1857 *Introduction to the Critique of Political Economy*, which, as part of a rather complex discussion, stated that 'it would be . . . wrong to let the economic categories succeed each other in the order in which they were historically decisive'.[51] In a way it is surprising that this took so long to emerge as an alternative since it had been around, not only in German (first publication 1903), but in English (1904),[52] for a long time.[53]

The assumption of many commentators, who rely on this as summarizing Marx's real view of the matter, is that he could not have changed his mind within a year or so, and that, therefore, Engels's promotion of a logical-historical method must be in error, and an unwarranted imposition on Marx's text. (P. Kain[54] and T. Carver[55] are prominent proponents of this view.)

Such a charge against Engels is put in question if we attend to the circumstances of the publication of the review. Marx was acting editor of *Das Volk* at that time,[56] and pushed Engels to do the review.[57] Submitting the first part to Marx, Engels specifically advised him that he could 'tear it up', or 'knock it into shape',[58] if he did not like it (doubtless it was taken for granted this would apply to the more controversial second article too). Thus it seems that the review had Marx's *imprimatur*. Many commentators miss this basic point; thus not only critics of Engels such as Carver[59] and Kain[60] but even Hunley,[61] Engels's defender, miss it. However, Meek, in the Engels corner, draws attention to it, as does Stedman Jones.[62]

If, then, because the review appeared under Marx's editorial aegis, we cannot say Marx disapproved of its content, we cannot, on the other hand, say it was a put-up job.[63] Marx did give advice; but for some reason Engels did his own thing. After asking generally for something 'briefly on the method and what is new in the content', Marx followed up with more precise instructions that it should not be forgotten '1. that it extirpates Proudhonism root and branch, 2. that the *specifically* social, by no means *absolute*, character of bourgeois production is analysed straight away in its simplest form, that of the *commodity*.'[64] Engels's review does not mention Proudhon, nor does it relate the commodity to bourgeois production. Of course, Engels might have been intending to come to these points in his promised third article on the 'economic content';[65] but before he could proceed Marx reported dolefully '*Das Volk* is no more'; the paper had collapsed, with Engels's second article in the last issue.[66]

To come now to the content of the review: Marx's book comprised two chapters, one on the commodity and one on money, together with the subsequently famous Preface with its sketch of historical materialism (the methodological *Introduction* written in 1857 was suppressed); the extraordinary thing about the review is that, without much evidence from the book, Engels in his second article (his first was on the Preface) situated Marx's work in the context of German philosophy, and more particularly Hegelian speculative science; he went on to foist on the book a 'logical-historical' method. Three puzzles arise: (a) was it useful to drag in Hegel? (b) was Marx's method 'logical-historical'? (c) if either of these are to be answered in the negative, why did Marx allow the review to pass (and exult when it was widely reprinted[67])?

On the first point: Terrell Carver has pointed out that the tradition that Marx's work should be approached through a study of Hegel was first established in Engels's review.[68] But, while this is so, it has to be added also that Marx himself adhered to this tradition in the second edition of *Capital*, in so doing appropriating from the review the metaphor of a rational 'kernel' in 'idealistic wrapping', where Hegelian logic is concerned. We can trace the origin of this metaphor backwards: *Capital* says (1873 edition) that 'the mystification which the dialectic suffers in Hegel's hands' can be corrected: 'With him it is standing on its head. It must be inverted in order to discover the rational kernel within the mystical shell [*Hülle*]';[69] Engels's 1859 review said that Hegel's thought 'reversed the correct relation and stood it on its head'; furthermore 'Marx was and is the only one who could undertake the work of extracting from the Hegelian logic the kernel containing Hegel's real discoveries in this field, and of establishing the dialectical method, divested of its idealistic wrappings [*Umhüllungen*]';[70] Marx himself again, writing earlier to Engels (January 1858), had expressed the ambition to make accessible 'in 2 or 3 sheets . . . the *rational* aspect of the method which Hegel not only discovered but mystified'.[71]

As for Hegel himself, he explained that since his dialectical logic was the system of pure reason 'this realm is truth as it is without a veil [*Hülle*]'.[72] As if anticipating Engels, Hegel wrote that in his philosophy the 'manner of presentation is not arbitrary, it does not stand on its head ... because it has got tired of using its legs'.[73]

In trying to explain why it was not useful as it stood, Engels characterized 'Hegel's method' as one 'which, according to its own avowal, "came from nothing through nothing to nothing".'[74] This is a surprisingly vulgar attack on Hegel. Possibly it is in part a caricature of Hegel's central category of 'absolute negativity'; but, in so far as the quotation can be identified with anything in Hegel, it seems to be a reference to Hegel's dialectic of 'Reflection' (in his *Science of Logic)* which is characterized in its purity, or abstractness, as the movement from nothing, through nothing, back to itself. The section introducing this concept, however, is part of a chapter on 'Illusory Being' (*Schein*), not therefore the standpoint of Hegel's own philosophy, but one he identifies with scepticism and Kantianism, and whose position he is concerned to undermine in order to make further progress.[75] (The formula is of such small importance that it is suppressed in his *Encyclopaedia* 'Logic'.)

But why did Engels bring Hegel into his review when Marx's text barely mentions him?[76] Apart from his own views on the matter,[77] Engels had the evidence of the above-mentioned letter from Marx, in which it is noted that Hegel's *Logic* was of assistance in 'the method of analysis'.[78] Marx discussed his work on a visit to Engels in May of 1858[79] and could well have infected Engels with his new enthusiasm for Hegel.[80] Officially, the trip was to enable Marx to recover his health after overwork on the *Grundrisse*. But, clearly, theoretical matters inevitably obtruded themselves. Specifically, we know that Marx discussed the projected 'chapter on capital' with Engels, valuing his opinion on the matter[81] – precisely the material on which Hegel's dialectic had been of assistance according to the January letter. Furthermore, as Engels noted in his review,[82] in the *Contribution* ... Marx freely employed the term 'contradiction', and in one place[83] compared the metamorphoses of commodities to the syllogism P:U:I, a figure which Hegel treated exhaustively in his *Science of Logic*.

All in all, I conclude that Engels was entitled to refer to Hegel.

However, what exactly was the lesson that Marx learnt from Hegel? It is necessary to distinguish between systematic dialectic (a method of exhibiting the inner articulation of a given whole) and historical dialectic (a method of exhibiting the inner connection between stages of development of a temporal process), of which examples of both are to be found in Hegel. The problem with Engels's account is that he conflated the two. It is clear that Marx was influenced in his work by Hegel's method of developing concepts from one another in accord with a logical principle. But in his review Engels tried to restore Hegel's reputation by pointing to his 'tremendous historical sense'.[84] Engels was thereby led to make the fateful step of inventing a method of exposition which, while 'logical', is yet 'nothing but the historical method, only stripped of . . . disturbing fortuities'.[85]

I say 'invent' because this is not something that can properly be derived from Hegelianism as Engels seems to imagine,[86] for Hegel, in his systematic dialectics such as *The Philosophy of Right*, is to be found developing logical orders differing from historical orders. Indeed, when Marx in his 1857 *Introduction* makes reference to Hegel in one place, he does so precisely on this question, pointing out that in his *Philosophy of Right* Hegel rightly developed the category of possession before that of the family although this made no historical sense.[87] Almost certainly Marx must have had at the back of his mind a passage from Hegel's *Philosophy of Right* in which the latter made the same point with this very example: 'It may happen that the temporal sequence . . . is to some extent different from the conceptual sequence. Thus, we cannot say, for example, that property existed before the family, although property is nevertheless dealt with first.'[88]

The *Logic* itself, although eminently dialectical, being indeed dialectic in its home sphere, could not possibly be 'also historical' of course. As if to emphasize this point Hegel equates it with an eternal pre-given form: the mind of God before the creation of the world.[89]

Extraordinarily, however, when he cited Hegel's books in evidence,[90] Engels ignored the *Logic*, the one book Marx himself told Engels had influenced him.[91] If Engels had taken seriously the *Logic* as a guide to method, then he would have been led to stress the *systematicity* of Marx's approach; instead, harking back to his youthful enthusiasm for Hegel's philosophy of history, Engels saw the unity of the text as established historically.[92]

Engels's view dominated Marx scholarship this century (e.g. Hilferding, Dobb, Meek, Howard and King, Mandel) but is now widely contested, for it flatly contradicts Marx's explicit statement in his draft 'Introduction' of 1857 (presumably unknown to Engels) that the categories should not be presented in order of historical evolution, but in accordance with the articulation of the existing system.[93]

However, Engels *did* have on file an extremely confusing outline by Marx of his projected book, in which he spoke of transitions which were 'also historical'.[94] Possibly the idea of a 'logical-historical method' may have occurred to Engels when trying to make sense of Marx's text because of this.[95]

Furthermore, Marx always intended to supplement his substantive treatment with a review of the history of economic thought. In the 1859 text we find three interludes on this literature, the first explicitly historical. This seems to have been why Engels stated that 'even according to the method won, the critique of economics could still be arranged in two ways – historically and logically'.[96] For he conflates the literature with its object: 'Since in history, as in its literary reflection, development proceeds by and large from the most simple to the more complex relations, the historical development of the literature of political economy provided a natural guiding thread with which the critique could link up, and on the whole the economic categories would thus appear in the same order as in the logical development.'[97] So the double exposition of the *Contribution* in which the substantive critique is followed by a survey of the relevant literature seems to have been interpreted by Engels as a straight comparison of logic and history since the literature was 'reflected history', so to speak.

The problem lies in the term 'reflection'. Marx gives the following example: 'Caught up in the ideas of the monetary system, Petty asserts that the labour which determines exchange value is the particular kind of concrete labour by which gold and silver is extracted.'[98] We see, then, that in a sense Petty 'reflects' an underdeveloped stage of capitalism; but this issues in a false theory, false even at the time. The presumption that money hoards alone constitute wealth reflects the fact that when bourgeois society was in its infancy trade was the basis of capital accumulation. However, Marx does not leave the matter there. When he comes to the attack on the illusions of the monetary and mercantilist systems mounted by political economy he says that in truth these old systems were not only historically excusable, they had validity in so far as they sought to express value in an adequate form.[99]

Nonetheless, in the *logical* development Marx follows classical political economy in concentrating first on money in its 'fluid' form before its 'crystallization' into hoards, whereas the history of the theory developed in the opposite direction because at first international trade bulked larger than industry.

What remains to be assessed is Engels's argument that the history has to be 'corrected'[100] in the light of the logic. What does it mean? Engels is not at all clear on this; however, whereas sometimes he speaks as if the exposition must start with something primitive ('with the moment when products are exchanged for one another – whether by individuals or primitive communities'[101]), in other places he says that the method requires that this *not* be done, but rather that commodities be studied 'in their complete development', and that, in general, each moment must be examined 'at the point of development of its full maturity, of its classical form'.[102]

The only way of making sense of this claim is to assume that the truth about commodities and money can only be established in their complete development, yet for some sort of unexplained reason one is entitled to read this back into their elementary forms, and that this would have historical relevance in so far as Engels was confident that on the whole history follows the same order as the logic.

Such a complex procedure is certainly not explained and justified in Marx's 1859 text. But Engels's reference to the complete development of forms *is* based on Marx's own exposition. For example, Marx says: 'The full development of the law of value presupposes a society in which large-scale industrial production and free competition obtain, in other words, modern bourgeois society.'[103]

But the true relationship of logic and history, if there is one, may be the inverse of Engels's assumption: Marx points out, in the suppressed 1857 *Introduction*, that the 'simple' category of labour-in-general only acquires 'practical truth' when capitalism is mature. (Likewise, it was not until Smith that the literature of political economy arrived at this pure concept.[104]) Again, he argued that it was necessary to deal first with capital as the predominant factor in modern bourgeois economies, as against land, however important the latter had been historically. On this basis Marx concludes it would be wrong to deal with economic categories in some historical order. But what is also apparent is that at this time Marx was by no means clear about the relation between logic and history; the piece has very much the feel of an exploratory discussion, and it was very possibly suppressed *just because* Marx felt the whole issue needed further thought. For when he directly posed the question as to whether simpler categories had historical existence before more concrete ones he replied 'that depends', and launched into a complex discussion of the matter.[105] While Marx's notes show that he differed from Engels's formulation of this relationship, I think Marx let the review pass, not just because of the urgency of deadlines,[106] but because he was still undecided about the relevance of his logical arrangement of the categories for historical research. However, what we can say is that if the relation to history of the logical development is variable, then we cannot, as Engels seems to think, take history as a *guide*. Rather we must take the inner articulation of this present system as our point of departure, evolve a purely logical method of treatment of the material to hand, and then we might *in addition* note transitions that are 'also historical' in some sense. But that would not be a necessary feature of the method as is implied by Engels's talk about 'constant contact' with the course of history.[107] So the present might provide hints for looking at the past, but this is different from identifying in it earlier instantiations of purely logical phases in the development of the categories of the capitalist economy.

What probably impressed Engels (and his followers like Meek) is that if one considers the basic forms of circulation, then the sequence commodity–money–capital could be both logical and historical; each cannot be understood without its predecessors, and with luck the concept of each could be derived from its predecessor through a dialectical development, while historical contingencies did indeed make this progression possible. But we should note that starting *historically* with the commodity would *not* mean starting historically with value in Marx's sense, because under the contingencies operative in underdeveloped forms of commodity exchange we would have price, to be sure, but not yet labour values (unless one means something relatively indeterminate by value) which, as Marx allows in the *Contribution* itself, require full industrial development. (I postpone elaboration of this argument about the law of value until the topic of 'simple commodity production' is reached in the next section.)

Let us now summarize how close Engels's review is to the method of the book it is reviewing. Meek was too generous when he claimed that 'what Engels says is accurate enough as a generalization of the method employed by Marx *in the book Engels was actually reviewing*.'[108]

On comparing the two texts we conclude:

(a) Engels was right to refer to Marx's dialectical development of categories, and to name Hegel as an important source for dialectical method. But he should have looked to Hegel's logic rather than to his philosophy of history;

(b) Engels was wrong to say that the literature of political economy provided Marx with his 'guiding thread';[109] on the contrary, Marx criticized the literature, for its vacillating between categories of different levels of analysis, in his final word on it;[110] he could only do this having *independently* grasped the hierarchy of categories with his own logical apparatus.

Before leaving the 1859 texts it is interesting to observe something Marx said in *Contribution* which Engels failed to pick up in his discussion of Hegel. In a section expressing ideas Marx will later term his theory of 'commodity fetishism',[111] he calls the system of commodity exchange 'perverted', not in a normative but a cognitive sense. In the value form the relation of persons is 'hidden by a material veil' (*'dinglicher Hülle'*),[112] which gives rise to *'Mystifikation'*.[113] Although labours are carried out privately they require some social mediation. This is achieved through their positing as identical in the value form. 'This reduction appears to be an abstraction, but it is an abstraction which is made every day in the social process of production.'[114] It determines labours as social but in a very peculiar sense because they are constituted by 'a specific kind of sociality' in which 'the social relations of individuals . . . appear in the perverted form of a social relation between things.'[115]

In his review Engels observed that in Hegel real relations elevated to the realm of 'pure thought' appear in an 'abstract distorted' manner, wrapped in an idealistic veil.[116] Is there not a striking parallel between this critique of Hegel and that mounted by Marx of commodity relations? In both cases, 'abstraction' is fatal; in Hegel's case his abstractions, 'distorted' forms of real relations to be sure, veil reality idealistically; in the case of commodity exchange a *real* abstraction gives rise to the value form and casts a 'material veil' over the reality of social production. If one wanted to relate 'literature' to real history one might find food for thought in *this* parallel![117]

After 1859 nothing more was said on the 'logical-historical method' while Marx was alive.[118] It is worth noting that in Engels's reviews of *Capital*, Volume I, this account of Marx's method was not mentioned. This may be considered very significant (although, as we shall see shortly, it seems to be applied in the Preface and the Supplement he wrote for his edition of Volume III[119]). But that he may still have hankered for it can be seen from his letter responding to proof sheets of the first part in which he said that 'the knowledge gained here dialectically could be supported by more historical examples, to make the test of history on it'.[120]

Before addressing the question of what sort of method is implicit in Marx's project, let us look at another relevant text of Engels.

SIMPLE COMMODITY PRODUCTION

In his 1859 review Engels at one point specified that, although both logical and historical methods were possible, the logical sequence was 'nothing but the reflection of the historical process in an abstract and theoretically consistent form, a corrected reflection but corrected in accordance with laws yielded by the actual historical process itself, since each moment can be examined at the point of development of its full maturity, of its classical form.'[121] The question arising from this is at what point *does* a moment attain 'its classical form'? – With regard to value itself, for example?

Engels came back to this question in his Preface to *Capital*, Volume III. He started there by referring to 'the misunderstanding that Marx seeks to define where he only explains, and that one can generally look in Marx for fixed, cut-and-dried definitions that are valid for all time'. He explained that 'where things and their mutual relations are conceived not as fixed but rather as changing, their mental images, too, i.e. concepts, are also subject to change and reformulation; that they are not to be encapsulated in rigid definitions, but rather developed in their process of historical or logical formation.'[122]

This passage is an excellent expression of the dialectical point of view, and it does indeed apply in full measure to Marx's *Capital*. However, in applying it himself Engels provided a particular interpretation of it which proved to be enormously influential. He said that in view of the above propositions, 'it will be clear, then, why at the beginning of Volume I, where Marx takes simple commodity production as his historical presupposition, only later, proceeding on this basis, to come on to capital – why he proceeds precisely there from the simple commodity and not from a conceptually and historically secondary form, the commodity as already modified by capitalism.'[123]

Although Engels did not refer to the 'logical-historical method' here, his coining of this concept of 'simple commodity production', and his claim that such a régime *did* exist, and instantiated the law of value, can be properly seen as an application of the method. In this passage Engels is again supposing that Marx's logical method is based on a historical process, namely that from the historical 'presupposition' of 'simple commodity production' to capitalist production.

In truth, Engels never completely clarified the point about *when* exactly value is a reality. Thus, when in response to *Capital*, Volume III, Conrad Schmidt put forward the thesis that the 'value' discussed in Volume I is a 'necessary fiction', Engels wrote to him arguing that 'the law of value and the distribution of surplus value according to the rate of profit . . . attain their most complete approximate realization only with the prerequisite that capitalist production has been completely established everywhere', but 'this condition does not obtain yet even in England . . .'.[124] However, the general thrust of his reply was to claim that, notwithstanding the point about its 'complete realization', value is real enough for practical purposes earlier, indeed at the outset of 'simple commodity production'. The day before writing to Schmidt, Engels had written to Werner Sombart in much the same vein, arguing that 'value had a *direct and real existence*' at the time 'when commodity exchange began', but 'this direct realization of value . . . no longer happens', for 'the value of the capitalist mode of production . . . is so thoroughly hidden'.[125]

So strongly did Engels feel about this that he wrote a special paper on the subject, which was placed as a Supplement to the second edition of *Capital*, Volume III. He was there concerned to dispel any doubt that 'what is involved is not just a logical process but a historical one'. After developing the point at length, he concluded that 'Marx's law of value applies universally, as much as any economic laws do apply, for the entire period of simple commodity production, i.e. up to the time at which this undergoes a modification by the onset of the capitalist form of production.'[126]

Of course, the context in which Engels became involved in the discussion of simple commodity production was that in which it seemed to many that in the third volume of *Capital* Marx had abandoned the law of value in favour of another principle of price determination. However, intelligent readers could see that in Marx's procedure values were a stage in the process of generating the Volume III 'prices of production'. Faced with the claim that, if such values were not *empirically* present because they were superseded in the presentation by these prices of production, then they had no substance, being, indeed, mere 'fictions', even if convenient or necessary fictions (as Schmidt argued), Engels reacted by interpreting the stages of Marx's presentation *historically* in order to ensure that the values were indeed empirically visible, but, of course, in the *past*, before capitalism 'modified' the relationships involved. But Engels conceded far too much to the sceptics by reorganizing Marx's conceptualization of value in such a fashion that these obsolete values were adjudged the pure form and the 'capitalistically modified' form the 'secondary' one. Sceptics could legitimately wonder if such superseded values had *any* present relevance.

Before discussing the merits of Engels's view, it has to be noted that there is precious little textual support for it. Marx certainly does not develop the idea of 'simple commodity production' at the point where it was supposed to be under discussion, namely the first few chapters of Volume I. This did not prevent Dona Torr, for example, indexing no less than twenty pages of Volume I under the head 'Commodity Production, Simple'[127] – striking testimony to the almost hypnotic power of Engels's influence on Marx's editors and commentators.

The truth is that *Marx never used the term 'simple commodity production' in his life.*[128] Likewise, it is certain he never referred to the capitalistically produced commodity as a secondary derivative form.[129]

The only occurrence of the term 'simple commodity production' in the whole three volumes of *Capital* occurs in Volume III, but this is in a passage given to us subsequent to Engels's editorial work, as he himself warns us in a note.[130] It is now possible to check this against the manuscript itself, which recently was published in the new MEGA. It is clear that the entire paragraph was interpolated by Engels (as, indeed, was the one on the next page about capital's 'historical mission').[131]

It is evidence of the enormous authority of Engels, as interpreter of Marx's meaning, that the standard textbooks for a long time repeated his view of the matter.[132] Generations of students have been taught Marxist economics on the basis of a distinction between capitalist production and 'simple commodity production'. Yet this approach descends from Engels, *not Marx*.

It is true that Engels was able to cite a passage from the manuscript of the third volume in which something like the content of the idea of a stage of simple commodity production was discussed by

Marx. Seizing enthusiastically on this, Engels claimed that 'if Marx had been able to go through the third volume again, he would undoubtedly have elaborated this passage significantly':[133] however, it is just as possible he would have decided it was a false trail and eliminated it![134] Certainly, odd references in *Capital* to pre-capitalist production are not used with any *systematic* intent.

Let us be fair to Engels: it is of course permissible to invent new terminology in an endeavour to make clear what a writer intended even if he himself failed to put it in such terms. The question is whether or not it gets closer or further from a sensible understanding. This is what will be addressed in the next section.

It may be noted that such an outstanding Marxist economist as Ernest Mandel remains firmly persuaded of Engels's opinion that Marx's *Capital* is relevant to simple commodity production, and that such a regime existed historically.[135] Nevertheless, just as with the 'logical-historical method' in general, this application of it is now contested.

Engels rightly drew attention to the fact that, in a dialectical movement, concepts must be grasped in their 'formation'. But *when* do we have a fully formed concept? When do we have a 'half-baked' one? I argue – to put it crudely – that 'simple commodity production' of value is a half-baked notion.

I shall not enter on a discussion as to the historicity of 'simple commodity production'; for there is a prior more interesting question from a theoretical point of view: does the model work *conceptually*? Does the law of value really attain its maturity at such a posited stage of development of commodity exchange, or rather, does it attain its complete development only with capital? Is it correct to view the 'simple' commodity as in some sense primary, and the product of capital as in some sense 'secondary', a derivative form presenting us with a less than 'pure' case?

The key question we have to answer is whether or not it makes sense to speak of value, and of exchange governed by a law of labour value, in such a pre-capitalist society, just as much, or perhaps more purely so, as in capitalism proper? The truth is that it does not, because there is in such an imagined society no mechanism enforcing such a law; there is no *necessity* for value to emerge as anything more than an empty form with the potential to develop a meaningful content with capitalism.

There are two cases to consider: either there is mobility of labour or there is not. In the latter case exchange in proportion to labour times expended could only occur on the basis of a *normative* principle. It might have been a widely followed rule, but not an objectively imposed law to be grasped in its necessity by science. Even if one could find historical examples of this rule, it is clearly *irrelevant* to commodity production in a market economy based on driving hard bargains. In the former case exchange at 'value' is supposed to take place because otherwise people would switch into the better rewarded occupation. As with the other case, it should be noted that this presupposes everyone knows what labour is expended by others; this is a very doubtful proposition historically.[136] However, even if it is accepted as an idealizing assumption it is still true that we have nothing like an objective law operative. For the assumption is here that the *only* consideration affecting the choices of individuals is avoidance of 'toil and trouble', as Adam Smith originally argued; equal quantities of labour are always 'of equal value to the labourer', he claimed.[137] This *subjective* hypothesis has little to do with Marx's argument that there exists in capitalism an *objective* law of value which makes exchange at value *necessary*. If one relies on a merely subjective perception of producers, then other subjective considerations to do with the trouble of learning new methods, or the preference for one occupation rather than another, may be operative also.

Why should there be any tendency to establish a socially necessary labour time? It is only in modern industry that competition within a branch, and the mobility of capital between branches, brings about the development of a common measure. Only in capitalist industry are tea-breaks timed to the second, and abolished entirely if possible. The heart of the matter is not an ideal type of rational economic man read back into the natural state, but the objective rationality of the system of capitalist competition. Marx makes this clear when he says that Ricardo 'is at least aware that the operation of the law [of value] depends upon definite historical preconditions'. Ricardo held that the determination of value by labour-time is valid for 'such commodities only as can be increased in quantity by the exertion of human industry, and on the production of which competition operates without restraint'; Marx comments that what is really meant by this is that 'the full development of the law of value presupposes a society in which large-scale industrial production and free competition obtain, in other words, modern bourgeois society.'[138]

Just because there is exchange of goods produced, this does not mean any law of value governs the ratio of exchange. Price in such a case could simply be a formal mediation, allowing exchange to take place but *without any determinate value substance* being present. According to Marx the law of value is based on exchange in accordance with socially necessary labour times, but in the case of simple commodity production there is no mechanism that would *force* a given producer to meet such a target or be driven out of business. When all inputs, including labour power itself, have a value form, and production is subordinated to valorization, then an objective comparison of rates of return on capital is possible and competition between capitals allows for the necessary enforcement of the law of value.[139]

If it is granted that value is not a substance given prior to exchange (as is use value), but one which develops only in and through the forms of exchange, then it is fully developed only when these forms have reached the point at which we can demonstrate that value has become a reality in both form and content, and that its logic has imposed itself on the movement of the economy to the extent that we can speak about a quantitatively determinant law of commodity production. For the reasons explained above this law cannot hold in the postulated model of simple commodity exchange.

In assessing the faithfulness of Engels's commentary on *Capital* to Marx's intentions, two distinct issues must be separated. First, do the early chapters of *Capital* refer to simple commodity production? Here, I think that the evidence is clear that from the very first line Marx is presupposing that his object is capitalist production and that the commodity is its basic unit of output whose conditions of existence he traces.[140] Next, notwithstanding this last point, namely that Marx was interested in the commodity as a product of capital, might it not be true that the laws adduced here can nonetheless be referred back to a real or imaginary stage of simple commodity production? Here, I have argued above that the law of value could not govern such a mode of production.

Thus, taking the two points together, Engels's view that the logical development of Marx's argument is a 'corrected history' of a development to capitalism out of 'simple commodity production' fails both at the textual and substantive level.

THE PROBLEM OF TOTALITY

Following Engels's lead the main dialectical theorists presented dialectic as a principle of movement, primarily of history. Left in the shade was the fact that dialectical argument is better suited to reconstruct the articulation of a structured whole, regardless of whether the whole is stable or likely to transform itself into something completely different. Yet if we look at Hegel and Marx it is clear that analysis of wholes through systematic dialectical argument is what is most important in their work. The problem I want to address is in what exactly consists the *logical* method of development of the argument of *Capital*? It must be adequate to its object: I argue that the object is a certain sort of whole. What sort? Well: it is not a mere *aggregation*; this we have in a pile of bricks where one brick is placed casually on another. It is, rather, a totality where every part clearly requires complementing with others to be what it is; hence internal relations typify the whole, such that the very essence of each element depends on its relation to others and the whole. A thing is internally related to another if this other is a necessary condition of its nature. We cannot say 'what it is' without reference to the whole context of its relations and determinants. If the elements are bound together in such a whole, we can even speak then of holistic causality bringing about a substantial transformation of the spheres involved.

The problem we face is that a totality cannot be presented *immediately*; its articulation has to be exhibited; we have to make a start somewhere, with some aspect of it. But in the exposition the argument can move through the reconstruction of the whole from a particular starting point because we can move logically from one element to another along a chain of internal relations; in strict logic if the very meaning of an element is at issue (which I would argue is the case in the value forms commodity–money–capital each of which requires the others to complete its meaning or develop its concept), or with a fair degree of confidence if material conditions of existence are involved (as with the relation of valorization to production).

This is why Marx and Engels got involved in methodological problems. As was noted above, Engels explains that one cannot generally look in Marx for fixed, cut-and-dried definitions that, once given, are valid from then on.[141] In a dialectical argument the meanings of concepts undergo shifts because the significance of any element in the total picture cannot be defined for good at the outset. In an analytical argument this last *is* the assumption, namely that the analysis of the whole into its elements results in a set of 'atomic facts', and then the whole is grasped as the aggregate influence of these elements on each other. But if, contrary to this, each element is significant only in so far as it is itself determined by its place in the totality, then, as the presentation of the system advances to more complex, and concrete, relationships, the originating definition of a concept shifts accordingly, normally towards greater definiteness, although sometimes new and broader applications of the concept come into view. Instead of foreclosing on reality, the dialectical method remains open to fundamental reorganizations of the material thus far appropriated, as it gets closer to the truth of things. For example, only when commodities are grasped as products of capital can the form of value be seen as infused with a determinate content under the force of valorization. A commodity is not at all the same commodity when viewed as a product, and again when viewed as a product of capital.[142]

For Engels, the value of commodities is real *from the start* of the exposition, and its truth is transparent at that point, only to become clouded when the later modifications impact on the initial posit. The reason I argue this logic is inappropriate is that at the core of capitalism is a totality which forms its elements in such a way that taken apart from it they are denatured. Thus value depends for its reality on the full development of capitalist production, and makes very little sense outside it. Yet this 'finished form' of value cannot be artificially held apart from its predecessors. From a dialectical point of view, when the movement to prices of production is undertaken the law of value is realized only in its negation, for the condition which grants it determinacy, namely capitalist competition, brings with it differences that transform actual values. But the law still holds in an important sense, even in the mode of being denied, because prices of production can properly be understood only as the *outcome* of this dialectical unity in difference: of the potential and realized values.

The law of value is not something lying at an *origin*, whether logical or historical; it is something that *comes to be* in the capitalist totality.

To conclude, let us address the problem posed by historical anticipations of capitalist relations. We have argued that the object of

Marx's investigation is a totality in a special sense. In this context we can now locate the problem of how to deal with the fact that elements of the totality pre-existed it; for we know that prior to the rule of capitalist industry there existed commodities, money, and even capital itself in the shape of merchant capital and usurious capital.

If one takes Marx's analysis of money one discovers that he introduced its functions in a quite unhistorical manner. Indeed, as Marx himself was aware, historically these functions were frequently performed by different objects, having been institutionalized separately.[143] What is distinctly different about capitalism is that the actualization of value as a totality of form determinations imposes a requirement for these separate functions to be integrated through the evolution of a single money commodity. Given a single, though complex, concept of money, then the exposition of the totality can develop its functions in the most appropriate *systematic* order, without any historical implications. Thus money has a key role *now* as an internal moment of capital; this gives it quite different determinations than any 'money' that performs some particular function (e.g. as circulating medium) in pre-capitalist formations.

Next: should one take Marx's derivation of M–C–M′ (i.e. the exchange of money for commodities followed by the sale of commodities for more money) as abstractly general or as introducing capital in a particular historical shape, namely merchant capital? Clearly, systematically it must be counted as the abstract form of capital with no such concrete reference.[144] Interpreted *concretely* it could be a description of the circuit of merchant capital, but Marx rightly deals with such capital late in his exposition because in this society merchant capital is subordinate to industrial capital. It has a quite new historical determination owing to its function of circulating and realizing values of industrial products and achieving a revenue based on this specific function. This is different from its earlier function of linking otherwise isolated centres of economic activity for the sake of a revenue based on arbitrage. The merchant capital is not now facilitating the circulation of pre-capitalist surpluses, and profiting from that, but it is dealing in goods produced *for the market*, and helps valorization of capital in general.[145]

The same lessons can be drawn for money-lending capital. We must distinguish first the usurer who originally set up to fund consumption, then the Shylockian lender to speculators and merchants, and finally modern banking, the bulk of whose lending goes to *businesses*. Thus the abstract form of interest-breeding capital, M–M′, covers very different functions according to the level of historical development of commodity production. So, again, simplicity demands the development of the exposition be systematic rather than historical.[146]

Marx explicitly concentrates, in *Capital*, Volume I, on industrial capital and produced commodities, whereas, historically, merchant capital and money-lending capital came earlier because they have fewer real presuppositions than industrial capital. Marx reached them only in Volume III because they now have a secondary status when functioning in the service of modern industrial capital, and, therefore, come later in his presentation. When Marx identified industrial capital as the dominant form in the bourgeois epoch this does not mean simply that it has pushed aside, as it were, other bases of unearned income such as land[147] and merchant capital, but rather that it is the overriding moment in a totality which restructures the context in which other elements operate, and thereby also fundamentally *transforms* them in their own determinacy and in the role they play in the whole and its reproduction. Thus the 'capital' that 'pre-existed' capitalism is not *the same capital* that exists now. Marx commented:

> Industrial capital is the only mode of existence of capital in which not only the appropriation of surplus-value or surplus product, but also its creation, is a function of capital . . . The other varieties of capital which appeared previously . . . are not only subordinated to it and correspondingly altered in the mechanisms of their functioning, but they now move only on its basis, thus live and die, stand and fall together with this basis.[148]

What I argue is that if capitalism is a totality that assigns every element its particular function, then elements in a pre-capitalist context have perhaps rather different determinations, and their nature is not the same, even if superficial similarities across time may allow some sort of nominal definition of them. But, now, their real definition is given by capital. Marx said:

> In every social formation there is a specific kind of production which predominates over all the others and whose relations therefore determine their rank and influence. It is a general illuminant tingeing all other colours and modifying their specific features. It is a special ether determining the specific gravity of everything appearing in it.[149]

In general, then, attempting to fit the 'logic' to the 'history' would be a misconceived enterprise, since the elements traced through the internal relations of the capital totality are not identifiable with similar elements operating in an earlier environment. If the significance of an element cannot be grasped apart from its place assigned by the totality, then even if nominally identical elements existed in earlier periods they are in truth different just because of the different context in which their effectivity is played out. As Marx put it: 'Even economic categories which belong to earlier epochs of production take on a specifically different, historical, character on the basis of the capitalist mode of production.'[150]

Although this self-relating, self-differentiating, self-grounding totality did not spring from nowhere, in so far as its elements preexisted it in some shape or other they cannot – just because they were *not* formed by the totality in question – then have had the same nature, form, function and law as they gain within it. As I indicated earlier (in the discussion of 'simple commodity production') this is true of the law of value itself.

CONCLUSION

In discussing the question of whether or not Engels was accurately retailing Marx's method, both those for and against him could find – and have found – suitable quotations to support each case. Although it is clear that in *Capital* he articulated the structure of a totality, I think that Marx himself never fully clarified the relationship of his own logical method to history. But I hope I have said enough to show that, while Engels was certainly sensitive to the demands of dialectical forms of exposition, it was not helpful to insist so strongly on the so-called 'logical-historical method'; rather, a strictly systematic dialectic is indicated, with caution exercised about relating the moments of the existing totality to pre-capitalist forms.

Truer to Engels's account of the dialectical exposition of concepts than treating the starting point of *Capital* as a historical presupposition, or as a simple model, would be to consider it as a provisional immature abstract moment of a complex totality. The exposition has to remedy the insufficiency of the starting point by showing how value, in its complete, finished form, does make good the promise of a law of value, by grounding it in the *developed* value forms – first money, then capital, then productive labour, finally circulation and accumulation of capital.

Engels was quite right in his intuition that to comprehend such a system requires, not a 'rigid definition' of value, but an *exposition* of its development, an unfolding of its forms, discovering deeper essential determinations at each stage. In such an exposition this system of forms must be grasped as a totality, not as a set of independent stages. Certainly history is the test, as Engels said, but it is *future* history because only when capital achieves a mature form does its inexorable law of accumulation take root.

We all owe Engels a tremendous debt for the work he accomplished after Marx's death in transcribing and editing the volumes of *Capital,* and organizing translations. I believe that much of the work he did on Volume I cannot be faulted. As for the work he did on the other two volumes, more research is required to reach a final verdict, but I have shown that he wrote 'simple commodity production' into Marx.

With regard to Engels's attempts to facilitate our understanding of Marx's method, I have argued that he was absolutely correct to indicate the importance of dialectic, but, instead of interpreting this largely in the light of Hegel's philosophy of history, he should have drawn attention to the importance of Hegel's *systematic* dialectic.[151]

Notes

1. An English translation may be found in Karl Marx and Frederick Engels *Collected Works* (hereafter *CW*) Vol. 3. For an illuminating study of it see Gregory Claeys, 'Engels' *Outlines of a Critique of Political Economy* (1843) and the origins of the Marxist critique of Political Economy', *History of Political Economy,* Vol. 16, 1984.
2. *Very* early times in fact, for Marx complains to Engels in a letter of 1856 about a journalist: 'It is exceedingly odd, the way he speaks of us in the *singular* – "Marx and Engels *says*", etc.' (1 Aug. 1856: *CW* 40, p. 64).
3. M.C. Howard & J.E. King, *The Political Economy of Marx,* Longman, Harlow, 1975, p. 46. I cannot trace this error-ridden paragraph in the thoroughly rewritten second edition of 1985.
4. Ibid., p. 48 = p. 56 in the second edition.
5. R.L. Meek, *Economics and Ideology and Other Essays* (1967), pp. 96, 98, 99ff.
6. *Studies in the Labour Theory of Value* (1956), 'Introduction to the Second Edition' (1973), p. xv.

7. All quotes below are on p. 210.
8. *CW* 20, p. 217.
9. Ibid.
10. Ibid.
11. *CW* 20, p. 208.
12. *CW* 20, pp. 224–5.
13. Letter of 7 Dec. 1867: *Letters on Capital*, pp. 121–3.
14. Neither J.D. Hunley (*The Life and Thought of Friedrich Engels: A Reinterpretation*, 1991) nor S.H. Rigby (*Engels and the formation of Marxism*, 1992), who both know Levine's work, mention, or reply to, this part of it.
15. Hunley defends Engels's editing work on the later volumes against Levine's criticism of it (op. cit., pp. 56–8). G. Stedman Jones cites this part of Levine's study but does not mention, or reply to, the mistaken charges against Engels as a reviewer ('F. Engels', in *The New Palgrave: Marxian Economics*, 1990, p. 163).
16. Levine says Mss. I of Volume II is 'missing' (*Dialogue Within the Dialectic*, 1984, p. 182). In fact it has now been published in *Marx-Engels Gesamtausgabe* (hereafter 'MEGA'), MEGA II, 4.1 (1988).
17. Levine, *Dialogue* . . ., pp. 201–2.
18. *Capital*, Volume III (Fernbach trans.), p. 91; *Capital*, Volume I (Fowkes trans.), p. 110.
19. *Le Capital Paris 1872–75*, trans. M.J. Roy; MEGA II, 7, p. 690.
20. Letter to Danielson, 15 Nov. 1878: *Letters on Capital*, p. 190.
21. *Capital*, Volume I (Fowkes trans.), p. 110.
22. Allen Oakley, *The Making of Marx's Critical Theory* (1983), p. 98.
23. The Pauls when translating (1928) from the fourth (1890) German edition deal with the different chapter numberings from the earlier translation by falsely informing the reader that earlier German editions of *Capital* had *more* chapters (Everyman edition, p. xliv).
24. Hal Draper, *Marx-Engels Cyclopedia Volume II, The Marx-Engels Register* pp. 28, 27, 188.
25. Talk of 5 Aug. 1986, published in *News & Letters*, November 1990, p. 4. Also see her *Rosa Luxemburg, Women's Liberation* . . . (1982), p. 139n., and her *Women's Liberation and the Dialectic of Revolution* (1985), pp. 254, 200, and 59.
26. Translated from the third German edition by Samuel Moore and Edward Aveling: see MEGA II, 9.
27. A 1954 edition, originating from Foreign Languages Publishing House of Moscow, continued with Engels's title. But in 1965, without notice, the same translation (now from Progress Publishers) had its title changed to correspond with the German: *Capital: A Critique of Political Economy*, Volume I, Book One, *The Process of Production of Capital*. The 1983 publication by Lawrence & Wishart, London, of this edition, printed in the USSR, is so titled; and in accordance with the above-mentioned reflections, I complied with the new format in preparing my Student Edition (Lawrence & Wishart, 1992) on the basis of this edition.
28. Letter to Danielson, 28 May 1872. See also Marx to Sorge, 27 Sept.

1877: *CW* 45, pp. 276–7. But note that Engels did not like the French (letter to Marx, 29 Nov. 1873).

29. Letter to Danielson, 15 Nov. 1878: *CW* 45, p. 343. It might be thought the same 'flattening' happened to the 1887 English version.
30. 28 Nov. 1878: *CW* 45, p. 346.
31. See my note in *Science & Society* (Summer 1990), using the French, for an important case where the Engels edition is to be preferred to the modern translation by Fowkes.
32. *Capital*, Volume I (1983 edn), p. 63; MEGA II, 9, p. 49. The *Apparat* volume to the MEGA edition of the first English translation of 1887 has an inventory of deviations of the translation from the third German edition on which it was based.
33. This debate was initiated by Althusser and Balibar in their *Reading Capital* (English trans. 1970). See the Index and Glossary under 'support'.
34. *Capital*, Volume I (1983 edn) p. 89; MEGA II, 9, p. 74.
35. *Capital*, Volume I (3rd German edn), MEGA II, 8, p. 112: *'als deren Träger sie sich gegenübertreten'*. *Capital*, Volume I (Fowkes trans.), p. 179.
36. MEGA II, 7, p. 64; MEGA II, 9, p. 74. In view of its interest, I restored the sentence in my Student Edition (p. 41), otherwise based on the 1983 edition published by Lawrence & Wishart.
37. MEGA II, 7, p. 790; MEGA II, 9, p. 739.
38. *Capital*, Volume I (1983 edn), p. 365; MEGA II, 9, p. 337; *Apparat*, p. 754. It *is* in the French: MEGA II, 7, p. 331.
39. *Capital*, Volume I (Fowkes trans.), translator's preface, p. 87.
40. *Capital*, Volume I (Fowkes trans.), p. 508.
41. *Das Kapital, Erster Band, Marx-Engels Werke, Vol. 23* ([Berlin, 1962] 1983), p. 407. M. Postone has already pointed out the omission in Fowkes (in *Time, labor, and social domination*, 1993, p. 338).
42. *Capital*, Volume I (1983 edn), p. 83; MEGA II, 9, p. 69; MEGA II, 7, p. 59. Another example is the note on Necker (*Capital*, Volume I, 1983 edn, p. 552; MEGA II, 9, p. 510) which is not in any German edition. See for Engels's editorial principles *Capital*, Volume I (1983 edn), Preface to English Edition, p. 14.
43. MEGA II, 5, *Capital 1867*, p. 147. In the French edition (MEGA II, 7, p. 162) the sentence is omitted, and replaced by other matter.
44. Rudolf Hilferding, *Böhm-Bawerk's Criticism of Marx*, trans. E. and C. Paul, ed. P. Sweezy (London, Merlin Press, 1975), pp. 141–3.
45. Ibid., p. 143n. It isn't clear why Hilferding did not use the fourth edition.
46. *Capital*, Volume I (1983 edn), p. 192; MEGA II, 9, *Capital 1887*, pp. 171–2. Fowkes, translating from the fourth edition, is faced with *'daher'* of course (*Das Kapital, MEW 23*, p. 212), and gives: 'This power being of a higher value, it expresses itself in labour of a higher sort . . .' etc. *Capital*, Volume I (Fowkes trans.), p. 305.
47. In Marx's main previously published work, *The Holy Family* (1845) and *The Poverty of Philosophy* (1847), Hegel is treated rather roughly.
48. Nos 14 and 16, 6 and 20 Aug. The original text is available in Karl

Marx, *Ökonomische Manuskripte Und Schriften 1858–61*, MEGA II, 2. I shall also give page references to the Peking edition (published as an Appendix to Karl Marx, *Preface and Introduction to 'A Contribution to the Critique of Political Economy'*, 1976), which is a modification of the English translation appended to K. Marx, *A Contribution to the Critique of Political Economy* (Progress Publishers, Moscow 1970), for the 1980 translation in *CW* 16 is inferior to the earlier one.

49. R.L. Meek, *Studies in the Labour Theory of Value* (1973), p. 148. The term itself is not in Engels but is fair to his text.
50. *The Economic Journal*, Vol. 86, June 1976, pp. 342–7. (A longer version of this paper is in his *Smith, Marx and after*, pp. 134–45.) He had already used the Engels review in *Economics and Ideology* (1967), p. 96, and *Studies . . .* (1973), p. 148.
51. *Preface and Introduction to 'A Contribution to the Critique of Political Economy'* (Peking edn), p. 40. This text is quoted, in the abovementioned challenge, by M. Morishima and G. Catephores ('Is there an "Historical Transformation Problem"?' *The Economic Journal*, Vol. 85, June 1975); and also very extensively in their response (Vol. 86, June 1976) to Meek's reply. Astonishingly, throughout the latter note they give the impression (e.g. pp. 348, 350–1) that Engels in his review was also reviewing this *Introduction* – but the latter was excluded from the *Contribution . . .*, as Marx notes in his Preface.
52. Appendix to *A Contribution to the Critique of Political Economy* by Karl Marx, trans. N.I. Stone (Chicago, Charles Kerr, 1904).
53. Indeed, in English it may well have predated an English translation of the Review. The first translation of the latter appears to have been published in 1935: Appendix D in F. Engels, *Ludwig Feuerbach and the Outcome of Classical German Philosophy* (Martin Lawrence, London, 1935).
54. *Marx' Method, Epistemology, and Humanism* [*sic*] (1986), p. 113
55. *Marx & Engels: The Intellectual Relationship* (1983), pp. 96–117.
56. Draper, *Marx-Engels Cyclopedia* (1985), Vol. I: *The Marx-Engels Chronicle*, p. 97; *CW* 16, Marx and Engels 1858–60 (Lawrence & Wishart, London, 1980), pp. xvii and 674.
57. Letters of 19 July 1859 and 22 July 1859.
58. Letter to Marx, 3 Aug. 1859. *CW* 40, p. 478.
59. In his biography of Engels, Carver acknowledges the point but cites his earlier work on the subject without comment (*Friedrich Engels: His Life and Thought*, 1989, p. 239).
60. Kain refers to Engels mischaracterizing Marx's method (*Marx' Method . . .*, 1986, p. 113). Yet, oddly enough, instead of excusing Engels on the grounds that he could not have been aware of Marx's 1857 *Introduction . . .* on method, Kain for some reason thinks Engels *was* aware of it (Kain, *Marx' Method . . .*, 1986, n. 24, p. 172). Carver too thinks Engels may have been aware of it but simply misunderstood it (*Marx and Engels: The Intellectual Relationship*, pp. 109–10). I think it certain Engels was not aware of it. It is clear from his correspondence that Marx never showed anyone his work until it was in proof.

61. For his discussion see *The Life and Thought of Friedrich Engels: A Reinterpretation*, 1991, pp. 89–90.
62. Meek, *Smith, Marx and after*, 1977, p. 136. Gareth Stedman Jones, 'F. Engels', in *Marxian Economics*, eds J. Eatwell et al. (Macmillan, London, 1990), p. 163.
63. When D. McLellan refers to the review he adds: 'the main points in which had been dictated by Marx': *Karl Marx: His Life and Thought* (Granada, St Albans, 1976), p. 310. Carver has already pointed this out: *Friedrich Engels: His Life and Thought*, p. 239.
64. *CW* 40, pp. 471 and 473.
65. Peking edn, p. 59; MEGA II, 2, p. 255.
66. Letter of 26 Aug. 1859. In this letter Marx says nothing about Engels's second article which appeared on the 20th (*CW* 40, p. 484).
67. See letter to Engels, 5 Oct. 1859 (*CW* 40, p. 502) and letter to Lasalle, 6 Nov. 1859 (*CW* 40, p. 518).
68. Terrell Carver, *Marx and Engels: The Intellectual Relationship* (Wheatsheaf, Brighton, 1983), p. 100.
69. *Capital*, Volume I (Fowkes trans.), p. 103.
70. Engels's *Review* . . ., Peking edn, pp. 54–5; MEGA II, 2, pp. 251–2.
71. Letter to Engels [16] Jan. 1858: *CW* 40, p. 249.
72. *The Science of Logic*, trans. A.V. Miller (George Allen & Unwin, London, 1969), p. 50.
73. *The Philosophy of Nature*, trans. M.J. Petry (George Allen & Unwin, 1970), Vol. 1, pp. 201–2.
74. Peking edn, p. 54; MEGA II, 2, p. 251
75. See *The Science of Logic*, pp. 400, 445, and 499.
76. In Marx's *Contribution* . . . Hegel is mentioned in its *Preface* respectfully but critically. There is no mention of anything to be learnt from him.
77. Perhaps it is worth noting that Engels was reluctant to do the review (letter of 25 July 1859), feeling very diffident about writing a theoretical piece after a long interval (letter of 3 Aug. 1859). So it is understandable if he fell back on old reflexes and continued the debates of the 1840s. (See Carver, *Marx and Engels: The Intellectual Relationship*, p. 115.)
78. [16] Jan. 1858: *CW* 40, p. 249.
79. *CW* 40, p. 618; Draper, Vol. 1, p. 90.
80. But Engels also was at that time using Hegel in beginning his researches on 'the dialectics of nature'. During his visit Marx must have promised to send Engels Hegel's *Philosophy of Nature*, for Engels complained in July that he had not received it (letter of 14 July 1858). One has to say the strictures in the 1859 review on the use of Hegel by the epigones apply only too well to the *Dialectics of Nature* of Engels himself.
81. *CW* 40, pp. 310–15, 368, 303, 623.
82. Peking edn, p. 58, citing material in *Contribution* . . . (*CW* 29, pp. 284–5).
83. *CW* 29, p. 331.
84. Peking edn, p. 54; MEGA II, 2, p. 251.

85. Peking edn, p. 56; MEGA II, 2, p. 253.
86. Peking edn, pp. 54–5.
87. Peking edn, p. 33.
88. See §32, Remark & Addition; English trans., p. 61.
89. 'It . . . is the exposition of God as he is in his eternal essence before the creation of nature and a finite mind': *Science of Logic*, p. 50.
90. Peking edn, p. 54; MEGA II, 2, p. 252.
91. In a late letter Engels refers to it: letter to Schmidt, 1 Nov. 1891. But in the review there is only the slighting allusion discussed above.
92. T. Carver (*Marx and Engels: The Intellectual Relationship*, p. 103) has already pointed this out.
93. Meek claimed Marx's *Introduction* . . . merely 'qualifies' Engels's account (*Smith, Marx, and after*, p. 138).
94. Letter of 2 April 1858. (Meek has already drawn attention to its importance: *Smith, Marx, and After*, p. 139n.)
95. Engels in his reply (9 April 1858) complained of 'a very abstract Abstract indeed', and of unclear dialectical transitions (*CW* 40, p. 304).
96. MEGA II, 2, p. 252; Peking edn, p. 55.
97. Ibid.
98. MEGA II, 2, p. 131; *CW* 29, p. 293.
99. *CW* 29, pp, 389–90.
100. Peking edn, p. 56.
101. Peking edn, p. 57.
102. Peking edn, pp. 56–7.
103. *CW* 29, p. 300.
104. Peking edn, pp. 95–6.
105. Peking edn, p. 33.
106. See letter of 13 Aug. 1859: *CW* 40, p. 482.
107. Peking edn, p. 58.
108. *Smith, Marx and after*, p. 139.
109. Peking edn, p. 55.
110. *CW* 29, p. 417.
111. Compare *Contribution* . . . (*CW* 29, pp. 272–6) with *Capital*, Volume I, Ch. 1, s. 4.
112. *CW* 29, p. 276; MEGA II, 2, p. 113.
113. *CW* 29, p. 276; MEGA II, 2, p. 114.
114. *CW* 29, p 272; MEGA II, 2, p. 110.
115. *CW* 29, p. 273 (trans. modified), p. 275; MEGA II, 2, pp. 111, 113.
116. Peking edn, p. 55.
117. See my previous work: *Dialectics of Labour*, and 'Hegel's Logic and Marx's Capital'. Also see L. Colletti's 'Introduction' to *Karl Marx: Early Writings* (Penguin, Harmondsworth, 1975), p. 39; and M. Postone, *Time, labor, and social domination* (esp. p. 81).
118. Marx's *Capital* of 1867 made numerous references to his *Contribution* . . ., but not to Engels's review of it, although three other works of Engels were praised. In the 1873 *Afterword* to the second edition Marx rightly said that his method 'has been little understood' (Fowkes trans. p. 99), but this *Afterword* raised more questions than it answered, especially with regard to some notoriously ambivalent and opaque remarks on Hegel's dialectic.

119. Incidentally, Engels's Preface to Volume II of *Capital* did not touch on the matter of logic and history. For purely external reasons he devoted it to an explanation of the uniqueness of Marx's theory of surplus value. Brilliantly making a parallel with the debate over the discovery of oxygen, he showed that, where others saw in surplus value only a *deduction* from the value of the worker's product, Marx saw an *addition* to the values productively consumed, namely surplus labour. He further clarified the point that labour as value-creating activity cannot have a value of its own. Note that the recent translation by D. Fernbach (1978) misses matter in this passage: 'labour-power for labour as the value-creating property' (p. 99) should read 'labour-power. By substituting labour-power for labour as the value-creating property . . .'
120. Letter to Marx, 16 June 1867: *Letters on Capital*, p. 103.
121. Peking edn, p. 56.
122. *Capital*, Volume III, p. 103.
123. Ibid.
124. Letter to Schmidt, 12 March 1895: *Letters on Capital*, pp. 287–8; *Marx and Engels Selected Correspondence*, pp. 481–5.
125. Letter of 11 March 1895: *Marx and Engels Selected Correspondence*, p. 481.
126. *Capital*, Volume III, pp. 1033 and 1037.
127. This was in a 1938 edition of *Capital* based on a reissue of Engels's edition.
128. If Marx did not use the term, what may have suggested it to Engels? There are two possibilities: in Volume I Marx refers to 'simple commodity circulation' in contrast to the circulation of money as capital (p. 253); also, in Volumes I and II there are chapters on 'simple reproduction' which deal with a supposed situation in which all surplus accruing to capital is consumed unproductively.
129. In his *Anti-Dühring* (pp. 225–6) Engels claimed to have found in *Capital* a discussion of the historical transition of commodity production into capitalist production. He cites at length a passage in which Marx presupposes the worker owned his own product (*Capital*, Volume I, Fowkes trans. pp. 729–30). He does not notice that this passage is written in hypothetical mode. I argue it is counter-factual in character in my 'Negation of the Negation in Marx's *Capital*', *Rethinking Marxism*, Winter 1993.
130. Fernbach trans., p. 370 and p. 371n.
131. Compare Marx-Engels, *Werke, Band 25*, pp. 271–3, with MEGA II, 4.2, pp. 334–6.
132. In the Introduction above it was mentioned that Meek, for example, cited Engels as if his words were Marx's own.
133. *Capital*, Volume III, p. 1034; the full passage from Marx is on pp. 277–8.
134. Morishima and Catephores also have said this (*The Economic Journal*, 1975, p. 319).
135. See Mandel's 'Introduction' to the Penguin edition of *Capital*, Volume I (Penguin, Harmondsworth, 1976) and his *Marxist Economic Theory* (Merlin Press, London, 1968).

136. Engels, Meek and Mandel think it is the case, but Morishima and Catephores argue against.
137. *The Wealth of Nations*, pp. 34–7. For Marx's criticism of Smith on this point see his 1859 *Critique* . . ., *CW* 29, p. 299.
138. *CW* 29, p. 300; the quotation from Ricardo is given in the original English of the third edition (1821, p. 3; Pelican Classic edition 1971 p. 56) whereas without notice *CW* 29, provides a retranslation. The Stone translation of the 1859 *Critique* . . . has it correctly, p. 69.
139. For a careful and devastating critique of Engels's view see John Weeks, *Capital and Exploitation* (Edward Arnold, London, 1981). Chs I and II.
140. *Capital*, Volume I (Fowkes trans.), p. 125. In the 1857 *Introduction* . . . Marx stresses that the subject he addresses is 'modern bourgeois society', and that therefore the succession of the economic categories, as well as the categories themselves, must express the form of being of this *specific* society. It follows that capital 'as the all-dominant economic power . . . must form both the point of departure and the conclusion' (Peking edn, pp. 39–40).
141. He made the same point also elsewhere: 'To science definitions are worthless because always inadequate. The only real definition is the development of the thing itself, but this is no longer a definition' (*Anti-Dühring*, p. 468).
142. Cf. Marx, *Resultäte*: *Capital*, Volume I, Appendix (Fowkes trans.), p. 949; and *CW* 32, p. 301.
143. Marx, *Contribution* . . ., *CW* 29, p. 312.
144. *Capital*, Volume I (Fowkes trans.) p. 216.
145. *Capital*, Volume III p. 444 ff.
146. On lending see *Theories of Surplus Value*, Volume III, p. 467; *CW* 32, p. 463; *Capital*, Volume III, p. 735.
147. For the example of land see *CW* 28, pp. 183–4; in particular note that after a digression on the history of land and capital he writes: 'But here we are concerned with bourgeois society . . . developing on its own basis' (p. 184).
148. *Capital*, Volume II (Fernbach trans.), pp. 135–6.
149. *1857 Introduction*, Peking edn, p. 39 (*Grundrisse*; *CW* 28, p. 43).
150. *CW* 34, pp. 358–9.
151. That the systematic approach need not lead to a premature *closure*, as Engels argued it had in Hegel (F. Engels, *Ludwig Feuerbach and the Outcome of Classical German Philosophy*, p. 23), I hope to show elsewhere.

References

Althusser, L. and Balibar, E. *Reading Capital*, London, Verso, 1970.
Arthur, C.J. *Dialectics of Labour*, Oxford, Basil Blackwell, 1986.
Arthur, C.J. '*Capital*: A Note on Translation', *Science & Society*, Vol. 54, No. 2, Summer 1990.

Arthur C.J. 'Hegel's *Logic* and Marx's *Capital*', Fred Moseley (ed.), *Marx's Method In Capital: A Reexamination*, New Jersey, Humanities Press, 1993.

Arthur C.J. 'Negation of the Negation in Marx's Capital', *Rethinking Marxism*, Vol. 6, No. 4, Winter 1993.

Carver, T. *Marx & Engels: The Intellectual Relationship*, Brighton, Wheatsheaf Books, 1983.

Carver, T. *Friedrich Engels: His Life and Thought*, London, Macmillan, 1989.

Claeys, G. 'Engels' *Outlines of a Critique of Political Economy* (1843) and the origins of the Marxist critique of capitalism', *History of Political Economy*, Vol. 16, 1984.

Colletti, L. 'Introduction', in *Karl Marx: Early Writings*, Harmondsworth, Penguin, 1975.

Draper, H. *The Marx-Engels Cyclopedia*; Vol. I: *The Marx-Engels Chronicle*; Vol. II: *The Marx-Engels Register*, New York, Shocken Books, 1985.

Dunayevskaya, R. *Rosa Luxemburg, Women's Liberation, and Marx's Philosophy of Revolution*, Atlantic Highlands, Humanities, 1982.

Dunayevskaya, R. *Women's Liberation and the Dialectic of Revolution: Reaching for the Future*, Atlantic Highlands, Humanities, 1985.

Dunayevskaya, R. 'Why post-Marx Marxists didn't become continuators of Marx's Marxism', *News & Letters*, November 1990.

Engels, F. *Ludwig Feuerbach and the Outcome of Classical German Philosophy*, London, Martin Lawrence, 1935.

Engels, F. *Anti-Dühring*, Moscow, FLPH, 1962.

Hegel, G.W.F. *The Science of Logic*, trans. A.V. Miller, London, George Allen & Unwin, 1969.

Hegel G.W.F. *The Philosophy of Nature*, trans. M.J. Petry, London, George Allen & Unwin, 1970.

Hegel, G.W.F. *Elements of the Philosophy of Right*, trans. H.B. Nisbet, Cambridge, Cambridge University Press, 1991.

Hilferding, R. *Böhm-Bawerk's Criticism of Marx*, published with E. v. Böhm-Bawerk, *Karl Marx and the Close of his System*, ed. P. Sweezy, London, Merlin Press, 1975.

Howard, M.C. & King, J.E. *The Political Economy of Marx*, Longman, Harlow, 1975.

Hunley, J.D. *The Life and Thought of Friedrich Engels: A Reinterpretation*, New Haven and London, Yale University Press, 1991.

Kain, P.J. *Marx' Method, Epistemology, and Humanism* [*sic*], Dordrecht, D. Reidel, 1986.

Levine, N. *The Tragic Deception: Marx Contra Engels*, Oxford and Santa Barbara, Calif., Clio, 1975.

Levine, N. *Dialogue Within the Dialectic*, London, George Allen & Unwin, 1984.

McLellan, D. *Karl Marx: His Life and Thought*, St Albans, Granada, 1976.

Mandel, E. *Marxist Economic Theory*, London, Merlin Press, 1968.

Mandel, E. 'Introduction', in Karl Marx, *Capital*, Volume I, Harmondsworth, Penguin, 1976.

Marx, K. and Engels, F. *Marx-Engels Collected Works* (50 vols) (cited as *CW*), London, Lawrence & Wishart, 1975– .

Marx, K. and Engels, F. *Karl Marx/Friedrich Engels Gesamtausgabe (MEGA)*; Berlin, Dietz Verlag, 1975– .

Marx, K. and Engels, F. *Letters on 'Capital'*, trans. A. Drummond, London, New Park Publications, 1983.

Marx, K. and Engels, F. *Selected Correspondence*, 2nd edn, Moscow, Progress Publishers, 1965.

Marx, K. *Ökonomische Manuskripte Und Schriften 1858–1861*, MEGA II, Band 2, Berlin, Dietz Verlag, 1980.

Marx K. *Preface and Introduction to 'A Contribution to the Critique of Political Economy'* (with a review by F. Engels), Peking, Foreign Languages Press, 1976.

Marx. K. *A Contribution to the Critique of Political Economy*, trans. N.I. Stone, Chicago, Charles Kerr, 1904.

Marx, K. *A Contribution to the Critique of Political Economy*, Moscow, Progress Publishers, 1970.

Marx, K. *Ökonomische Manuskripte 1863–67*, MEGA II, Band 4, Teil 1, Berlin, Dietz Verlag, 1988.

Marx, K. *Ökonomische Manuskripte 1863–67*, MEGA II, Band 4, Teil 2, Berlin, Dietz Verlag and Internationales Institut für Sozialgeschichte, Amsterdam, 1992.

Marx, K. *Das Kapital Erster Band Hamburg 1867*, MEGA II, Band 5, Berlin, Dietz Verlag, 1983.

Marx, K. *Das Kapital Erster Band, Hamburg 1872*, MEGA II, Band 6, Berlin, Dietz Verlag, 1987.

Marx, K. *Le Capital, Paris 1872–75*, MEGA II, Band 7, Berlin, Dietz Verlag, 1989.

Marx, K. *Das Kapital Erster Band, Hamburg 1889*, MEGA II, Band 8, Berlin, Dietz Verlag, 1989.

Marx, K. *Capital: A Critical Analysis of Capitalist Production, London 1887*, MEGA II, Band 9, Berlin, Dietz Verlag, 1990.

Marx, K. *Das Kapital Erster Band, Hamburg 1890*, MEGA II, Band 10, Berlin, Dietz Verlag, 1991.

Marx, K. *Capital: A Critique of Political Economy,Volume I*, London, Lawrence & Wishart, 1983.

Marx, K. *Capital: A Critical Analysis of Capitalist Production* (a reprint of Engels's edition of 1889 with supplementary material, trans. Dona Torr), London, George Allen & Unwin, 1938.

Marx, K. *Das Kapital, Kritik der politischen Ökonomie, Erster Band, Marx-Engels Werke 23*, Berlin, Dietz Verlag, 1983.

Marx, K. *Das Kapital, Kritik der politischen Ökonomie, Dritter Band, Marx-Engels Werke 25*, Berlin, Dietz Verlag, 1964.

Marx, K. *Capital: A Critical Analysis of Capitalist Production, Volume I*, Moscow, Foreign Languages Publishing House, 1954.

Marx, K. *Capital, Volume I Der Produktionsprozess des Kapitals*, trans. Eden and Cedar Paul (1928), London, Dent, 1972.

Marx, K. *Marx's Capital*, A Student Edition, ed. C.J. Arthur, London, Lawrence & Wishart, 1992.

Marx, K. *Capital, A Critique Of Political Economy,*Volume I, trans. B. Fowkes, Harmondsworth, Penguin, 1976.

Marx, K. *Capital,* Volume II, trans. D. Fernbach, Harmondsworth, Penguin, 1978.
Marx, K. *Capital,* Volume III, trans. D. Fernbach, Harmondsworth, Penguin, 1981.
Marx, K. *Theories of Surplus Value,* Volume III, London, Lawrence and Wishart, 1972.
Meek, R.L. *Economics and Ideology and Other Essays,* London and New York, Chapman & Hall, 1967.
Meek, R.L. *Studies in the Labour Theory of Value,* 2nd edn, London, Lawrence & Wishart, 1973.
Meek, R.L. 'Is There an "Historical Transformation Problem"? A Comment', *Economic Journal,* Vol. 86, 1976.
Meek R.L. *Smith, Marx, & after,* London, Chapman & Hall, 1977.
Morishima, M. and Catephores, G. 'Is there an "Historical Transformation Problem"?', *Economic Journal,* Vol. 85, June 1975.
Morishima, M. and Catephores, G. 'Is There an "Historical Transformation Problem"? A Reply', *Economic Journal,* Vol. 86, 1976.
Oakley, A. *The Making of Marx's Critical Theory,* London, Routledge & Kegan Paul, 1983.
Postone, M. *Time, labor, and social domination,* Cambridge, Cambridge University Press, 1993.
Ricardo, D. *Principles of Political Economy and Taxation,* 3rd edn, Harmondsworth, Pelican Classics, 1971.
Rigby, S.H. *Engels and the formation of Marxism,* Manchester, Manchester University Press, 1992.
Smith, A. *The Wealth of Nations,* Chicago, University of Chicago Press, 1976.
Stedman Jones, G. 'Friedrich Engels', in *The New Palgrave: Marxian Economics,* eds J. Eatwell, M. Milgate and P. Newman, London, Macmillan, 1990.
Weeks, J. *Capital and Exploitation,* London, Edward Arnold, 1981.

Index